AND SMITH *DID* SCORE

The Gordon Smith Story

Gordon Smith
&
Norman Macdonald

BLACK & WHITE PUBLISHING

First published 2005
by Black & White Publishing Ltd
99 Giles Street, Edinburgh EH6 6BZ

ISBN 1 84502 074 X

Copyright © Gordon Smith & Norman Macdonald 2005

A CIP catalogue record for this book
is available from The British Library.

Cover photograph courtesy of
Mirrorpix

Printed and bound by Creative Print and Design

CONTENTS

FOREWORD · v

1 AND SMITH *DID* SCORE · 1

2 A BALL AT MY FEET · 22

3 A BOY AMONG MEN · 35

4 FROM HAMPDEN TO THE CLASSROOM · 52

5 TREBLES ALL ROUND · 72

6 LIKE A DEATH IN THE FAMILY · 91

7 TRICKED INTO TRANSFER TALKS · 109

8 UP BRIGHTON EARLY! · 123

9 LIFE IN THE CITY · 145

10 SOCK IT TO ME, BOSS! · 161

11 I NOSE WHAT A FOUL IS · 179

12 SAINTS AND SINNERS · 186

13 THE CAP OBVIOUSLY DIDN'T FIT · 210

14 THE NEGOTIATOR · 220

15 JUST HOW DO WE MANAGE? · 242

16 MY MATE, PAUL . . . · 257

17 BOXING CLEVER · 278

FOREWORD

It was a strange but satisfying experience to not only relive my life and times but commit it so openly to print. I didn't always enjoy my football career but at least I have all kinds of memories to share with my family, friends and now the general public.

Experience has taught me that it's people not circumstances that let you down. Sometimes they do it consciously but often it's because they have not thought about the consequences of their actions and how these might affect the life of another human being. I bear no grudges because I have had the willpower, determination and self-belief to overcome these negative situations and move on with my life.

Marlene has been at my side through everything that has happened. She's had a rougher time than me in coming to terms with all the changes in circumstances and moving about this resulted in. I love her dearly and have taken tremendous strength from her support. I sincerely hope that she feels that I have given her a good life despite everything I put her through.

I am delighted with my kids and how they have developed as people. They have adopted the principles my parents passed on to me of honesty, fairness and giving respect to others – where it is due.

Finally, I would like to thank all those who have been positive, helpful and influential in my life but have not been mentioned or suitably credited in this book. I apologise for that but extend my gratitude to you for your support and I dedicate this work to you. You know who you are.

Gordon Smith

1

AND SMITH *DID* SCORE

It was a roasting hot day, the sun was splitting the sky and my team mates were relaxing on sun loungers around the hotel swimming pool. Only now and again would you hear a splash as someone summoned up the energy to dive into the water to cool off.

It really was quite humid that day in Kuala Lumpur, Malaysia, and, eyes closed, I lay full stretch and felt the heat of the sun make my skin tingle. 'It's hard to believe,' I said to myself, 'we're in the middle of January and here I am getting a suntan.' Being a professional footballer can have its advantages.

I was just about to nod off when, in the distance, I heard the youngster's voice plead in a Far East accent, 'Autograph, autograph.'

I squinted my eyes open, put my hand up to shade them from the sun and gazed to the far end of the pool. I could see a lad, about thirteen years old, wandering between the sun loungers collecting autographs from the players.

After a few minutes he made his way to where I was lying and addressed me in a similar fashion. 'Autograph, autograph,' he pleaded.

'No problem,' I said, leaning up on one elbow to take the book and pen from the lad. I signed my name and handed it back to the boy then lay back down and closed my eyes thinking he would move on to the next player, add more names to his collection and away he'd go to proudly show off the autographs to his pals.

But, after a few seconds, I became aware that the boy was still hovering above me and then he asked, 'Are you Gordon Smith?'

'Yeah, that's right,' I answered.

'How you miss that cup-final goal?' he said.

My team mates were howling with laughter and all I could think of saying to him was, 'Cheers – thanks for reminding me.' At that, the boy shook his head as he wandered off, delighted to be able to tell everyone he'd met the footballer responsible for the most famous – or infamous – miss in the history of the FA Cup.

In that instant I suddenly realised that my miss in front of goal in the last minute of extra time in the FA Cup final at Wembley was never going to be forgotten and it would follow me around like a shadow for the rest of my life. I began to appreciate what the phrase 'you'll never live this down' was going to mean to me.

It had been almost two years since I played for Brighton against Manchester United in the FA Cup final, on 21 May 1983, and here I was on the other side of the world with some kid asking me how on earth I hadn't scored a goal that would have made history. Of course, I should have realised what it was going to be like with a worldwide television audience of 150 million watching the final and me missing that goal.

By then I had been transferred from Brighton to Manchester City and in January 1985 we took part in a four-game tour of Malaysia. In January of that year we had been put out of the FA Cup in the third round when Blackpool beat us 2–1, so there was a free week when the fourth-round ties were being played.

That day by the poolside was a signal that for evermore my Wembley miss and the commentator's prediction, '. . . and Smith must score!' would never be far from the spotlight. Even in America I couldn't escape. I was doing some coaching out there in the summer of 1985 and I was introduced to an American guy who asked who I had played for. When I mentioned Kilmarnock, Rangers, Brighton and Manchester City he said, 'So you're the Gordon Smith who played for Brighton.'

I looked at him as if to say, 'How on earth do you know me?' And he added, 'I saw that cup final on television – you missed that chance at the end.'

Back in England, every time I played an away game, the home team's match day programme would mention my name along with the obligatory 'who missed a goal in the last minute of extra time in an FA Cup final' or 'who could have won the FA Cup for Brighton'. It was like a label that had been stuck on to me.

That phrase in the commentary, 'and Smith must score', has been used countless times on television, radio, newspapers and even as a question in pub quizzes since then. Normally you'll hear it over the TV pictures of me just 12 yards out, shooting for goal and my effort being saved by the Manchester United goalkeeper Gary Bailey in the final minute of extra time with the score at 2–2. But that phrase was never uttered by the TV commentator John Motson that day. It was said by Peter Jones on the BBC radio commentary of the match.

What happens now is that the television people broadcast the radio commentary along with the TV pictures of the incident. In fact, on one of these occasions, I was in John Motson's company and he was at pains to let me know he never said 'and Smith must score'! Never in my wildest dreams – or should that be nightmares? – did I think that, more than twenty years later, that miss in front of goal would still be getting replayed on television and mentioned in the media wherever I go.

Years after that cup final, some Brighton fans started a football fanzine and they called it *And Smith Must Score*. I never had any grief from the Brighton fans over the miss and when they were starting the fanzine, they phoned me to ask if I was OK with them using that title. They said the fanzine title was really a tribute to what I had helped achieve for Brighton as that game was the only time in the club's history they had reached an FA Cup final. They even asked me to write a column for the fanzine and I was happy to do that for them.

But of course, the Scottish media turned it round and tried to make out that this was the Brighton fans having a go at me. Nothing could have been further from the truth.

When I was playing with Manchester City, we went to the Goldstone Ground to play Brighton. We were on the team bus and as we drove up to the stadium, the lads turned to me and said, 'There's a crowd of Brighton fans, Gordon. They're waiting to get you.' To be honest I did feel a little trepidation because I had no idea what kind of reception I would get. But, when I stepped off the team bus to walk into the dressing room, there was a tremendous round of applause from the Brighton fans. The Manchester City players couldn't believe it.

Then there was a video of sporting mishaps presented by TV quizmaster Nick Hancock and his programme which uses that other famous piece of football commentary, *They Think It's All Over*. There were loads of different incidents from a variety of sports but what do they call the video? – *And Smith Must Score*.

It's never going to go away – not that it bothers me – and, every so often, the miss is played on television when there's a programme about the FA Cup. In 1997, the BBC were doing a one-hour special on the history of the FA Cup to celebrate 125 years of the famous competition and, sure enough, the phone rings and it's the producers wondering if I would like to appear on the programme.

I couldn't believe it. They had 125 years of cup finals to cram into a one-hour-long programme and they wanted to interview me. I was right up there with the Stanley Matthews Cup final and I hadn't even won the trophy.

There was one good thing about having to relive that cup final on the programme and that was when they showed all the goals from the game. I had people phone me to say they hadn't realised I had actually scored the first goal.

My Wembley miss has also featured on the TV programme *A Question of Sport*. And, talk about quizzes, I've even made *Mastermind*. Just last year, the final question on the famous BBC programme asked for the name of the football fanzine named after an incident in the 1983 FA Cup final. Needless to say, the contestant got it right and the guy won *Mastermind*. At least somebody connected to my miss has eventually won a trophy!

In 1988, I came out of football for a time and worked as a financial consultant in London. I had just started and my boss was on the phone talking to someone when I heard him say, 'Gordon Smith, the ex-footballer, has just joined us . . . yeah, that's the one.'

When he came of the phone, I asked him if the guy on the other end of the phone had asked if I had missed a goal in the last minute of a cup final. The boss said he had and I thought to myself, 'This is not going to go away, right enough.'

Like many stories do over the years, the facts have tended to get lost in the mists of time. Many a time I've been introduced as 'Gordon Smith – the man who missed an open goal in the FA Cup final' or even 'the footballer who missed a penalty in the last minute of a cup final'. Neither of which is true.

I've also lost count of the time people have said to me, 'Would it not have been great if you had scored at Wembley in the cup final?'

And I always reply, 'I did score.'

And they would say, 'No, you didn't. You missed – I watched the game on the telly.'

Sure, they saw my miss but what they also would have seen – and everyone seems to forget – was me scoring the first goal for Brighton in that cup final. It's amazing that, when someone tries to use the miss to bring me down or wind me up, that when I ask what the score was and who the scorers were, they don't know.

I was on a Radio Scotland phone-in one night talking about someone not scoring with an easy chance when this guy came on the line and said, 'You'd know all about missing a goal. How can you criticise anyone about missing a goal after what you did in the cup final?'

'So you know all about my miss?' I said. 'Tell me about it. What did I do? Did I put it over the bar or past the post?'

'Past the post,' he said.

'Well,' I replied, 'we'll just finish the conversation there because the goalkeeper saved my shot and you obviously don't know what you're talking about. You've made an idiot of yourself on national radio – so cheers and goodbye.'

It's very rarely that I get annoyed when someone raises the incident. Only when someone is trying to have a go and they don't know the full facts about what went on during that cup final, can't remember what went on or have never even seen the game does it make me angry. There was one time, though, when I put my lawyer on to a magazine and threatened to sue them.

The British Airways in-flight magazine, *High Life*, had an article about sporting blunders and it described in detail me 'missing an open goal' in the cup final. That did make me angry because it wasn't an open goal – the goalkeeper saved my shot.

The people at the magazine stonewalled my lawyer's letter and basically said they would see us in court if we took it further. In the end, it wouldn't have been worth me spending the money on lawyers' fees. I thought the least they would have done was admit their mistake and offer me a couple of free flights!

Another thing that intrigues me is when Rangers fans say to me, 'What about you missing the FA Cup final goal?'

I always ask them if they remember that I scored the winning goal for Rangers against Celtic in the League Cup final in 1978. It was my first cup final and the score was 1–1 with two minutes to go and I scored the winning goal. I also scored one of the goals that won Rangers the league title and the treble in the last game of the same season. We were playing Motherwell, at Ibrox, and had to win that game to win the league

When this happens, I say to myself, 'If you're a Rangers fan, you shouldn't be talking about my miss in the FA Cup final – you should want to know about the goal that won the League Cup against your greatest rivals, Celtic, and how I scored a goal in the 2–0 victory over Motherwell to win the league title.'

I've also had a right few laughs over the years talking about the cup final miss. A couple of years after the final, I was in a pub with some of my Manchester City team mates. A City fan came up to me and said, 'Are you Gordon Smith?'

'Yes,' I replied.

'I thought as much,' he said. And, as he shook my hand, he added, 'That's great. You're the guy who scored against Manchester United in the cup final.'

The other players started laughing and the fan asked what was so funny. I told him, 'You're the first person ever to bring up the subject of that cup final and mention the fact that I scored a goal.'

In general, other players were pretty sympathetic to my plight as they recognised that Gary Bailey had made a good save and it's not that easy to score at Wembley during a cup final.

Only once did another player try to put me down on the park by slagging me off about the Wembley miss. It was during a reserve game between Brighton and Swindon and there was a bit of argy-bargy going on between the players. I had got myself involved and one of their players – hadn't a clue who he was – chipped in with, 'What about that sitter you missed in the cup final at Wembley, then?'

'Did you see it, then?' I asked.

'I saw it all right, don't you worry,' he replied.

'Were you there or did you see it on the telly?' I enquired.

'I saw it on the telly,' he said.

'Well, what was it like? 'Cos, see when you're playing in a cup final, it seems totally different from just watching it on television like you did,' I said.

Suddenly he realised I was just making a fool of him and he told me to f*** off. My parting shot was, 'You watched it mate. But I was there.' Playground stuff, of course – but he started it!

It surprised me that this was the only occasion when another player used the miss to try to wind me up on the park. And I must have had hundreds of arguments and verbal spats on the park with players over the years. I think it's a respect thing among footballers. Everybody makes mistakes. It's just that, for most people, it isn't at Wembley in the last minute of a cup final.

I also get a few laughs myself during my after-dinner speaking routine. I always do a line about my cup final miss and say that some people think that my career was ruined but, on the contrary, it made me loads of money. 'The following season, I received a record-breaking sum of £10,000 from football boot manufacturers Adidas. But only if I wore Nike boots!'

But, for me, there was much more to that cup final than missing a chance in the last minute of extra time. What happened that season on the road to the final was an exciting, amusing and sometimes amazing journey.

It began, for me, not in Brighton but back in Glasgow with Rangers FC – the club I was with before I moved down south. I was asked to come back to Ibrox on a month's loan to play in the Scottish League Cup final, in December 1982. It wasn't a happy reappearance for me as we lost 2–1 to Celtic.

And there's another pub quiz question involving my career. Which footballer played in cup finals in two different countries in the same season? The answer, of course, is yours truly.

I was still on loan with Rangers on 8 January 1983 when Brighton played their first cup tie against Newcastle at home in the third round. The score was 1–1 and the following Wednesday, Brighton won the tie 1–0 up on Tyneside.

However, I was back at Brighton – and back in the team – for the fourth-round tie on 29 January against, ironically, Manchester City. We won 4–0 and I played really well, laying on a couple of goals.

I missed out on the next round of the cup with a calf muscle strain. And what a game to miss. No one gave us any chance against the mighty Liverpool at Anfield and the only person at Brighton who seemed happy at the pairing was our manager, Jimmy Melia.

The draw was made on a Monday lunchtime and the television cameras were at the club to watch the players' reaction. When

8

we were drawn with Liverpool, who were the current league champions, you could hear the groans from the players – they were the last team we wanted to come up against at that stage.

But Jimmy Melia – who is from Liverpool – was at the front giving it a big 'Yesssss . . .' to the cameras and the smile on his face showed he was obviously delighted to be up against the Merseyside giants.

After the camera crew had left, our team captain, Steve Foster, pulled Jimmy aside and asked him why he was so delighted to be up against Liverpool when everyone knew it would be a really difficult game for us.

'I was just thinking,' said Jimmy, 'there's a family get-together that weekend and I'll be able to go after the game.' There was me, the players and all the Brighton fans thinking Jimmy had a masterplan to beat Liverpool and he'd got the chance to put it into action when, in reality, he was just happy to be able to go to a family party back home on the Saturday night. So, despite my absence on 20 February, the lads got through the fifth-round tie by beating Liverpool 2–1 – a superb result.

I played in the quarter-final tie at home against Norwich on 12 March and we got through that game, winning 1–0. Against the odds, we were creeping ever closer to the FA Cup final. In the semi-final on 16 April, we played Sheffield Wednesday, at Highbury. Although I didn't score, I had a great game in the 2–1 victory and was voted man of the match. I should have scored, however, and I was raging with my team mate Mick Robinson who stole the ball from off my foot as I was about to slot it into an empty net.

The television pictures show me shouting at Mick as he scored and I was still bawling at him as he was running around celebrating. After all, I had done all the hard work – taking the ball through on the goal, shooting, goalkeeper saving it, me picking up the rebound and jinking round the keeper ready to roll the ball into the net – and just as I was about to strike the ball, in came Mick to steal all the glory. But that was us in the final of the FA Cup and facing Manchester United at Wembley on Saturday 21 May. For the next month in the run-up to the final, the whole of Brighton was caught up in cup-final fever. And no one seemed to notice – or, if they did, they weren't too bothered – that we had been relegated to the second division.

It was incredible. You would meet fans everywhere you went and all they wanted to talk about was the FA Cup final. The fact we had been relegated wasn't even mentioned. We had been playing some really good football but never really getting the breaks. But there's no doubt that, if you're going to get relegated, it should be in the same year as you're in a cup final and then you won't get any grief from the fans. It wasn't until the fixtures came out for the following season that it really sank in to the players that we would be playing in the second division.

The players enjoyed every minute of the run-up to the final. We all did the usual rounds of newspaper, radio and TV interviews with the money for them going into the one pot for all the players to share. It even led me to me appearing on *Top of the Pops* – a programme I had watched avidly as a youngster.

It was *de rigueur* for any team playing in a cup final in those days to make a record. So, not to be outdone, we recorded a song and made a video to go with it. Our cup-final record was a rap song called 'The Goldstone Rap' and the B-side was a version of The Drifters' hit 'On Broadway' – this time called 'In Brighton'.

Normally, players make a bit of money out of their cup-final songs but we never made a penny. Most of the team did have a right good bevvy before, during and after the recording session and our goalkeeper, Graham Mosley, was sick in superstar Elton John's private lift at his recording studios. And according to our commercial agent, Howard Kruger, all the profit went to pay for the lift being redecorated.

We recorded the song in Elton John's studio in London and the whole first-team squad left Brighton in a hired bus at about 8 a.m. After two hours and a right few beers from the carry-out the lads had brought on the bus, we arrived at the studios. I was never a great drinker but I had a beer or two on the way to London. Unfortunately, some of the boys didn't know when to stop and they were really in the mood to party when we got to the recording studios.

Everyone piled off the bus and into the studios and, to many of the lads' delight, even more beer was waiting to be drunk in a room next to the recording area. It was for medicinal purposes only, you understand – just to help lubricate the vocal chords.

We were hanging around for some time before we were told what was happening and a lot of lubricating was going on. Eventually, we were played the backing track and given the lyrics to learn. The producers listened to everyone singing and they eventually choose five of us who were actually going to do the singing on the record. I was one of them and I think the criteria for getting the tap on the shoulder and being asked to leave the recording booth was either a) you couldn't sing, b) you'd had too much to drink or c) both.

So the rest of the lads went off to enjoy what was left of the drink in the studio and, when that was finished, they headed off to the pub across the road. Meantime, the five of us left in the studio sang the song as well as we could then had our voices over-dubbed a few times to make it sound like there was a choir singing on the record.

We also recorded a follow-up song which was going to be released if we won the cup. The producers must have thought I wasn't too bad at the singing because they chose me to do the lead vocal on that track.

The recording process takes a long time and, by the time we were finished, everyone had started to wander back into the studio in time for filming the video. These videos are always the same – fifteen or so guys, who wished they could hold a note as well as they could hold their drink, being filmed standing with headphones on miming to the song.

What we didn't know on the day was that, after coming back from the pub in the afternoon, Graham Mosley had got lost in the studio and ended up in Elton John's lift, which took you to his private apartments above the studio. Thankfully, Elton wasn't there that day because Graham was sick in the lift, which was very lavishly decorated with expensive carpet and suede wallpaper.

Graham never let on this had happened and we only found out after the cup final when we had a meeting with Howard Kruger to divide the money amongst the players. We looked at the accounts and asked Howard why there was no profit from the record. He claimed that all the profit had gone on the cost of cleaning and redecorating Elton's lift after Graham had been sick in it. We couldn't believe it and, although Graham admitted he had been sick but couldn't remember where, he claimed it couldn't have made that much of a mess.

I really enjoyed being in the recording studio as I already had a huge interest in music and played the guitar. The cup-final song brought another fantastic opportunity for a music fan like me and that was appearing on *Top of the Pops*.

The week before the cup final Howard Kruger revealed that the record was selling well and two of the squad were to be interviewed on the famous BBC pop programme before the song and our video was played. Jimmy Case and I were chosen to appear.

The pair of us were picked up in a big limo and driven to the BBC studios in London. We were in the green room chatting to Bananarama, who were also on that night, when one of the *Top of the Pops* production team pulled us aside ten minutes before the showed started and broke the news that they weren't going to be playing our song on the programme. He claimed they had just realised that our sales were regional and they were only allowed to feature songs which had a national sales impact. Even worse, he said they were going to play the Manchester United song instead and asked if we would still agree to be interviewed on the show.

I had a strange mix of feelings standing in that green room.

On the one hand, it was incredible to think that we were going to be on *Top of the Pops* but, on the other, I was also really disappointed they weren't going to play our song.

We did the interview with Radio 1's Gary Davis – who was a Manchester United fan, would you believe? – and he was asking all about Brighton's preparations for the final. So after the nation heard from Jimmy Case and Gordon Smith, who play for Brighton, they cut straight to the Manchester United song.

After the show, Jimmy and I looked at each other and said, 'What was all that about?'

However, it's not every day you get to appear on *Top of the Pops* and my wife Marlene likes to remind me that I was wearing a rather fetching tank top on the show. Well, they were fashionable in the 80s – honest.

The reaction to my appearance on *Top of the Pops* was amazing. Lots of people were calling to let me know they had seen me and, back home in Scotland, my mother was also getting loads of calls from people. 'I saw your Gordon, on that pop music programme the other night.' She was dead chuffed.

Jimmy and I may even have had a *Top of the Pops* first – appearing on the show and someone else's song being played.

So, with my flirtation with pop stardom over, it was down to the serious business of playing in the FA Cup final. You could also say that my miss at Wembley cost me a new career in music because, after we lost the replay, the follow-up record with me singing lead vocal was never released.

On the day of the cup final, we arrived at Wembley in style. The squad flew from Brighton to London in a helicopter. And it was the same helicopter that had transported the late Pope John Paul II around Britain a year earlier.

Nobody gave Brighton much of a chance in the final but we had decided, whatever the outcome, we were going to enjoy the occasion. I suppose, in a way, arriving by helicopter was a bit of psychology on our part and, when we were in the tunnel, we surprised our opponents by chatting away to them. They certainly weren't expecting that. They were obviously a bit uptight about playing in a cup final and here we were, relaxed as you like, telling them about the helicopter ride, saying how much we were looking forward to the match and wishing them all a good game.

The United players couldn't handle that and, when we walked on to the park, we were waving to our wives and families in the stands. I found out years later that big Gordon McQueen, who was playing centre half for United that day, had been telling everyone how we had tried to psyche them out in the tunnel and Gary Bailey had said that flying in by helicopter had been us playing mind games. They were spot on.

There were 100,000 cheering fans in Wembley that day and we certainly silenced the Red Army when I scored in fourteen minutes. Gary Howlett fired a diagonal cross towards the far post and I drifted in behind their defence to head the ball back across goal, beating Gary Bailey at his left-hand post to score the opener. Yes, folks, Gordon Smith *did* score at Wembley in the FA Cup final!

We were well organised that day and, at half-time, we were still one up. As we trooped off the park, I looked at the giant Wembley scoreboard, saw my name as the scorer and thought that maybe, just maybe, we could pull off a shock result and I would be a hero for scoring.

But, in fifty-five minutes, United equalised when Frank Stapleton forced a Mike Duxbury cross over the line. Then, in the seventy-second minute, Ray Wilkins put them into the lead with a superb shot from about 20 yards out which curled into the top corner of our net.

We might have been down at that point but certainly not out. During the game we had always been dangerous from set pieces and, with three minutes to go, I forced a corner. Jimmy Case took the corner and passed low to the outside of the box for Tony Grealish to hit the ball hard into their penalty box. Gary Stevens managed to control it and fired it past the United defenders and keeper into the net for the equaliser.

Extra time came and went without much incident until the

final minute of the game. Jimmy Case picked the ball up in the centre circle and sent down a long through ball for Mick Robinson to chase. He beat their defenders to the ball, shrugged off Arnold Muhren, turned the ball inside to beat Gordon McQueen and saw that I had matched his run on the right and was in the penalty box unmarked.

As Mick squared the ball to me, I was already thinking that I'd take a touch to control it. The goalkeeper was coming out to close the angle and I was going to hit it hard and low at his feet because that's a difficult shot for a keeper to save when he's standing trying to make himself big in front of an attacker. But, just before I struck the ball low and hard, Gary Bailey did what I didn't expect him to do – he dived. And, not only that, in goalkeeping terms, he dived the wrong way. The ball hit him on the legs and squirmed slightly behind and, before I could get to it, he was able to smother it with his arms and pick it up.

My first thought was, 'I can't believe he's dived as early as he did. He shouldn't have dived – that's the wrong thing to do.' Well, for me, it certainly was but, for Gary Bailey, it was the right thing to do – he saved my shot and also saved his team from losing a cup final. If I had thought the keeper was going to dive so early, I could have chipped the ball over him into the net, like I'd done countless times before. But, because I thought he was going to come towards me, close the angle and stand big as most goalies do, I hit the ball reasonably well, low and hard.

My first reaction was shock and disbelief that he had managed to save the shot. Then, as I started to walk back up the park, I was thinking that I should have chipped the keeper. I would have reacted just the same if it had been a practice match I was playing in and failed to score. I didn't immediately think that I could have scored the winning goal in the cup final. However, a few seconds later, the biggest shock of all was about to hit me – the final whistle.

Immediately after the save, I was angry with myself for not scoring and, in a strange way, I felt annoyed at Gary Bailey for doing the unorthodox thing and diving early. At that point, I was thinking I'd missed a chance of scoring and was ready to get on with the game. But it was only when the final whistle went, I realised the enormity of what had just happened.

Not only had I missed a goal – I had missed the goal that would have won the FA Cup for Brighton for the first time in the club's history. That was when the full impact hit me. 'Shit!' I said to myself. 'That would have been the last kick of the game. I could have won the cup for Brighton.' And, in true Victor Meldrew fashion, I kept saying to myself, 'I just don't believe it!'

As I trudged back up the pitch with the referee's final whistle still echoing round my head, the first of my team mates to say anything was Tony Grealish who was standing in as captain for Steve Foster who had been suspended for the game. Tony said, 'You were unlucky there – you nearly did it.'

The next person I spoke to was Steve Foster who had come on to the pitch and thanked me for not scoring. 'Cheers, Smudger,' he said, 'that means I'll get a game in the replay. I'll get to play at Wembley after all.'

Both teams did a lap of honour together round the pitch, soaking up the cheers and adulation of the fans, but I still couldn't get that miss out of my head and the consequences were beginning to sink home even more. None of my team mates gave me a hard time. A few of them said that Gary Bailey had made a good save but most of them were just saying 'well played' to each other.

By the time we got into the dressing room and spoke about the game, I was more critical and harder on myself than any of them could have been, although I never lost any confidence in my ability, particularly since I had played quite well that day and had scored the first goal.

And, when I did take the shot that Gary Bailey saved, I was quite calm and composed and knew exactly what I wanted to do with the ball. Not for a second did I think I was going to get slaughtered by any one of my team mates – and I never was.

The worst thing about it was that I kept going over and over in my mind what I would do differently when the pass came to my feet. You can't recreate that moment again. In my head I can imagine me chipping the ball over Gary Bailey and see it hit the back of the net but I'm stuck with that moment and there's absolutely nothing I can do about it.

We headed back to Brighton in the helicopter and were due to attend a civic reception later that night. Meanwhile, the players' families and friends were heading back on a hired bus and Marlene was in tears all the way to Brighton. It must have been an incredibly emotional time for her that day because it was the first anniversary of her dad John's death. He was a lovely guy and sadly he passed away on a visit to see us.

The bus to the civic reception was leaving from my house and, while everyone was waiting to go, there were three or four policemen – who were there to escort the bus – sitting in the lounge with their helmets at their feet drinking cups of tea and eating potato scones with my mother-in-law Annie and Marlene's Aunt Lizzie.

At one point Marlene came into the lounge and our son, Grant, who was only three at the time, was sitting with one of the policeman's helmets on his head. He turned to her and said, 'Mum, sure it wasn't Dad's fault?'

At the civic reception, the television people wanted to interview Brighton's manager Jimmy Melia and me about the game. They had set up a TV monitor so we could watch incidents from the match and comment on them. Naturally, the big talking point was my miss and they were replaying it on the monitor.

I started to talk about it as it was shown for the umpteenth time when Jimmy Melia – who hadn't yet seen a replay of my shot – butted in as I was saying that I really should have scored. 'Oh, no,' said Jimmy. 'That's a good save by the goalkeeper. That's not as bad as I thought it was. I thought it was an easier chance but it was a good save – you can't blame Gordon for that.'

It was really good of Jimmy to defend me like that and he wasn't the only fellow pro to do that. Years later, Jimmy Case was being interviewed about the cup final and my last-minute miss when he said, 'Of all the players I've played with, if I'd want to put anyone in that position at that stage of the game, it would have been Gordon Smith.' Whether he meant it or not, it was a fantastic thing for him to say.

Bryan Robson won an FA Cup medal in that game playing for United and years later he asked me if I was still getting stick for the miss. When I told him I was, he said, 'Anyone who has ever played the game would never give you stick for that. They would know, playing in a cup final and everything that goes with it, how difficult it must have been.'

The club chairman, multi-millionaire Mike Bamber, had a laugh with me about the miss at the civic reception. 'You could have won the cup for us and been a hero in Brighton for ever more,' he said. It was probably this remark that made me think about the long-term consequences of the miss and he was right. If I'd scored, I probably would have been elected Mayor of Brighton every year for the rest of my life.

With the replay coming up the following Thursday, there was a constant stream of sports journalists from newspapers, radio and television beating a track to the Goldstone ground – and guess who they all wanted to interview? I featured in every interview and they all asked the same question – how did I feel about missing the goal in the last minute?

It didn't bother me. I was very honest with my answers, admitting that I should have scored and saying I was disappointed not to score, especially for the fans, but we had another chance in the replay. I wanted to let the fans know that I was just as sick as they were when I missed the goal but we were looking forward to the replay and thought we still in with a chance of lifting the trophy.

The papers were saying that I should have scored and won the cup for Brighton and they were right. That's fact and there was nothing I could do about it except make up for it in the replay.

The Brighton fans I met in the run-up to the replay were great.

They would mention the goal I scored and say I could have won the cup for them but it was a great save from Manchester United's keeper.

The pundits were split on our chances. Some of them went with the old adage that the smaller club only gets one chance of being a giant killer and others were saying that Brighton had played well on the Saturday and we shouldn't be ruled out.

I was handling the situation just fine but, when the replay came along, I wasn't quite as relaxed as I had been for the first game. I knew I had let people down and I was desperate to make amends. I just wanted to get on that park and score another goal or even two.

I realised that this replay was more important to me than to the rest of the team. If we lost, they would get away with it but it would come back to haunt me because of the miss on the Saturday.

For the opening spell of the game we played well and had the upper hand although we just never got any breaks. But United hit us with three goals before half time, with Bryan Robson getting a double in the twenty-fifth and forty-fourth minutes and Norman Whiteside scoring in the thirtieth minute. That was a real body blow and, in the dressing room at half-time, there was a stony silence.

I thought that someone had to break the silence so I piped up, 'What's the record defeat in a cup final?' That broke the ice and everyone started laughing. It also made them realise that our pride was at stake and we had better get out there and make sure we weren't on the wrong end of a drubbing.

Eventually we lost 4–0 after Arnold Murhen scored for United in the sixty-second minute and that was that.

The media really went to town talking about my miss in the previous game and they pointed out that I would always be remembered for missing the goal that would have won the cup for Brighton and that my miss will go down in FA Cup history. That was the first inkling of just how big this was going to get –

although I didn't think, for the life of me, that it would go on for more than twenty years.

Although, obviously, I would rather have scored with that chance in the last minute of the final, the notoriety which has come with missing the chance has had a few benefits. Up until then, I had had quite a low profile in England but that all changed after the Wembley final. It has made me better known down south and, if I ever contact a manager over a player I represent as an agent, they know who I am when I mention my name and they recognise that I played at a high level in the game. It hasn't done me any harm in that respect.

And, while I regret missing the chance, I don't regret that it happened. If it was a choice of getting beaten by Manchester United 4–0 in the first game or drawing 2–2 with them and me missing in the final minute, I'll take the latter every time.

I find it amazing that my miss is still so well known after all these years but I don't get fed up with people asking me about it. There's not much more I can say after all this time. 'Yes, I could have scored, should have scored, didn't score, lost the replay and didn't win the FA Cup.' That's about it in a nutshell.

It was one split second in a football-playing career that spanned seventeen years with league winner's medals, cup medals, goals in cup finals, the lot. I've never thought of myself as a failure because of that miss. I've played in plenty big games and scored other vital goals so I can deal with it. But I'm sometimes annoyed that people seem to sum up my entire football life as one miss or a good save from a goalkeeper.

I have always been mentally strong and, in some ways, I am glad it was me who missed the goal and not one of my team mates. I knew I could handle the aftermath and, to this day, I can have a laugh and a bit of banter about it. Yes, because the lads I played with that day were a great bunch of guys, if anybody had to endure the disappointment, I'm glad it was me. And, to put everything in perspective and answer those who say that miss must have changed my life, I'll tell you a sad and tragic story.

I swapped shirts with the Manchester United winger Alan Davies after that cup final. That poor lad, who got his hands on the FA Cup that year, tragically committed suicide in 1992. So, if anyone thinks missing a sitter in a game of football is going to change my life, well, they're over-estimating the importance of not scoring that goal and they should think again because what happened to Alan Davies puts everything in perspective.

That FA Cup Final miss at Wembley certainly got me noticed but there's a lot more to Gordon Smith than that one game. So, let's start at the beginning . . .

2

A BALL AT MY FEET

A group of young lads has gathered in the church car park. One of them is playing keepie-up with a football. There's a bit of pushing and shoving between another pair but mainly the boys are in a cluster talking excitedly about the game ahead. The chat is about tactics, tackles and who's going to take a penalty if their flying winger is brought down in the box. A shoulder bag with the Pan-Am airline logo on the side suddenly flies into the air followed by another bag, this time with the BEA airline motif, and a bout of pretend wrestling between two of the youngsters breaks out. But the jostling comes to an abrupt end as the Morris Oxford motor pulls into the car park.

Out steps the team manager-cum-team-driver, Mr McMillan, and shouts the boys over. 'Right, lads,' he says. 'We're running a bit late so let's all pile in.' Within seconds there's a mad scramble, arms and legs everywhere, as eleven young footballers squash and squeeze themselves into the car.

I hold back for a minute with my pal Davy Patterson and let everyone else dive into the front and back seats. We've worked out the physics of it all. If we're last in, we'll be on the top of everyone else and we won't have the breath squeezed out of us by a pile of squirming boys.

Now, I've played for some of the country's biggest football clubs, stayed in the swankiest of hotels and travelled in luxury tour coaches all over Europe but this is how my football career started. I was a gangly nine-year-old inside-left playing for the 3rd

Stevenston Lifeboys and this was the scene every second Saturday morning going to away games during the football season. Eleven of us – there were no substitutes in those days – waiting at the High Kirk at Stevenston Cross for Mr McMillan – or Mac the Knife as we used to call him – to pick us up in his car at 9.30 a.m. and drive us all over North Ayrshire to places like Irvine, Dalry, Ardrossan and West Kilbride to play our games.

How on earth eleven of us managed to get into that Morris Oxford, I'll never know. It would never be allowed in this day and age but, back then, it was a great laugh and no one thought anything of it.

Big-time football it certainly was not. We had to bring our own football shorts and socks with us as the only kit the Lifeboys provided was the top. Nevertheless, it was the first time I had played in any organised football matches and every game was like a cup final to us all. So there I was, nine years into my young life and literally kicking off a career that would eventually become a dream come true for me.

I was born on 29 December 1954 at Buckreddan Hospital, Kilwinning, although my parents, Bill and Edith, stayed in Stevenston in Ayrshire. It may be that things will come full circle when I'm older because Buckreddan is now an old folk's home. Perhaps one day I'll be seen shuffling around the grounds at Buckreddan kicking a ball while grasping on tightly to a Zimmer frame!

My parents named me Gordon Duffield Smith – and, if we can get the laughs about my middle name out the way here and now, that would be just fine, thank you. I was named Gordon after the legendary Hibs and Scotland footballer Gordon Smith – which is fair enough – but the Duffield middle moniker came from my maternal grandmother's maiden name. I've never liked Duffield because to me it sounded daft as a middle name and people have always laughed at it throughout my life.

I'm listed on the FIFA website as Gordon Duffield Smith and people have written to me, 'Dear Mr Duffield'. I suppose, if I ever wanted to come across all posh one day, I could add a hyphen and call myself Gordon Duffield-Smith. However, having been brought up in a council house in a staunchly socialist working-class family, I doubt that will ever happen.

My grandfather on my father's side was a professional footballer, playing for Kilmarnock in the 1920s as an inside-right. Matthew Smith – or Mattha as he was better known – is the only player to have lifted the Scottish Cup for Kilmarnock in both 1920 and 1929. Old Mattha was the team captain in 1929 and I'm very proud that my grandfather made the history books of the club all my family supported as I was growing up.

Sadly, Mattha died of heart problems in 1953 and I never got to meet him. It's also a shame that he wasn't around to pass on his knowledge and experience as a professional footballer when I was trying to make it at senior level. By all accounts, he was very good and, after his playing career was over, he carried on coaching youth teams.

My dad was also a bit of a player and turned out for various junior teams in Ayrshire, including Ardrossan Winton Rovers. That's where he met my mum. She lived round the corner from the Rovers ground and would regularly watch them play. Obviously, the young Bill Smith caught her eye and the rest, as they say, is history. I had a great football background in the family with my grandfather being a professional player, my dad playing at junior level and my mum being a fan.

My mother's dad, George Bullock, was English and came to Ayrshire after the First World War. I was really interested in history at school and had a great fascination with the Great War. My grandad Bullock fought at the Somme and Gallipoli with the Border Regiment but wouldn't talk about his time there, however hard I tried to get him to describe the horrors of that conflict.

In those days the regiments were made up of families and friends from the same area and, if a regiment was devastated in battle, it would be family and friends who had died. A lot of his family were killed in these battles and I think that's what stopped him talking about it.

When I was born, I had an older brother, Matthew, who had been born in February 1952, and we lived in a terraced house at 3 Smithfield Terrace, right in the middle of Stevenston. At one time, my grandfather Smith had owned a garage, a shop and a pub and obviously had a bit of money. He owned the property in Smithfield Terrace and had given the house to my mum and dad, although my dad's brother Matthew had a half-share in it.

It was certainly no luxury pad and we had an outside toilet in the garden – just a shed out the back. Many people nowadays would throw their hands up in horror at the idea of having an outside toilet but, at the time, it was no big deal. The house was on the main road and, as a three- and four-year-old, I would sit at the front window and watch the cars going by.

One of my earliest memories is of me kicking a football back and forward to my dad's brother, James Smith, in the back garden of his house which was also in Smithfield Terrace. I would be about four and there would just be the two of us out in the back garden and he would show me how to kick a ball properly by side-footing it back and forward. It felt quite natural kicking a ball around and, thankfully, it was a sign of things to come.

In 1959, we sold the house and moved to one of the new council houses, which had just been built at the top end of Hayocks Road in Stevenston. We stayed at number 72 and it was a typical late-50s, back-and-front door, two-bedroomed council house – but at least it had an inside toilet and bath.

Downstairs was the living room – no such thing as lounges in those days – with a coal fire which my dad would light first thing in the morning and a small kitchen with a Formica-top table where we would have our meals as a family. We had a black and white television in the living room and the whole family were great telly watchers.

Westerns were my favourite – I loved *Bonanza* and *Rawhide*. And my fascination with all things cowboys and Indians has stayed with me throughout my life. One of my ambitions is to go to the site of Custer's Last Stand where the Battle of the Little Bighorn was fought, on 25 June 1876, along the ridges, gentle sloping hills and ravines above the Little Bighorn River, in Montana. It's a fascinating story and I've read a few books about that famous battle. I'm determined that one day I'll go there. It has all stemmed from watching those cowboy programmes on television in my mum and dad's living room when I was a wee boy.

The upstairs had two bedrooms – one for my mum and dad and the other was for my brother Matthew and me to share. We got on fine but it was strange because we never had anything in common. I was always out on the streets with my pals playing football whereas Matthew would prefer to study and was into things like stamp collecting.

Probably the major difference was that Matthew didn't play football and had no interest in the game. But, as I was growing up, that was all that mattered to me. So we were almost like strangers, never played together and never really palled about when we were young. We've got more in common now because we're part of the same family and we've both got kids.

Like my dad, who was a big Labour man and a councillor in Stevenston, Matthew was also interested in politics. He became Britain's youngest councillor when he was twenty-one and he was elected to serve on Stevenston Town Council.

In November 1961 my younger brother Billy was born and that meant three of us sharing the same bedroom. This wasn't a problem for me as, even to this day, I've never had a bedroom to myself. Before I got married I was living with my parents, sharing a bedroom with my brothers.

I went to Stevenston High Primary School up until Primary Six when they built a new school nearer our house – Hayocks Primary. I was always pretty good at school and I listened to what the teachers had to say. I was never disruptive in class and always gave the teachers respect – that was something my mum and dad drummed into me. My favourite subject was arithmetic and I was pretty good at it.

Of course, every playtime and lunch break we would be playing football in the playground and, if we didn't have a full-size plastic football, then a tennis ball had to suffice. When I started primary, the older boys would play football in the main playground and the younger ones, like me, either had to watch and hope we'd get the chance to kick the ball back when it went astray or find our own wee corner of the playground for a kick-around. But by the time I was eight, the older lads were letting my best pal, Davy Patterson, and me play in their games which was a sure sign we were a lot better than most kids our own age. It wasn't too long before Davy and I had gone from being last pick when the teams were being chosen to us actually picking the teams.

There was obviously plenty going on in my life as a youngster but the defining moment for me at that tender age was the day my grandpa Bullock and my uncle James took me to my first senior football match to see Kilmarnock versus Rangers, at Rugby Park. That's when I stood on my tiptoes on the terracing behind the goals to the right of the main stand and first laid eyes on one of Scotland's greatest-ever footballers – Jim Baxter. And that was when I became a secret Rangers fan.

This was 1963 and I was nine years old. It was my first real football match and, all Saturday morning, the colony of butterflies nesting in my stomach were flying around like nobody's business. My grandpa and uncle lifted me over the turnstile and I'll never forget the roar of the crowd when the two teams ran on to the park. Now, like all my family, I was a Kilmarnock supporter but it wasn't long before I couldn't take my eyes off the master of ball control, passing, dribbling and shooting that was Slim Jim Baxter, the Rangers and Scotland left-half.

I was supposed to be there to watch and cheer on Kilmarnock but I was fascinated by this mop-haired, skinny guy who would strut around the park with an air of total authority and do things with a football I'd never seen before. I was awestruck.

You just know when some life-defining moment like that is upon you. I loved everything about Baxter. Everyone is influenced by someone at some point in their career and they think they can be like that person. Luckily my influence struck me at a very early age before I had even started playing organised football. That day I watched Baxter and thought, 'Maybe I look like him. He's skinny just like me. I love the Beatles haircut. I might be able to play a bit like him. No, I'm going to play just like him.'

As the game went on, I became more and more entranced with his abilities on the park and more determined to model myself on him. But then it struck me, 'He plays with his left foot and I'm right-footed but that's the player I want to be. So I've got to start playing with my left foot like Jim Baxter does because that's what makes Jim Baxter so special – his left foot.' There and then I decided I was never going to kick a ball with my right foot again.

As soon as I got home, I got hold of Davy Patterson and told him that, from now on, I was only going to kick a ball with my left foot. And for more than a year that's exactly what I did. Any time I touched a ball, whether in the street playing keepie-up or in the school playground with my pals, I only ever kicked the ball with my left.

I knew I had to learn to kick a ball from scratch but it didn't take as long as I first thought it would because I discovered I could naturally do the same things with a ball with my left foot that I had been doing with my right. Nobody I was playing football with complained about me not being as good as I used to be when I started kicking with my left foot. The same skills I had in my right foot very quickly developed in my left, which was just as well because I was determined I was going to be the next Jim Baxter.

It was only when I started playing organised football with the Lifeboys that I began to kick with my right foot again. I remember people saying I should try to kick with my right foot because I was too one-footed. Little did they know that, a year or so earlier, that's all I did. And this rather unusual idea of only kicking with my left gave me amazing benefits later on in my career. It turned me into a two-footed player, which meant there was a greater variety in my attacking play. I could go down the left wing and cross the ball with my left foot or cut inside and take a shot with my right.

After seeing Jim Baxter play in that Kilmarnock–Rangers game, I was desperate to see him again but the opportunity didn't come until the following year when Dundee beat Kilmarnock 4–0 in the semi-final of the Scottish Cup to set up a final against Rangers at Hampden.

I had been at that Kilmarnock–Dundee semi-final at Ibrox with my dad and grandpa and after the game I asked them if they would take me to the final. They thought I had been impressed by that great Dundee team at the time that had Alan Gilzean up front but, really, I wanted to see Jim Baxter playing again.

I was a secret Rangers fan and I wouldn't dare tell anyone in my family. They were all ardent Kilmarnock supporters and, with my grandad having played for them it would seem like a real betrayal to support anyone else.

My dad was never a big fan of Rangers or the sectarianism that went along with them. He was a real Labour man – he was a councillor in the old Stevenston Town Council for several years – and hated the whole bigotry thing. Even when I was older, I was never allowed to go to an Old Firm game. The first-ever Old Firm game I attended was one I played in.

The odd time I was taken to a senior game it would be to see Kilmarnock and I just went along with that. At the time, I didn't go to that many senior games as the junior side Ardeer Thistle was my local team. Davy Patterson and I used to sneak into their ground without paying. Davy had discovered that part of the corrugated iron fence round the ground had come loose and we could pull it back just enough for us to crawl through.

I wasn't yet old enough to be picked for the school team but playing for the 3rd Stevenston Lifeboys was enough to whet my appetite for organised games on full-size football parks. And it was in my second season with the Lifeboys that I was cheated out of my first league championship medal.

As the season drew to a close, we kept asking how we were doing and if we were at the top of the league. All we were told was that we doing 'fine'. What we should have been told at the end of the season was that we had actually won the league, but they kept this from us. It was only when we started playing again the following season that some of the players from other teams mentioned we were the league champions. That was my first league championship win and I never knew anything about it.

I've no idea why they never told us we had won. One of the theories we had was that the Lifeboys didn't want to spend money on buying us medals. Maybe they couldn't afford the medals or maybe they just didn't want us getting carried away with ourselves. But I think it was wrong of the people running the Lifeboys not to have told us we had won the league. We were aghast when we eventually found out from other lads the following season. You would think there would be some recognition of that achievement. Even a mention during the church service when the minister reads out intimations would have been nice and they could have said congratulations to our Lifeboys for winning their league. But not a word was said. I definitely feel we were cheated out of not only a medal but the recognition and satisfaction that we had achieved something and we were winners. We were cheated out of that fantastic feeling of winning something.

In recent years, I've handed out a lot of trophies at youth football awards nights and, occasionally, I've found out that the team haven't actually won anything. People are giving youngsters medals for everything – best player, player's player, best sportsman, best trainer and a medal for just turning out and playing for the team. Youngsters must have their own trophy cabinets these days and I think it is a bad thing. Every medal or award I got since I started playing as a boy was for winning something and that's how I think it should be. Giving medals out to everyone to make them feel important is a bad thing.

People say sport should be a lot less competitive and I totally disagree with that. For me, that's what sport is. It's a game where you have an opposition and you are trying to win. Sure, we have to show kids how to deal with losing and how to handle not winning with dignity. But the way to do that and prepare them for life shouldn't be about making them all winners because life is simply not like that.

Making everyone a winner can hold back the youngster who wants to win and you are also not encouraging a winning mentality, which is what sport and, in many cases, life are all about. We should reward real achievement and teach kids to be winners as well as teaching them how to deal with losing and how to learn from that experience and become better sportsmen and sportswomen – and better people.

I remember reading an article by a sports psychologist who said that life is like sport and that there are three different types of people – those who don't mind losing, those who hate losing and those who like winning. He said that contrary to what most people think, the strongest category is people who like winning rather than people who hate losing. To hate losing is a negative attitude and it's better psychologically to teach people to like winning because those who like to win can deal with losing.

But back to boyhood days. When it came time for Davy Patterson and me to start playing for the school team, it gave my mum the ideal opportunity to make sure I stuck in and did well at school. She told me I would be *banned* from playing football if I wasn't in the top three in the class when it came to tests and exams. My mum was desperate for me to do well with my education and, from the very beginning, encouraged me to do well. Fortunately, I always brought home good report cards and I always was in the top three. The top spots in class were usually contested between Sandra Dowie, Margaret Reid and me and the threat of no football certainly kept me on my toes.

At the time, I thought it was a bit harsh of my mother but, at that age, you don't analyse things too much and you just accept the rules and regulations you have to live by. I might not have been so relaxed about mum's rules if I had slipped out of the top three. 'C'mon mum, I was fourth in the class. Let me play – please.' Somehow I can't see my mum giving in to my pleading. Thank goodness it never got to that.

It wasn't long after Davy and I had started playing for the Hayocks Primary School that we were more or less managing the team as well by manipulating the teacher who organised it. Mr McAulay was very enthusiastic about running the school team – and good on him for that – but he didn't know a lot about football. If we were near the opposition's goal during a game, he would shout 'score' instead of 'shoot'. Davy and I were able to manipulate him by just having chats with him about the games and telling him that 'So-and-so shouldn't be playing' and 'He's a better player in that position'. Because he didn't know any better, he would soak it all up and, when he announced the team, everything would be as we had suggested.

After this happened a few times, we realised how little Mr McAulay knew about football and tactics so we would talk to him even more about how the team should line up and he would always pick up on our suggestions. The team was being run the way Davy and I wanted it and, although we were quite a small school, we did manage to get to the final of the North Ayrshire Cup.

Davy and I watched all the football there was on television at the time and listened to the commentators so we knew all the terminology. I think that was one of the reasons we were able to persuade Mr McAulay do things our way.

On the home front, in 1962 the family moved house again, this time to 14 Hawthorne Drive, which is right at the top of Stevenston and had nothing but countryside at the end of our cul-de-sac. This was great for me. Not only was I closer to my pal Davy but there wasn't a lot of traffic and that meant more space on the street for playing football. And play we did, for hours and hours on end.

We were at the top of the cul-de-sac and there were two pillars at the entrance to our driveway which made excellent goalposts. Every day, a group of us would be out there playing beat the goalie – someone crossing the ball and the others trying to score.

My sister Elaine was born in February 1964 and, three years later, the family moved to our new home at 1 Bute Court, Stevenston, which was closer to the town centre. But it was still football, football, football as far as I was concerned – nothing else came close to being so important in my life. Playing for the Lifeboys and the school, Davy and I began to realise that we were better than the other kids. We scored most of the goals and our team mates began to rely on us to win games for them. Davy was a real good player. He played inside-right and I played inside-left.

Davy was a hard tackler and loved that physical side of the game. Me? I couldn't have tackled a fish supper when I was playing in a game – I never tackled anyone. I had a bad attitude towards that side of the game because all I wanted to do was score goals and create goals for other people. In many ways, Davy and I were a good balance and complemented each other in the team. We had an almost telepathic understanding and awareness of what the other was doing on the park. I would beat a couple of players and, nine times out of ten, who would be in the perfect position to take the pass? – Davy. The funny thing was, though, away from the organised games, Davy and I would spend hours in his garden playing one-on-one and I was all for going in with full-on tackles then.

It was the same playing for the Lifeboys – Davy and I would score a barrowload of goals. But my first 'transfer' saw the break-up of that football partnership – in Boys' Brigade football, anyway.

Davy and I were due to move up to the 3rd Stevenston Boys' Brigade Company but, before the football season started, I was 'tapped' by some older lads who were with the 1st Stevenston BB and they asked me to join them and play with their team. 'Come and play with our BB team,' they urged me. 'We've already got a good team but, if you come, we could have a great team.'

I knew the 1st Stevenston had the best football players in the area and I wanted to play with the best. So, I decided I would give it a go and I joined up with them, playing in an age group two years above what I should have been. It was big thing joining another BB company because you also had to change your church and it was something I had to get permission from my parents to do. They said they were OK with it as long as I promised to go to Sunday School every week at the new church.

Strangely, Davy left the 3rd Stevenston at the same time but he joined another BB Company – the 2nd Stevenston. I never did find out why he did that.

Looking back to my early years, I would say I had a happy but strict childhood. I was brought up to be respectful of authority and to be well behaved. I was afraid to step out of line and get into trouble with my parents. I also had a very religious background as my parents were at the kirk every Sunday and they took religion seriously. So much so that observing the Sabbath meant I was not allowed out to play on a Sunday. We only left the house on a Sunday to go to church and, in the afternoon, to visit my granny and grandpa Bullock, who stayed in Ardrossan.

It was only when my younger brother got older that I was allowed out into my granny's back garden with him. Not being allowed out with my pals on the Sabbath sure made for a boring Sunday but I just accepted it, even when I was in my early teens and still not being allowed out on a Sunday. That was the family convention and I never fought the conventions at that early age.

It was only later on in life I started fighting conventions. And that got me into a few tight corners in my time.

3
A BOY AMONG MEN

The steam from the roasting hot water in the giant bath filled the air along with the usual banter from a group of footballers winding down after a hard day's training.

As usual I was keeping quiet and not getting involved in the rough and tumble of the verbal abuse they were giving each other. I slipped into the water for a quick wash before heading off home to pinch myself again in case I was dreaming that the fourteen-year-old Gordon Smith was sharing the same Kilmarnock FC dressing room and training pitch as some of the best-known names in Scottish football.

A couple of the guys slid to the side to make room for this skinny schoolboy they had nicknamed Casper, who had landed in the middle of their very adult world of professional football. I stretched my arm over to the side of the bath where I'd left my bottle of shampoo and flicked open the top. I poured a good measure into my hand and started rubbing the shampoo into my thick mop of black hair.

Within a few seconds the shout went up, 'Would you look at the state of him?'

And another player chimed in, 'He's washing his hair with shampoo. See you, Casper? You're nothing but a big poof!'

By this time the whole team had joined in giving me dog's abuse about shampoo only being for girls and, if I was half a man, I would use the carbolic soap like the rest of them. But I hated carbolic soap. It would come into the dressing room in a foot-square block and then be cut up into small squares. There were no showers in those days so everyone jumped into the communal bath for a wash. All the players used that awful-smelling carbolic – even to wash their hair.

But no matter how much of a slagging I took for using shampoo, there was no way I was going to go back to using the carbolic. After a week or two of being told I was like a big lassie for using shampoo, things began to change.

'Here, son – give us a wee drop of that shampoo you've got there,' one of them would say when we were in the bath after training.

'Aye, throw the bottle over. I'll have some of that as well,' said another.

Before I knew what was going on, the whole team were borrowing my shampoo and one bottle was only lasting about two days. I'd gone from being a poof for using shampoo to wash my hair to the sole supplier to the rest of the team. It was costing me a fortune.

I soon got wise to this, though. Instead of buying bottles of shampoo I would buy sachets and only take one into the bath with me. When I think back to those days and look at footballers now with their toilet bags crammed with shampoo, shower foam, skin cream, deodorants, hair gel and bottles of men's fragrance – how times have changed.

I got my nickname – Casper – after Kilmarnock's Scotland international fullback, Billy Dickson, said to his team mates one day, 'Here comes the ghost,' when I walked into the dressing room. That soon became Casper after the cartoon ghost character. I was called that because I used to move about the dressing-room planking myself down beside a group of players to hear what they were saying but not daring to utter a word myself. I was just a schoolboy and these guys were the professional footballers I'd been watching from the terracing just a few months previously. There was no way I was going to butt into their conversations but I was desperate to lap up every last word these guys spoke.

The Casper nickname stuck with me all the time I was at Kilmarnock and newspapers used to say that I was called that because of the way I ghosted into the opposition penalty box to score a goal. If only. I had gone from being a lippy teenager at school to almost total silence as I was giving these players my total respect in their own environment. Who was I to start a conversation?

Those summer months of 1969 were a real eye-opener for me after I had signed an S-Form with Kilmarnock in March of that year. But, although I was on my way to becoming a professional footballer, I was still a schoolboy having to negotiate my way through troubled waters infested with teachers – who doubted my unswerving belief that I would be a footballer – exams and a growing personality trait of standing up for myself, speaking out and not kowtowing to authority.

Any time a teacher would ask the class what they wanted to do when they left school, I would say I wanted to be a professional footballer. And always the reply would be, 'C'mon, be serious. You'll have to come up with something more realistic that you can do for a real job.'

I suppose I was a bit naive in continually setting myself up for that kind of criticism from teachers. I couldn't understand their reluctance to accept that I was going to make it as a footballer but they obviously didn't realise my determination and self-confidence that was going to get me there. And, to be fair, the teachers probably knew better than me how difficult it is to make it in the professional game and they must have heard the 'I'm going to be a famous footballer' line from starry-eyed schoolboys a million times before.

I was in the top class, taking Latin and French, when I went to Stevenston High School and, although the work was a lot more difficult than primary, I was still passing exams comfortably. I was a good listener in class and was able to get away with a few hours' swotting the night before an exam to get me by. I was very lucky that way and I was getting away with murder by not spending night after night poring over my schoolbooks.

Incredibly and to my mother's astonishment, I passed all seven 'O' Grades I sat without doing much studying at home – which is just as well because my mum was still threatening to stop me playing football if I didn't pass my exams. Even after I had signed with Kilmarnock and was playing in their reserve team every Saturday, she would warn me that, if I didn't do well at school, the football would stop. And I believed my mum could stop me playing for Kilmarnock reserves – even after I had signed a contract with them and they were paying me money. What drove me on at school was that I loved my football so much that I didn't want to put her threats to the test by failing exams and finding out if she really could stop me playing.

In my early teenage years at school, I began to have problems with a few teachers who seemed to have taken a dislike to me. I was the type of boy who wouldn't be afraid to speak up – and worse, talk back – in class. Because of how well I was doing at football and particularly being signed up on an S-Form by a professional football club, I had become more confident.

If a teacher said something or asked me to do something and I didn't think the reasoning or their argument was logical, I would question what they were saying. Some of the teachers didn't like their authority being challenged like that. Before long, the teachers began to look on me in a different light. The word had obviously got round the staffroom that I was a pupil with an attitude problem.

Maybe I was too full of myself although I certainly didn't intend to come across as arrogant. I knew that some teachers didn't like me and I didn't want to do anything to make that situation worse. But I wasn't going to be a shrinking violet at school. If I thought I was in the right I would stand up for myself and say so. No doubt the teachers thought I was arrogant because of my single-mindedness and continual declaration that I would become a footballer. There might also have been a bit of envy on their part as well or they might have resented a lippy schoolboy refusing to take their advice on having something to fall back on.

I suppose my attitude came partly from my upbringing. Because my parents were socialists, there was always debate in our house and I was brought up to question the establishment and authority. I was taught to respect authority as long as it is fair and just and to believe that, as long as people treat you fairly, you give them respect and I have always done that. These lessons have stayed with me all my life. I give people respect until they act in a manner that loses my respect and that's when I sometimes take an attitude towards them.

That's probably what happened between me and some of my teachers – they didn't treat me with proper respect, so I reciprocated. And that didn't just stop with schoolteachers. It has been the same with all the football managers I have played for. I respect them to start with but, depending on how they react and treat me, my attitude towards them could, and often did, change.

Although I lived in a family of socialists, I was never a socialist as a teenager but, whenever I would be involved in a discussion about politics at school, I would argue the socialist case because I had heard all the left-wing viewpoints at home. I was probably apolitical until pushed. For some reason, when I started playing football seriously, I thought it would be better not to get involved in politics. I thought you either played football or got involved in politics.

To this day, I still argue with my older brother about the Labour Party. I am a socialist but a questioning socialist. I don't accept that the Labour Party has all the answers but it is, for me, the closest party to what I believe in. I vote Labour because of my background and most of what Labour stands for is the fairest way to go about things. This questioning, arguing, challenging Gordon Smith might be fine and well in adulthood but, in school, it just wasn't going down well at all.

One incident in particular from when I was in second year shows exactly what the problem was. I was walking in the school playground minding my own business when a teacher shouted me over and demanded that I pick up some litter from the ground and put it in the bin.

'Excuse me,' I said. 'It's not my litter and I never dropped it there. It's not my job to go around picking up other people's litter.'

'Listen, son,' the teacher replied, 'when I tell you to pick up litter you'll do it.'

I refused and, of course, got into trouble for it. But, if the teacher had asked me, instead of ordering me, I would have gladly picked up the litter. It was because of the way he treated me that I stood my ground and refused.

I had no trouble with the teachers who took the school football teams and, in first year, both Davy Patterson and I played in the Under-13s, Under-14s and Under-15s age groups. I found it great playing against older boys because I had to work a lot harder during the games. I wouldn't get it all my own way as the older boys were that bit stronger and better. And, because I was coping with playing at the older level, when I played for my own age group, I was that much further ahead of everyone else.

I think it's a great thing for young players to be up against older boys. If you just play in your own age group, you won't improve as quickly as you might and your potential won't show through at an early stage. When I played in my own age group, I was an inside-left, but when I played in the older age group I was on the right wing. I could dribble and pass the ball well and I was always good for a goal.

Every year, our school won the North Ayrshire Schools League through all the age groups I played in. The only trophy that I missed out on was the big one – the Ayrshire Schools Cup which was for all the schools in Ayrshire and not just our part of the county. Twice we got to the final and both times we were beaten in the final by St Joseph's, from Kilmarnock. It was still a big achievement for us because we were a small school.

Just as we had done with the teacher who took the football team in primary, Davy Patterson and I were soon influencing the secondary school teacher who took our team. Ian Proctor was a music teacher, very posh, but a great football enthusiast. He knew that we were good players and seemed to like us so he let us talk a lot about football to him. We even managed to persuade him that we needed new school strips and that, since Brazil were everyone's favourite team at the time, it had to be Brazil strips for us. We were the only team in the league running around in brand-new Brazil strips.

Although it seems a million miles away from being a maverick schoolboy and wanting to be a professional footballer, both Davy Patterson and I were in the school choir. This was down to Mr Proctor who was a great teacher, able to transfer his enthusiasm for music to the pupils and made his classes interesting for us. He even had the class going to operas at the theatres in Glasgow. Imagine a bunch of unruly kids from North Ayrshire heading up to the King's Theatre to see *Die Fledermaus* but we were taught how to appreciate the music and we enjoyed it.

However much we liked Mr Proctor, Davy Patterson and I couldn't help having a laugh at his expense. The teacher would be sitting playing his piano and the school choir would be singing their hearts out. We would be fine for a few minutes but then start to deliberately sing out of tune. Mr Proctor's face would screw up as he wondered what was happening and he would get up from the piano and walk along the lines of pupils singing in the choir. When he came close to us we would go back to singing in tune. He would shrug his shoulders and think he must have been hearing things but, as soon as he was back at the piano, we would start the out-of-tune singing again. This would drive him crazy as he could never find out who was out of tune. Sorry, Mr Proctor. You were one of the good guys but I was always a better footballer than a singer.

After fourth year, a new school, Auchenharvie Academy, was built in Stevenston and I transferred there in 1971 from Stevenston High. Unfortunately, so did the teachers. I must have been the only school sports champion who was banned from taking PE for two years. And I wasn't to blame – honest.

Up until we were in fourth year, Davy Patterson and I had never taken an interest in sports other than football. Davy was always quite scathing of the school sports. 'We're the football team and that's that,' he would say. But, by the time I was sixteen, I had spent more than a year training with Kilmarnock two nights a week and full-time during the school holidays. This gave me a massive lift in my physique and my fitness level. No one else at the school was going through that amount of fitness training.

I suggested to Davy that we should go in for the school sports and, at first, he said I shouldn't be so daft. Then, after he had thought about it, he came up with a ruse that both of us should enter the school championship 1500 metres race. We were to sprint from the start, which was too fast a pace to keep up for the whole race, and, halfway round, we'd drop out. He reckoned that everyone else would try to keep up with us and, after we'd chucked it, we could watch them all struggling to finish the race.

So we were all lined up on the running track and off we went, with Davy and me haring away round the track at breakneck speed. We got round one lap and discovered nobody had come with us. We were well ahead of everyone else who had gone at the normal pace.

'What'll we do now?' asked Davy as we pounded round the track.

'We'll just have to keep going now,' I replied. So we did and I won the race and Davy was second.

The following year, I was even fitter and stronger as I was playing for Kilmarnock reserves every Saturday along with the normal two nights a week training stints. So I decided I would enter more than one event in the school sports championships, which was split into two sections. The 100 metres, 200 metres, 400 metres and the 800 metres were held at night at the Ardeer Recreation Juniors' stadium. The other half of the events – field athletics and field events like the 1500 metres, javelin, shot putt, long jump and the cross-country – were held at the school playing fields earlier on with the winners being announced on the night of the Ardeer section.

That year I broke the school record for the 1500 metres, running an even faster time than the year before with our sprint start. I also won the cross-country, javelin, shot putt and long jump. I wasn't going to enter any of the events at the big sports night at the Ardeer Rec but I had still won enough points from these earlier events to be the overall school sports champion. It was announced on the night and I picked up the trophy without even having to change out of my school uniform.

Because I had won the school cross-country championship, I was entered for the Ayrshire schools cross-country event, which I also won. A few months later, in September of that year, the head PE teacher, Andrew Walker, took me aside and said I had been entered into the Scottish Schools Cross-Country Championships, representing Ayrshire, in two weeks' time.

But, by this time, I was playing regularly in the Kilmarnock reserve team and the cross-country championships were being held in Kirkcaldy, Fife, on a Saturday morning. There was no way I could run a cross-country and then turn out for Kilmarnock the same day.

So I told him, 'I can't run on a Saturday.'

'You're running for Ayrshire,' he said.

'But I can't,' I replied. 'I play for Kilmarnock reserves on a Saturday and I can't run the cross-country and play for Kilmarnock on the same day.'

'You're running in that race. You'll be there,' he said, walking off before I could say another word.

Well, the Saturday came and went and so did the cross-country race that I didn't go to. There was no way I was going to jeopardise my football career for a schools cross-country race.

Then on the Monday morning, as sure as night follows day, I was called in to see Mr Walker. I could see he was raging with me. 'You didn't turn up on Saturday,' he said.

'I told you I couldn't run in the race,' I replied. 'I was playing for

Kilmarnock who pay me to play and I'm under contract to them.'

He ended the short but sharp conversation by announcing, 'You're banned from PE.'

What a farce. I was the reigning school sports champion, playing football for a First Division club and wasn't being allowed to take part in PE lessons for the last two years of my schooling. While everyone else was at PE, I was sitting in an empty classroom reading, catching up with homework or even just sitting daydreaming about football glories I hoped would come my way.

The ironic thing is that Andrew Walker's assistant in the school PE department was George Maxwell – one of my Kilmarnock team mates. I used to travel to training with George and we even went out to the dancing together on a Saturday night. Although George was four years older than me, we were great pals. I asked George what the problem was and he said there was nothing he could do. 'He's really not happy with you,' George said. Oh, really? I'd never have guessed!

I think Andrew Walker knew I couldn't run in that race because I was playing for Kilmarnock the same day. He wanted to get me into a position where he could nail me for not turning up for something he had told me to go to. There are people like that in life who, because they are in a position of power, want to bring you down a peg or two.

He probably didn't want me at PE since I would be a total inconvenience to him. Although still a schoolboy, I was a professional footballer and he couldn't have the same control over me as he had with the other pupils. In any case, I didn't really need PE at school as I was doing much more physical exercise with Kilmarnock two nights a week and on a Saturday afternoon than I would ever get at school.

I don't think he particularly liked me before the cross-country race incident, anyway. When I was in third year, he used to carry on with the boys and pretend he was going to hit them on the head. They would cover their heads and he would slap them somewhere else on the body. Teachers could get away with things like that in those days and it wasn't really a big deal. But I never played along with him and I refused to flinch when he made to slap me on the head. That obviously annoyed him.

Around about the same time, we were having practice for the school dance – learning all the Scottish dances like the Gay Gordons and the St Bernard's Waltz. There was a bit of a carry-on in the gym hall and he lined everybody up against the wall and said we were all a disgrace. Then he pointed a finger at me and said, 'And the main one who's a disgrace is you.' Still pointing at me he said mockingly, 'And you, you want to be a PE teacher?'

At one point, I had said to people that, if I didn't have a lengthy career as a footballer, I would probably be a PE teacher and this news had obviously got back to him. I looked over at him and, more than likely with just a hint of a sneer, replied, 'Me, a PE teacher? I don't think so.'

You can imagine how that went down with someone who was a PE teacher and wasn't used to pupils talking back at him. Once again, by being outspoken, I had marked my own card with the teachers. I bet he had a field day in the staffroom after that little outburst from yours truly.

Oddly enough, his daughter Margaret Walker was in my class all the way through secondary and she was a really nice girl. We were great friends and we would have a laugh about her dad not liking me.

Although I might have been unpopular with some school-teachers, I seemed to be popular enough with my fellow pupils. So much so that they voted me in as head boy when I was in fourth year. This was much to the chagrin of certain teachers who said that, if it had been a teachers' vote, I would never have been head boy.

The following year, there was a new head boy but I was still a prefect. That was when the school's headmaster, Mr Wilson, tried to pin the blame on me for a maths supply teacher resigning because of unruly behaviour in class. I was called to the headmaster's office and he told me I should take the blame for the teacher resigning. 'You're the leader in the class,' said Mr Wilson. 'And you're very much the perpetrator of this whole thing. You should admit to this because, otherwise, there are other boys from good backgrounds who will get the blame.'

I protested my innocence but it was to no avail. Mr Wilson continued to say that I was the leader and I should take all of the blame. All this stuff about me being the leader surprised me because I never saw myself in that role but, obviously, the teachers did. Again I said it had nothing to do with me but, along with three other boys, I was suspended from school for a week.

The incident which led to the teacher resigning was really not a big deal – especially not compared to the problems teachers face in today's classrooms. There was a bit of shouting and making noises behind the teacher's back – just generally giving the guy a hard time. He let them away with too much at the start and it just got worse as time went on. I thought the pupils carrying on were pretty immature and their behaviour quite childish. I certainly didn't try to stop them but I didn't have anything to do with what was going on.

If I had taken the blame, I would have been the only boy suspended but I was angry at the headmaster's suggestion that I should take the blame because the other boys were from 'good backgrounds'. It was as if he was saying that I wasn't from a 'good background' – what he appeared to suggest was that, because I was from a council house and the rest of the boys would be from private houses, I must be at fault. The reality was that the boys guilty of misbehaving in class were all from so-called 'good backgrounds'.

But you can imagine the heavy footsteps walking home with a letter in my pocket to my parents saying I was being suspended from school. My mum and dad were none too pleased, despite my protestations of innocence. I was made to find out where the teacher who had resigned lived and go with my dad to apologise to him.

When we got to his house in Saltcoats, he opened the door and said, 'Hi, Gordon, what are you doing here?'

I told him I had been suspended from school for being disruptive in his class but he said it had nothing to do with me.

'Will you tell my dad, then?' I said. 'My parents don't believe I had nothing to do with it.'

But, despite all the trials and tribulations that school may have brought me, I was still having the time of my life in my early teens. No amount of grief from teachers could take away the excitement and anticipation of being signed up by a senior football club. And, when I was signed up, it came right out of the blue.

I was still only fourteen when the first phone call from a football scout came. I was out at the time and my dad answered the phone. It was a scout from Celtic but he was telling my dad that Rangers wanted to sign me on S-Form. I've never found out why a Celtic scout was calling to say their greatest rivals wanted me. During the conversation, my dad happened to mention to the Celtic scout that he would have preferred me to go to Parkhead because he thought I would get a better chance of making it into the first team and youngsters were better treated there. I don't know how my dad would know that but that's what he said.

The Celtic guy was a bit taken aback at this and said he thought I wouldn't be allowed to sign for Celtic rather than Rangers because I was a Protestant. Nothing could have been further from the truth as there was never a hint of sectarianism in our house. The Celtic scout said that was good news and he would get back to my dad about getting me up to Parkhead on an S-Form.

The following day a Rangers scout phoned my dad and said they were interested in signing me on the S-Form and that someone would be in touch to confirm all the details. When my dad told me Rangers wanted to sign me, I was very excited. I still hadn't told my dad that I was a closet Rangers fan and the thought of going to Ibrox had me thrilled to bits.

A few days later, I was sitting in the living room and the phone rang. It was always kept in the hall and my dad got up out of his chair to answer it. I could hear him talking and, from what he was saying, I soon realised it was something to do with football and me. When he finished the call, he came into the room with a satisfied look on his face. 'That was Kilmarnock on the phone,' he said. 'They want you to sign with them.'

'But what about Rangers?' I asked.

Then I got the best piece of advice I could have been given. My dad said that there was more chance of me getting into the first team at Kilmarnock than at a bigger club like Rangers who had so many more players to choose from. 'If you've got what it takes, you'll be in the first team and bigger clubs will notice you and that's when you'll get the chance to sign for a bigger club and get straight into their first team,' he told me. It would have been harder for me to break through into the Rangers first team at that time so I listened to my dad and signed for Kilmarnock.

Although my dad was delighted at his son signing for the same club his father had played for with such distinction, he was always very critical of me when he saw me play either with the school or the Boys' Brigade. I still can't understand why he was always so down on my performances. It got so bad that my mum told him, 'Stop going to watch the boy if you can't say anything good about him.'

I would know when he had been at a game and, back home, I would wait anxiously to hear what he thought of my performance. If I thought I'd done particularly well, I would ask him how he thought I'd played. He would list a series of things I'd done wrong. He was wrong to do that because, as I've learned from my experience of coaching youngsters, the best way is to praise them first and then you can tell them what they did wrong. That way, they can handle the criticism better.

Being constantly criticised by my dad definitely put that wee bit of uncertainty in me. I was disappointed that my dad wasn't saying good things about me because a youngster always wants to have parental respect and approval. But I knew I was good because everyone else was telling me how good I was and I compared favourably to other boys of my own and older age groups. I had a lot of self-confidence but I just thought it would be nice if my dad recognised that and gave me some praise now and again. Eventually, he would say, now and again, that I had done well in a game and that gave me a magnificent feeling. He was always talking about how good his dad was and it was great that he was praising me as a footballer as well.

At the time, I thought my dad not praising me was his way of making me determined to be a better player. But, only last year when my dad and I were being filmed together for a programme about football in the community, I turned to him during the filming and asked, 'When you watched me as a kid playing football, did you ever think I would make it as a professional?'

He said, 'No. You were too gangly and I didn't think you would make it.'

While we were still being filmed, I replied, 'Well, I'm glad you never told me that because it could have had a massive effect on me.'

When I think about it now, before I signed with Kilmarnock, my dad never encouraged me to be a professional footballer. Maybe he didn't want me to be disappointed with my life and, if he thought I didn't have what it takes and wouldn't make it as a professional, then his attitude makes more sense. However, when eventually I did sign as a professional footballer, he backed off and stopped the criticism. It was almost like I had become his father who he idolised because I had made it as a professional footballer. And he probably got a surprise to see his gangly kid starting to fill out with muscles because of the training we did at Kilmarnock.

I've never sat down and analysed with Dad why he was so critical but it's fair to say it's just as well I had strong self-belief or I might never have achieved what I have done in my football career. Ironically, his criticism prepared me for the professional game, because there's plenty criticism going around there, but I was almost immune to it because of what my father had said to me when I was younger.

Not so long ago, Dad commented that he's spent half of his life being Mattha Smith's son and the other being Gordon Smith's father. So, whatever his reasons for being so critical of me, I had – and still have – a good relationship with my father. After all these years, I don't really care why he was hard on me. I made it as a professional footballer and I've had a successful career in the game.

Anyway, in March 1969, the criticism I had been getting from my dad was furthest from my mind as he drove me to Kilmarnock's Rugby Park to sign a schoolboy form for the club my grandpa played for and my whole family supported. The schoolboy S-Form, as it was known, had been launched that year and I was the second boy to sign these forms with Kil-marnock. The first was goalkeeper Jim Stewart who went on to play for Scotland.

I was going straight from school and was still in my school uniform as we drove to Kilmarnock. We were both excited but, like me today, my dad never showed it that much. He spoke about his father playing at Rugby Park and what he had achieved with Kilmarnock. I was asking questions about what the Kilmarnock manager, Walter McCrae, was going to say and my dad was telling me that I'd have to wait and I'd find out soon enough.

We reached the ground and were shown upstairs into the manager's office. Walter McCrae came round his desk to greet us and shook our hands. 'Sit down,' he said. 'We've had Gordon watched and we want to make him one of our S-Form signings.'

I asked if I could still play for my school team and he said I could. But the Boys' Brigade football would have to stop because he wanted me to play boys' club football.

He then said, 'We're going to have you in here training twice a week – Tuesday and Thursday nights. We'll get your fitness levels up and you'll get proper coaching. We'll try to improve you with a view to calling you up. If things go well, we'll pull you in here before you are eighteen.'

The words 'before you are eighteen' stuck in my mind. It seemed a long time away but I was determined to grab this opportunity and literally kick off a career which would lead to me making a living as a professional footballer.

That was me on my way and that's how a fourteen-year-old schoolboy ended up sharing a dressing room and the team bath with players who were known the length and breadth of the country.

Walter McCrae may have thought it would be a few years before the boy sitting in front of him would be playing first-team football – but that boy had other ideas.

4

FROM HAMPDEN TO THE CLASSROOM

The team sheet was neatly written out and the Kilmarnock substitute for the reserve game at home against Dunfermline was down as a young lad called Jones.

The tall, athletic-looking fifteen-year-old sat in the Rugby Park dugout watching his team mates. Every so often, he would jump up and run to the back of the goals, warming up, while, at the same time, keeping a watchful eye on the team coach just in case he got the call. It was a big game for the lad – he would make his professional debut if he got on the park.

Into the second half, that call did eventually come and he slotted into central midfield. He played well and didn't look out of place playing with and against footballers who were twice his age with certainly more than twice his experience in the game.

The match finished 2–0 to Kilmarnock and the teenager trooped off the park wishing the final whistle had never been blown. He would have played on until midnight if they had let him. But he was satisfied with his debut, especially with the chorus of 'Well played, son' ringing round the dressing room.

The youngster couldn't wait until the next midweek when the local paper, the *Kilmarnock Standard*, would hit the streets. He wondered what the match report would say and if he would get a mention. The sports reporter didn't let him down. He read the report over and over. 'I must have done well,' the lad thought to himself. 'It says it here in black and white.' The article described how the substitute, Jones, came on to the park, looked a capable player and did very well on his debut . . . a good prospect.

*****

Looking back all those years, the Jones boy must have been very proud of pulling on the Kilmarnock jersey for the first time. I should know – because it was *me*!

I was only fifteen, still on an S-Form and, according to the rules, not allowed to play in reserve matches. Kilmarnock had other ideas and wanted to give me a taste of the real thing but had to give me another name on the teamsheet. I don't know who it was but some wag thought it would be a laugh to call me Jones since my real name was Smith.

After being signed on an S-Form in 1969, Kilmarnock farmed me out to the Under-15 and then Under-16 teams with Prestwick Star youth team, for a couple of seasons, although two nights a week I was training with the professionals at Rugby Park.

That day, when I was called up to play in the reserves, early in season 1970–71, was another leap forward in my career which I was able to take without too much difficulty. Each time I had taken a step up in football, I found it very refreshing and a great challenge. I always managed to cope and actually play better than I was doing before. It was a mixture of the excitement of playing in bigger games and playing alongside better footballers. That same season, while still playing for the Under-16s – by this time Kilmarnock had taken over Prestwick Star and the team was called Kilmarnock Star – I was given another outing with the reserves, this time to Ibrox to play Rangers, but I never got on during that game.

We made a little bit of youth football history with Kilmarnock Star, winning the first of the well-known Eastercraigs International Tournaments in Glasgow, and I scored two goals in the final of a 3–2 win against Eastercraigs who had future Aberdeen and Scotland star Willie Miller playing centre forward. The Kilmarnock Star coach, Bill Beattie, was a great enthusiast and gave me a lot of confidence by the way he encouraged me and told me how much he expected of me.

When I was in at Kilmarnock training full-time during the

school holidays, I would be mixing with well-known names like Tommy McLean, Sandy McLaughlin, Andy King, Jim McLean, Ally Hunter, Eddie Morrison, Jackie McGrory, Davie Sneddon, Ross Mathie, Jimmy Cook, George Maxwell, Brian Rodman, Billy Dickson and Frank Beattie.

I'll never forget walking into the dressing room with all those Kilmarnock football legends milling around. I was just fourteen and had only seen these guys before from the Rugby Park terracing. Now I was in the same room as them, getting changed with them, running alongside them and playing football on the training pitch with them. You can imagine how awestruck I was and it was little wonder that I would just float around the place, not saying a word. It was amazing and I have to admit I felt out of place to begin with.

During the school holidays, starting in the summer of 1969, shortly after I'd signed the S-Form, I was at the ground for 10 a.m. sharp. One of the Kilmarnock squad, Cammy Evans had spoken to my dad and said he would take me along with George Maxwell, also from Stevenston, to Kilmarnock every morning and back home again.

Most of the work was done either around the running track at Rugby Park or on the training ground which used to be across from the stadium. I never missed a single session or practice game. I was able to do everything the first-team squad did – running, sprinting, sit-ups, press-ups, burpees, the lot.

The only time we left Rugby Park was when we were taken for a cross-country run round Annanhill Golf Club, in Kilmarnock. After the morning session, the squad would get lunch in the clubhouse and that was a real eye-opener for me. One week, I'd been queuing up for school dinners and, the next, I was having lunch served to me in a golf club.

The senior players were great to me when I arrived at the club and were quite encouraging when I played in the practice games. Of course, because I was just a boy, I was last pick when they were choosing the teams. I hadn't been last pick for football since

I was in primary school and wanted a game with the older boys.

Only once did I have a problem with one of the senior players and that was with – surprise, surprise – Jim McLean. Yes, he could lose the rag even in those days when he was playing. I was fifteen and had just finished a running session round the track at Rugby Park. Everyone was walking across the concrete to the training pitch for a practice match and the metal studs on my only pair of football boots were going clink, clink, clink on the ground. Jim McLean heard the noise I was making and he turned to me and said, 'Where are you going?'

'I'm going over to the park,' I replied.

'Not with them on,' he said pointing to my boots. 'You're not going to play with these studs on – you'll hurt somebody.'

'But these are the only boots I've got,' I protested.

'Doesn't matter,' he said. 'You're not playing wearing boots with screw-in studs.'

I honestly didn't mean to be cheeky – I was only looking for some help and advice – but I then asked if he could see about me getting a pair of rubber moulded-sole boots. Suddenly, he just erupted in fury and was shouting at me and pointing his finger into my face. I thought he was going to hit me as he warned, 'Don't you talk to me like that – I'm not getting you anything.'

Quickly, the other players moved in and pulled me away and Jim's brother Tommy told him, 'Away you go and leave the boy alone – you're out of order.' Wee Tommy then turned to me and said, 'Don't worry, son. He's off his head.' That was the only time I had any problems with the senior players at Kilmarnock. After that, I bought myself a pair of moulded-sole boots – just in case Jim McLean decided to check my boots any time in the future.

Although facing the wrath of Jim McLean was a terrifying experience for a young lad, some of the Kilmarnock players were very good to me and gave me every encouragement. John Gilmour – who sadly died a few years ago after battling cancer – was especially good to me. He would walk with me back and forward to training from the dressing room giving me encouragement. John would say, 'How're you getting on, Casper? See you and me? We're the best two players at this club.' He was a lovely guy.

I realised I was lucky to have been given the chance to be a professional footballer and I wasn't going to squander it. When the rest of my pals were trying to get into pubs for a fly under-age pint, I steadfastly refused. For me, smoking and drinking were no-nos and I stayed a teetotaller until I was twenty-six. As a teenager, I would stand outside pubs kicking a ball against the wall as I waited for my pals to come out after managing to get served. I was so completely consumed with the idea of becoming a footballer that I wasn't going to let a few pints of lager come between me and realising my ambitions.

One of the more unusual aspects of Kilmarnock Football Club in the late 60s and early 70s was its mascot – Angus the sheep. Yes, a real, live sheep wandered around Rugby Park and the training ground. I knew about Angus because, whenever I would go to watch Kilmarnock with my grandpa, he would point Angus out to me.

For the first few weeks I was at Rugby Park training, I thought some of the players were a bit eccentric to say the least. I would hear them talking about going to see Angus and having a cup of tea with him in his room. A sheep who has its own room and drinks tea with the players? I couldn't believe this but it must be true, I told myself, because I'd heard the players mention it several times.

Eventually, I discovered who Angus really was and thankfully I never opened my mouth and embarrassed myself with the rest of the players. The Angus they were having a cuppa with was certainly not the sheep – it was Angus Rodger, the Kilmarnock groundsman. I had seen him around the place but I hadn't thought to ask his name.

What I did soon realise, though, was that Angus Rodger was a superb groundsman and he really knew his stuff. Rugby Park had one of the best – if not *the* best – surfaces in Scottish football.

The pitch was in fabulous condition and I can't remember a match being postponed because of the state of the park all the time I was there. A perfect pitch and Angus made sure it stayed that way. Woe betide anyone who stepped on to the grass except on match days. One foot on the park and, if Angus caught you, he'd give you dog's abuse.

After the summer holidays, it was back to the classroom and training two nights a week with the part-time and youth players. There were also a lot of players training at Kilmarnock who lived in the area but played for other clubs. There were players from Queen of the South, Stranraer and other assorted clubs training with us and that meant there was a real crowd on a Tuesday and Thursday night.

The practice matches after the running and exercise session were a real farce. There were so many of us it was about twenty-a-side and you were lucky to get a kick of the ball. If you did get the ball, you had to be good to make sure no one took it off you. That was good dribbling practice for a Saturday when there weren't so many players to beat.

However, that was the only time during training we saw a football. Walter McCrae and trainer Jock Murdoch took the view that training was there to get you fit and that was it. That was the general attitude with a lot of football clubs in those days. Starve the players of the ball at training and, during the game on a Saturday, they will be desperate to get a kick at it. That's total nonsense. You practise the things you are expected to do on a Saturday so that they're second nature to you.

I was lucky to be playing with these professionals. Davy Patterson had signed an S-Form with Rangers and he never got near a first-team player. Unfortunately, Davy was released by the Ibrox management along with a lot of boys when he was sixteen. After that he played junior football.

My wage from Kilmarnock as an S-Form footballer was £1 10 shillings (£1.50p) a week, rising to £2 10 shillings (£2.50p) the second season, but I was also selling potatoes and doing a paper

round which I had started a few years before. I was making about
£1 10 shillings a week from selling potatoes round the doors in
Stevenston and 10 shillings (50p) for delivering the Sunday
papers for Sawers newsagent's shop. Add all this together and
you got a tidy sum – especially for a youngster still at school.

Stone and half-stone bags of potatoes would be delivered to
our house in Bute Court for me coming home from school on a
Thursday. I would deliver the potatoes round the houses on the
Thursday night, transporting the load in a wheelbarrow. On the
Friday night, I would collect the money but not everyone could
afford to pay you even though it was just a few shillings they
owed. One of the things I did begin to appreciate was that,
although we were a working-class family, we were reasonably
well off. I saw that some of the poorer people I delivered potatoes
to didn't have carpets or soft furniture in their homes. They didn't
have a settee or an armchair – they sat on hard chairs and had
linoleum on the floor.

At the start of season 1971–72, I was sixteen and still at school
when I was called up from youth football to play in the
Kilmarnock reserve team. This meant I was now on a proper
professional contract and getting paid £15 a week. The first game
Gordon Smith played for Kilmarnock reserves – not counting
the debut by the Jones boy – that season was against Dunfermline,
in August 1971.

I was playing on the left wing for the reserve team, which was
run by Norrie McNeil and the trainer, Jock Murdoch. Like most
Scottish coaches of their day, they weren't the type to encourage
you with praise when you did something right. I felt they tended
to put players down and this held back my progress. Sometimes,
before a match, they would tell me, 'Don't take on this fullback
today – you'll never beat him.' After a few months of this, my
confidence did begin to wane and my form suffered, although I
was still getting a game every week.

But everything changed when left back Billy Dickson fell out
with Kilmarnock manager Walter McCrae and was dropped from

the first team and came into the reserves. He's not slow in telling people that he's the person that turned Gordon Smith into a good footballer. And he's not far wrong.

He would be playing behind me and, all during the game, he would be urging me to try things and keep going forward. He'd pass the ball to me and shout, 'Go on, Casper. Take him on, son. You can skin him.' And that's exactly what I did, thanks to Billy's encouragement.

It was incredible the difference in my performances with Billy Dickson urging me on every chance he got. It shows the power of psychology. I was in the doldrums because I was being put down every week. Along came Billy, telling me I was good enough to beat everyone, and, before you knew it, I was flying again. When you are young and somebody gives you a boost, it can spur you on to greater things.

I then started to analyse the situation myself and thought, 'Hang on a minute. I was doing nothing until Billy Dickson came along and started to encourage me. I can do this because Billy's making me feel good about myself. I'm a better player than they were telling me.' Billy sure did turn my world around and set me in the right direction – more often than not towards the opposition goal. I was regularly scoring in the reserves and making a lot of chances for others as well.

At the start of the following season, 1972–73, I was seventeen and about to start my sixth year in school, having got B passes in two Highers – History and English. But there was a pleasant surprise awaiting me that summer in football terms. Kilmarnock were going to the Highlands for a couple of pre-season games against Ross County and Brora Rangers, who were both in the Highland League, and, much to my delight, I was in the first-team squad.

My first game for the first team was in the centre of midfield against Ross County, at Dingwall, and I also played against Brora Rangers. Then, when we got back to Ayrshire, there were more pre-season friendlies but, much to my disappointment, I didn't feature in any of them and I didn't get a game when the season proper started with the section games in the Scottish League Cup.

Then, completely out of the blue, I was pitched into the starting line-up to play Wolverhampton Wanderers in the Anglo-Scottish Cup. Wolves had Derek Dougan and Mike Bailey playing for them and Mike was to be my manager in years to come. It certainly was an exciting time in the Smith household.

If my first few games in the first team had seen me on cloud nine, then my league debut for Kilmarnock brought me back down to earth with a bump. We played Celtic at Hampden, in September 1972. The game was at the national stadium because the main stand at Parkhead was being rebuilt. I was now being played in my favourite position – the centre of midfield – and, before I had even kicked the ball, we were 3–0 down. It was some team Celtic had in those days and they were in the middle of their nine-in-a-row league championship era. I was up against some of the famous Lisbon Lions – Billy McNeill, Jim Craig, Bobby Lennox and Jimmy Johnstone.

Celtic came at us like a whirlwind and I was overwhelmed. I had never been on a football park with players as good as these Celtic bhoys. The match finished at 6–2 to Celtic – although I did play better in the second half. In the dressing room after the final whistle, I was expecting the worst from manager Walter McCrae, dreading being told my career in the first team had come to a short and abrupt end after such a drubbing. But Walter actually singled me out for praise. He said, 'Well done, son. You were one of the better ones today. If everybody had played as well as you, we wouldn't have had such a hammering.' I was relieved because my only concern was staying in the team and that's exactly what I managed to do.

Everybody was telling me to expect that I would be dropped after a few games, that someone as young as me would be rested or my form would dip and I would be replaced in the team and then be brought back in. But, thankfully, that never happened and I stayed in the Kilmarnock first team for the rest of that season.

FROM HAMPDEN TO THE CLASSROOM

So I went from playing Celtic at Hampden on the Saturday to sitting in a school classroom on the Monday morning and hardly anyone said a word to me about it. That's what it was like all through sixth year – I would be playing big games on a Saturday and, on the Monday morning, not a word would be said. No autograph hunters and no girls queuing up to speak to me – well, some people might say not even being a professional footballer would make up for my looks!

I suppose it's a very Scottish trait that you'll never be a prophet in your own land. It didn't bother me because I was doing what I had always dreamed of doing and that was being a professional footballer. I was getting recognition outside school in the media. Strangely, I was getting more mentions in the national papers than the local press – the *Kilmarnock Standard* and the *Ardrossan & Saltcoats Herald*.

Looking back, it does seem a bit spooky that I was playing teams like Rangers and Celtic at the weekend and nothing was being said about it by my teachers or fellow pupils two days later. If that were to happen today – a schoolboy playing against the Old Firm – it would never be out of the media.

Although it was *de rigueur* in most clubs for young footballers to carry out the boot-cleaning duties, Kilmarnock had staff to do that for you. I never had to do a stint in the boot room with the dubbin. But, when manufacturers like Adidas or Puma gave a supply of boots to clubs like Kilmarnock for the players, they would never hand over the top-of-the-range stuff. The boots I was being given weren't as good as the ones I had been buying. I found this strange as we were playing at the top level in Scottish football and I would have expected that the players would get the best boots available. But that simply wasn't the case.

And, when we were handed out boots by the Kilmarnock physio, Hugh Allan, if they were too tight, Hugh would say, 'They'll stretch.' And if they were too big, he would say, 'They'll shrink.' I decided I would carry on buying my own boots.

By this time, finances had forced Kilmarnock to go part-time, which was a benefit to me because it meant I was getting the chance to establish myself in the first team much earlier than I would normally. I had just started to become a regular in the first team when we pulled off a great result by beating Rangers 2–1 at Rugby Park. I didn't score – Eddie Morrison got our two goals – but I played really well.

It wasn't a bad performance for the Kilmarnock team, which had a lot of youngsters playing – me, Jim Stewart, Alan Robertson, Bobby Stevenson and Ian Fleming – because a lot of the full-timers had moved on. And, after all, Rangers had won the European Cup Winners Cup a few months earlier. But doing my best to defeat the team I had secretly supported as a boy wasn't a problem for me.

When I was playing with Kilmarnock, I was a Kilmarnock fan. And it was the same with all the other teams I have played for in my career. The team I'm playing for is the team that matters most to me at that time. So I didn't have any qualms about being delighted with a victory against Rangers in only my fifth or sixth first-team game.

I just lived for a Saturday when I could leave the school uniform and the classroom behind and become a professional footballer in the Kilmarnock first team. I loved it. The excitement of going to the ground, being in the dressing room, running on to the park and playing in front of thousands of fans was fantastic. The strange thing was that I found it easier playing in the first team than I did in the reserves. I'm not sure why that was. Maybe the atmosphere or playing with and against better players made me raise my game. I couldn't wait to get out there. I was aware of the crowd cheering if I beat a few players and went on a run and that gave me a real buzz.

I had been scoring regularly in the reserves and, although my performances were good, I hadn't hit the back of the net for the first team after about eight or nine games, but I was still being picked. I had always fancied myself as being able to score goals from midfield and, now and again, I would wonder if my lack of goals would see me out of the starting line-up. When my first goal did eventually come, it gave me a fantastic feeling of elation and it wasn't a bad goal, even if I say so myself. We were playing Airdrie, at Rugby Park, and I was running up the park towards their penalty box when the ball was crossed in from the right flank. I controlled it with my left foot and edged the ball away from the defender who was marking me. I had made just enough space for myself to tee up a shot and I let fly with my right foot. The ball soared into the top corner of the net and off I went celebrating my first goal for the big team.

The worst thing for me during that period was having to go to school. I wasn't enjoying school much at that stage and it seemed like it was just a nuisance having to go back to the classroom when I thought that I was gaining nothing from being there as I was doing what I had always wanted to do – playing football.

Because Kilmarnock had gone part-time, I was sure I would eventually move on from Kilmarnock to a bigger team and achieve the next stage of my ambitions to play full-time football. Walter McCrae was very much an old-style manager who picked the team and gave out the state-of-the-nation speeches before a match and at half-time. And some of Walter's traits obviously stemmed from his army background. He could be quite gruff and a bit like a sergeant major. When he had anything to say, he sort of barked at you and, as a young lad, I did what I was told. He certainly had more authority over me than most of the schoolteachers I had come across.

It would be fair to say that perhaps Walter was sometimes on a different plane to some of his players. During one of his pre-match team talks, when we were about to play Aberdeen at Pittodrie, Walter warned us we would have to be aware of counter-attacks by the opposition. He said, 'We will have to be careful today. We will have to raid judiciously.' It wasn't exactly the language of the average footballer and, after he left the dressing room, there were more than just a few blank looks and questions of 'What the f*** was he talking about?' But that was Walter for you.

I also began to realise that I wasn't really getting proper coaching on tactics, positional play and the technical skills needed to improve while I was at Rugby Park. But at least the physical side of my game was coming on leaps and bounds because of the hard training regime and I was beginning to fill out with the increased muscle weight I was gaining.

I might have been a regular in the Kilmarnock first team but that didn't stop me kicking a ball around the street or out my back door at night in my spare time. I was determined to hone my skills and, if I wasn't getting the chance to do that at training in Kilmarnock, I would head down to the lock-ups near my house. There, I would kick the ball off a wall and practise controlling it with both feet. Nobody ever said anything to me about it as they were used to me kicking a ball around these lock-ups – I had been doing it for years.

I would also spend hours in our back garden playing keepie-up. But I would make it more difficult and test myself by making sure I stayed on the same small concrete slab all the time while I kept the ball in the air for up to 400 times. I didn't dare tell my team mates that I was doing this practice at home but I was desperate to improve myself as a footballer.

My first season in the Kilmarnock first team ended in disappointment as we were relegated to the Second Division. You could say that I had an up-and-down career with Kilmarnock. In my five full seasons at the club we were either being relegated from the First Division or promoted back up again. But I was still enjoying being at Rugby Park and, like most football clubs, there was always a lot of banter going on in the dressing room. One of the biggest jokers was midfielder Jim McSherry who got his comeuppance one day when some of the players drove his car through the double doors of the main entrance and into reception. The club wasn't too happy but we all thought it was a great laugh. My mum would have been appalled if she had known the language and the kind of stories her wee boy was hearing in the dressing room.

At the start of the next season, with Kilmarnock playing in the Second Division, Walter McCrae was sacked as manager and Davie Sneddon took over as caretaker manager for one game. We were playing St Johnstone and Davie said he wanted to play me on the left wing as he thought their fullback was a bit slow and I could run him ragged down the left flank. I played well in that game but, unknown to me, the manager-in-waiting, Willie Fernie, was sitting in the stand that day watching my performance out on the wing.

When Willie took over he played me out wide and, after a few weeks, I went to see him. I told him left wing wasn't my best position. 'That's where I want you to play,' he said.

'But I don't want to play there,' I replied.

'Doesn't matter what you want – that's where you're playing,' was how the conversation finished.

So, that was me stuck out on the left wing whether I liked it or not. Willie's tactics talk to me was, 'Stay out wide on the touchline – I want to see chalk on your boots.' I would try to explain that I could vary my game and cut inside and try a shot at goal but it was all to no avail.

I even got a row for coming inside and scoring during a game. We were playing Alloa away from home and won 1–0. At one point in the match, instead of heading for the by-line as usual, I turned with the ball to the inside of the fullback, made a run into their box and scored with a decent shot.

At the next training session on the Tuesday night, Willie turned to me and said, 'About your goal on Saturday . . .'

I was thinking, 'At last, a compliment from the boss. He's going to say it was a great goal.'

But I was stunned when he said, 'I don't want you doing that.'

'You don't want me doing what?' I asked.

'I don't want you coming off the touchline.'

'You mean you don't want me running in and scoring the winning goal like I did on Saturday?'

'No, I don't.'

'Surely, if I see an opening, I take it?'

'No, that's not your job. You stay wide.'

By this time, I was well up for the debate. 'That might be someone else's job but they weren't doing it on Saturday so I decided to do it and won the game for us,' I countered.

But, as usual, the manager had the final word and he told me to stay on the wing and that was the end of it.

It appeared to me that Willie had something against me although I was only ever dropped once from the team and was back in the following week after we were defeated in that game. Even my team mates would say that Willie didn't like me but I could never work out why. I was playing well for him week in, week out.

It was only years later that Hugh Allan told me that Willie took a dislike to me because when he arrived at the club everybody, from the directors down, kept telling him how good our goalkeeper, Jim Stewart, and I were. For some reason, he took umbrage to that and Willie gave both Jim and me a hard time.

By the time Willie Fernie had taken over at the start of the 1973–74 season, I had left school with another two Highers – a B in Physics and a C in Maths – as well as a B for Sixth Year Studies History. I had then enrolled at the Glasgow College of Technology to do Business Studies. But, even at that age of eighteen, my mother was still trying to influence my life. I applied for the two-year HND course in Business Studies because I expected to be playing full-time football in the not-too distant future. During the summer break, I had got a job at the Vibroplant plant hire company in Irvine, cleaning the machines. One night I got home and my mother informed me, 'I've seen an advert in the paper for a Business Studies degree course at Glasgow College of Technology.'

'What about it?' I said.

'I've got you on it. They're looking for people with four Highers and you've got four Highers so I've got you on the course.'

'But I've already applied for the HND course,' I protested.

'It's OK,' she said. 'I've spoken to their office staff and it's all been changed over. You start your degree course in September.'

So, thanks to my mother, I was on the four-year degree course. I decided just to go along with it but all the time thinking there was no way I was going to finish the course because, sooner rather than later, I would get a transfer from Kilmarnock to a bigger club and full-time football.

In my second year on the course, the guys in my class decided to enter a team in the college's annual five-a-side football tournament and they asked me if I would play for them. I told them that I would get into big trouble with Kilmarnock for playing but they said it wasn't a big deal – just a bit of a kick-about and nobody would find out – so I agreed.

In the first few rounds, I wasn't playing full-out but was doing just enough to make sure we got through. Before the quarter-finals were to be played I was in one of the toilet cubicles and I overheard some other students who had come in discussing the games.

'We've got Business Studies in the next round and they've got that guy Gordon Smith playing for them,' I heard one say.

'Don't worry about it,' another one replied. 'I've seen him playing in the earlier games and he's not very good.'

I was raging and it was a different Gordon Smith they saw in the next games. I scored four goals in the quarter-finals, three in the semi-finals and three in the final which we won.

When I was the tender age of nineteen, I also met my future wife, Marlene McVie. I had always been quite shy with girls and felt a lot more comfortable if they made the running and spoke to me first. I had never had a steady girlfriend until I met Marlene. But she would have to turn detective before becoming my one and only girlfriend as well as my wife a few years later.

I would go to plenty of pubs and discos with lads like my team mate George Maxwell and that's who was with me when we walked into the Kiwi Lodge, between Kilmarnock and

Glasgow, one Saturday night after we had lost to Hibs in the Scottish Cup.

There had been a feature on me in the *Daily Record* that morning and, as I walked up to the bar, I noticed a rather attractive girl standing there with a friend. As I passed her, Marlene turned to me and said, 'Was your picture not in the *Kilmarnock Standard* this week?'

'It might have been,' I replied. 'But it was in the *Daily Record* this morning – maybe that's where you've seen it.'

Later on that night, our paths crossed again and I somehow managed to get her phone number. I've no doubt Marlene must have offered it to me because I would have been too shy to ask for it. I called Marlene a week later, asking her to come with me to a function, but she couldn't make it that night. I thought that was that and I'd never see her again.

But unknown to me, Marlene was kicking herself for not getting my phone number and she had started to go places where she thought I would be. Then she got the phone book out and started calling all the Smiths living in Stevenston. Marlene phoned twelve Smiths before finding one of my relatives who told her where I stayed. But, even then, when she called to ask me out to a function, I couldn't make it that particular night so Cupid's arrow missed again.

A fortnight later, after training one night, as I was walking through Kilmarnock, I turned a corner and literally bumped into Marlene. There's no doubt Marlene was a very pretty girl and I wasn't going to pass up another chance to ask her for a date and she agreed to come out with me the following Saturday night. Marlene obviously knew I was a footballer and I always give her stick by saying she recognised my potential but got the shock of her life when she discovered she was earning more money than me. I'm glad to say we've been together ever since.

I was going along from one season to the next with Kilmarnock and, disappointingly, no big team wanted to sign me – or so I thought. Another disappointment was that I hadn't been involved in the full international scene. I was becoming more and more frustrated at the lack of progress in my football career and I began to wonder if I'd ever go full-time. Little did I know there was a host of big clubs showing an interest in me but it appears that Kilmarnock kept knocking them back.

In my first year at Kilmarnock, there had been some talk in the papers about Liverpool being interested in signing me but nothing came of it. Years later, I met up with John Joyce – one of the lads who had played for St Joseph's against me in the Ayrshire Schools Cup final. He had signed with Liverpool and had come back to Scotland to play with Motherwell. He told me that their legendary manager Bill Shankly had asked about me and was interested in taking me to Anfield.

Only three years ago, I was at a dinner in Glasgow where former Manchester United boss Tommy Docherty was the guest speaker. During his speech, he said, 'It's nice to see Gordon Smith here tonight. I tried to sign Gordon when I was at Manchester United.' Marlene was there that night and she looked at me. I just shrugged my shoulders. After the dinner, I asked Tommy if he really did try to sign me and he said he did but Kilmarnock had told him I wasn't for sale.

While I was still only twenty and with Kilmarnock, I became friendly with a footballer called Harry Kirk whose dad, Joe, was a scout in Scotland for Sheffield United. I was talking to Joe one day and he said he knew of some clubs who were interested in signing me. He told me Sheffield couldn't afford to buy me but he had heard Everton were in for me. I knew nothing about this and, while I was in Joe's house, I called the Everton scout and he confirmed they had a bid in for me but he knew that Rangers had as well. Nothing came of this and I went to see Willie Fernie and asked if there had been any bids for me. He said he didn't know anything about other clubs trying to sign me.

I walked out the room without saying another word because there was nothing I could do about it. In those days, when you signed for a club, they held your registration and you could only leave when they wanted you to leave.

On another occasion, there was a story in the papers saying that Newcastle were coming to watch me play. I asked Willie Fernie about this and he confirmed that they were sending somebody to see me. During the game, I played quite well and scored a goal. On the Tuesday night at training, I asked Willie if anything was happening on the Newcastle front and he said they weren't interested.

A few months later, Joe Harvey, the Newcastle chief executive, was being interviewed for an article about spiralling transfer fees and the example he gave to show that prices were getting out of hand was that Newcastle had offered Kilmarnock £80,000 for Gordon Smith and the bid had been rejected. I was told by Kilmarnock that there was no interest from Newcastle and, a few months later, their chief executive was saying they had offered £80,000 for me.

The day I eventually signed for Rangers, Jock Wallace said to me, 'Welcome to the club – it's taken a while.'

I asked what he meant and he said, 'I've been trying to sign you twice a year for four years.' He had seen me in the Scotland Under-18 trial at St Mirren Park and he had wanted me in his team since then.

It was getting even more ridiculous the more managers I spoke to. After I signed for Rangers we played Aberdeen and I scored a hat-trick in a 6–1 win. After the game, Aberdeen's manager, Celtic legend Billy McNeill, pulled me aside and said, 'You did well. Well played.' I thought that was really good of him to say that, especially as his team had taken such a heavy defeat. He then asked me why I had signed for Rangers and not Aberdeen. I told him I had no idea Aberdeen were in for me.

'I thought you knew we had asked for first refusal if Kilmarnock were selling you,' he replied. And, to put the icing on the transfers-that-never-were cake, Billy revealed that Celtic had been in for me as well.

So, in all my years at Kilmarnock since I was a seventeen-year-old, there appears to have been clubs like Manchester United, Liverpool, Newcastle, Sheffield United, Everton, Aberdeen, Rangers and Celtic all showing an interest in signing me and I never knew a thing about it. Who knows how my career would have gone if I had been sold to any of these clubs while I was still a teenager?

I was eventually sold to Rangers at the beginning of the second week of the new season in August 1977. And my move only came a week after I had told Willie Fernie that I had got my Business Studies degree, had started a new job and that was going to be my priority from now on. Kilmarnock was going to have to take second place, I told him. But, a week later – literally out of the blue – the call came that would at last see me playing for one of the country's biggest clubs. But before we head up the A77 to Glasgow, there's one lasting memory I have playing with Kilmarnock.

Now, I've played all over the Continent in big European matches. I scored the winning goal for Rangers against Italian giants Juventus and I scored the goal that won the League Cup for Rangers but my best-ever goal was against *Cowdenbeath*! Yes, it came at Central Park in my second season playing for Kilmarnock's first team. We won a free kick on the halfway line and George Maxwell touched the ball to me. I started on a mazy run, beating players more than once as they tried to get the ball off me – and probably dribbling round my own team mates as well. I have no idea how many players I dribbled round until I got into their box and slotted the ball home. It was definitely not the most high-profile goal I've ever scored but it was the only one where the opposition players applauded me as I ran back to my own half. The Cowdenbeath players were clapping and saying, 'That was some goal.' I've played in some really big games but being applauded by the opposition after you've scored against them does it for me every time.

71

5

TREBLES ALL ROUND

The entire Rangers squad are crowded round the mouth of the Ibrox tunnel, jostling for a better view across the park. On the other side of the halfway line, two of us are crouched in the traditional runner's starting position for the big race. I'm on the outside lane of the running track and our giant of a goalkeeper, Peter McCloy, is on the inside.

We rock back and forward like the real athletes do, preparing ourselves for that burst of speed at the start to get an edge on each other. After all, there's a lot of money riding on this contest. Finally the shout 'Go!' from the rest of the players echoes round the empty stadium and we're off. We pound down the track at the far side of the stadium, matching each other stride for stride round the first bend. We're still neck and neck behind the goals and I'm feeling good – plenty left in me for the final push to the winning line. We come to the final bend before the home straight in front of the main stand and that's when I make my move.

My legs are going up and down like pistons as faster, longer strides take me away from Peter yard by yard. By the time I cross the finishing line, I'm 20 yards ahead and the current Rangers running champ had just lost his crown.

There are groans from all the players – except one, of course. Winger Davie Cooper dives on top of me, hugging and kissing me as if I'd just scored the winning goal in the European Cup final.

That was the rather bizarre start to my second week as a Rangers player but one which would see me get a place in the starting line-up the following Saturday.

It all began with a routine training session – running round the track at Ibrox with the players in groups. The morning's efforts had ended and I was in the dressing room getting my gear off, ready to go into the showers. Davie Cooper had been in my group and I could hear him telling the assembled players in a loud voice, 'Don't get in his group for running,' as he pointed at me, 'he's an unbelievable runner, by the way. Believe me, you don't want to be in his group for running.'

A few of the other players were casting doubt on Coop's observations on my running power. 'Aye but he'd never beat big Peter. He's the real good runner in here.'

Coop hit back, 'I'm telling you he'd beat Peter and I'd put money on him to do that.'

Within seconds, Coop was going round the dressing room taking bets off people on who would turn out to be the better runner. I could hear guys saying 'I'll have £20 on Peter' and 'Put me down for a tenner on McCloy' and so on. This was only my second week at Rangers so I was keeping well out of the arguing and, more importantly, the betting. I stepped into the shower and was just about to get lathered up when a crowd appeared at the entrance telling me, 'Right, get out of there, get dried and get back into your training gear – we've got a race on.'

I came out of the shower and got my training gear back on as Coop told me, 'You're going to race big Peter 200 yards – halfway round the track. And I've got about £150 worth of bets that you'll win.'

As Peter McCloy and I walked across the pitch to the far side to start our race, I was already thinking about getting a psychological advantage over the big man. Peter said, 'We'll toss a coin to see who gets the inside track.' Whoever was on the inside lane would have had an advantage because they would have slightly less distance to run on the bends. But I said, 'You have the inside.'

Peter looked puzzled and said, 'You sure you don't want to toss for it?'

'No,' I assured him. 'You have the inside.'

So, despite the big man's inside track advantage, I still won the race and Coop was delighted with his winnings, although I never made a penny out of it as I hadn't put a bet on myself. I wasn't sure if I would win the race because Peter McCloy had a reputation as a good athlete. They used to call him Big Juantorena after the famous Cuban runner of the time, Alberto Juantorena.

After getting showered for a second time and getting dressed, I was walking out the main door at Ibrox when I heard the gruff tones of our manager, Jock Wallace coming from the top of the famous marble staircase. 'Smithy,' he shouted, 'my office.'

I walked up the stairs and stood just inside his door wondering what kind of trouble I was in. 'Sit down,' ordered Jock. 'How come you didn't tell me you could run like that when I signed you last week?'

'You never asked,' was the only thing I could think of in reply.

'I saw your race, there,' said Jock. 'That was impressive. You're playing on Saturday. You're in the starting line-up.'

As you can imagine, I was a more than just a little surprised at what I was hearing. I had been dragged out the shower to run a race so one of my team mates could win £150 betting on me to win and now, because of that race, I was being handed my first start with Rangers in the next game.

A week earlier I had taken the phone call which turned my world around completely and, like many things in life, it came when I least expected it to.

It was in August 1977, on the Monday following the first game of the season after Kilmarnock had been relegated – again – and I had all but given up hope of getting signed by a big club. I had got my Business Studies degree that summer and had started a job developing the marketing strategy for a company called Edward McNeil Ltd, which sold branded plastic bags to shops and businesses. Their business was along Paisley Road, not far from Ibrox, and I was earning £60 a week on top of the £26 a week wages from Kilmarnock as a part-time player.

I was sitting in the office poring over the Yellow Pages, looking for leads for our sales people and redefining their territories. The phone rang and the switchboard girl said, 'A Mr Willie Fernie wants to talk to you.'

I had no idea why Willie would be phoning me at my work but I took the call and Willie said, 'It's the boss here. Just to let you know we've sold you to Rangers and you've to go to Ibrox right away and meet Jock Wallace.'

'Right now?'

'Yes, right now. I'm coming up to Ibrox and I'll meet you there before we go in.'

I had played for Kilmarnock against Rangers in a pre-season friendly and had put in a good performance – although we lost 2–1. On the first day of the competitive season, Kilmarnock had drawn 1–1 with Morton and Rangers had lost 3–1 to Aberdeen. There had been a small story in the papers on the Monday about Rangers being interested in signing me but I more or less ignored it and thought to myself that I'd heard it all before.

I went to see my boss at Edward McNeil's and told him I would need to disappear for a couple of hours as I was going along the road to Ibrox to sign for Rangers. That was fine and off I went along Paisley Road West, my heart pumping with excitement at the thought of signing for a big club like Rangers – at last, something good was happening for me on the football front.

I sat in the foyer at Ibrox waiting for Willie Fernie to arrive and, when he did, we climbed the stairs to Jock Wallace's office. We sat down and Jock started to go through the contract and the terms Rangers were offering me. I was to get a signing-on fee of £2000 and wages of £90 during the close season and £100 a week when we were playing. It was some jump from getting £26 a week as a part-timer at Kilmarnock and I was about to say, 'Yes, that's great, Mr Wallace – where do I sign?' when Willie Fernie asked if he could have a word with me in private.

Jock Wallace left the room and what Willie said next came as a real shock. 'We'll give you £3000 as well,' he told me. I couldn't believe it – after all the run-ins with the board that the Kilmarnock players had about the win bonuses not being enough. They were going to give me £3000 out of the £65,000 transfer fee and I thought that was very good of them. That made a total of £5000 just for signing on – the most money I had ever had in my life. When Jock came back in, I told him everything was fine with the two-year contract and I signed on the dotted line.

As we shook hands, Jock Wallace said, 'That's taken a while – I've been trying to sign you since you were eighteen. I saw you playing for the Scottish Youth team.' I turned to look at Willie Fernie and gave him my best 'Oh, is that true? – I never knew that' look but he never said a word.

It was at that point that I asked Jock what position he was going to play me in. 'You've just signed Davie Cooper who's a left winger and you've already got Tommy McLean and Bobby McKean who play wide on the right. These are the positions I play.'

'I'm not going to play you there,' said Jock. 'I see you as a midfield player that can score goals. You'll get goals playing for Rangers. I'm building a team here and you're the last piece of the jigsaw.'

Jock then told me that, as I'd been a part-time player, I wouldn't be in the team until I had proved that my fitness was as good as the rest of the squad. But then he made an already brilliant day even better by telling me I'd be on the bench for the European Cup Winners Cup game against Young Boys of Berne at Ibrox two days later.

After leaving Ibrox, I headed back to Edward McNeil's and to say I was on cloud nine wouldn't describe how high I felt. It was fantastic and I was in another world – it was a dream come true.

There were no such things as mobile phones in those days and I had to wait until I got back to work before I could phone my mum at home and tell her about signing for Rangers. She was delighted.

Shortly after that, I went in to see Joe Kingsley and his son Sam, who ran the company. I told them I was going full-time with Rangers but I would like to stay on with them in some capacity and work in the afternoons after training. I know this sounds daft but I had been given a new Datsun 120Y company car that I liked and I was keen to hang on to it. We negotiated a part-time work package with a reduction in wages.

My first day at Ibrox got off to rather a strange start when I met the team captain John Greig. I was walking into the ground when I met Greigy and Sandy Jardine at the entrance. Both of them shook my hand but Greigy's first words to me were, 'I don't know why we've signed you. We've got Davie Cooper and he plays on the left wing.'

I told him that I wasn't going to be playing on the wing and he just shrugged his shoulders and walked through the front doors. Sandy Jardine was a bit more hospitable and said, 'Welcome to the club.' I found it quite strange that the captain of Rangers would say that to me as I was about to join him at the club on my first day. As far as I knew, I'd had never done anything to get on the wrong side of Greigy. I think it was just his way. He was top man at Rangers – a legend. He could just about do and say anything he liked at Ibrox. Maybe he really was simply puzzled that Rangers had just signed Davie Cooper to play on the left wing that summer and here was I – another left winger as far as he knew – being signed as well.

His comment didn't really have a negative affect on me. I was so elated about joining Rangers, I just let it wash over me. All the other players were great with me and I was now a team mate of some of the most successful Rangers players of that era – Peter McCloy, Tommy McLean, Tom Forsyth, Derek Johnstone, Colin Jackson, Derek Parlane and Alex McDonald. The first day's training was quite low-key, a warm-up and a game of five-a-sides – nothing too strenuous since there was a European tie the following night. Little did the rest of the players know that, as soon as training was over, I was going to Edward McNeil's to put in an afternoon's work.

The following night, Jock Wallace was as good as his word and I was on the bench against Young Boys of Berne. I came on with twenty minutes to go but didn't really do anything spectacular although we won 1–0. I couldn't really show what I could do because they were sitting in for a tight result and keeping plenty of men behind the ball. We had lots of possession in midfield but there was no space to attack.

I was on the bench again on the Saturday for the game against Hibs, at Ibrox. I came on in the second half but couldn't do anything to stop us getting beaten 2–0. That was two league defeats in a row – a rather inauspicious start to the season 1977–78.

Then came that fateful race around the track with Peter McCloy which Jock Wallace witnessed from high up in the main stand. He was impressed by my running power and I was in the starting eleven against Partick Thistle at Firhill the following Saturday. And that's how I got my starting debut with Rangers, courtesy of the gambling-mad Davie Cooper.

I was playing in the centre of midfield against Thistle and, in the first half, I was brought down in the box by my former Kilmarnock team mate Ronnie Sheed and we went in at half-time 1–0 up after the resulting penalty was converted. In the second half, I scored two goals and we ended up comfortable 4–0 winners. That was me, up and running – two goals in my starting debut and there was more to come.

I was kept in the team for the away tie in Berne the following Wednesday and we were getting beaten 2–1 until I scored to equalise and put us through to the next round.

As the season went on I became very friendly with Davie Cooper – I was his best pal after he made all that money out of me – and fellow midfielder, Bobby Russell. The three of us would regularly go to lunch in a small restaurant called the Farmhouse Grill, in West George Street, Glasgow. It was the last place you would think of finding footballers having their lunch. I used to go there when I was a student – but we had lunch in there several times a week.

Davie Cooper was the most talented player I ever played with and one of the nicest. He was one of the few players I'd known who would praise your performance. He would say, 'You were brilliant today. See that goal you scored? What a goal!' Normally players are very cool about praising each other, but Coop was different. He would rave about other players' performances and he wasn't slow to tell them.

Bobby Russell was another lovely guy. He came to Rangers from Shettleston Juniors, which was amazing. But he was a bit naive about the ways of the professional football world, to say the least. The week after the Partick game, we were travelling to East End Park to play Dunfermline and were all on the team bus driving through to Fife. Bobby had taken his shoes off as he stretched his legs. Big mistake. First lesson – never take your shoes off among a crowd of footballers because they won't be in your possession for much longer. Sure enough, his shoes disappeared.

We were about five minutes from Dunfermline and Bobby decided he'd put his feet up on the table in front of him. Second mistake. Colin Jackson and Tom Forsyth grabbed his ankles, whipped his socks off and threw them out the skylight window. We pulled up outside East End Park and, as we all got off the bus and headed on to the park to have a look at the pitch, Bobby was searching under every seat and in every overhead locker for his missing shoes. When we got back to the dressing room, Jock was about to start his team talk when he noticed Bobby was missing. 'Where's Russell?' he asked.

'Don't know where he's got to, boss,' someone said. 'Last time I saw him, he was on the bus.'

At that, the door opened and in came a sheepish-looking Bobby Russell wearing his collar and tie and good suit but no shoes or socks. He'd walked all the way from the bus across the road and pavement, past scores of fans, in his bare feet. Of course, his shoes were now lying on the floor in front of the place where he was to get changed.

AND SMITH *DID* SCORE

'What are you like?' asked Jock.

'Somebody's stolen my shoes and socks,' protested Bobby.

Amidst the hoots of laughter, you could just about hear Jock say, 'You've got a lot to learn, so you have.'

Poor Bobby even failed his driving test because of what some of the senior players had told him. They claimed that a lot of the instructions the examiner gave you were there to trick you. 'When the examiner tells you to do something, you're really meant to do the opposite,' they told Bobby. Sure enough, the examiner told Bobby to take the next turning on the left and Bobby took the next on the right because the boys had told him to do the opposite of what the examiner said. Some of the stuff they got up to with Bobby was really funny. He was a lovely lad, but as Jock said, he had a lot to learn.

As the season went on, I was going great guns – never out of the team and scoring regularly. I notched up sixteen goals in my first seventeen games for Rangers and that included two goals in my first Old Firm game.

That game was at Ibrox and we were down 2–0 at half-time. And as we trooped, heads down, into the dressing room I was expecting we would get a right good bollocking from Jock Wallace. But I was shocked when the bawling and shouting I had expected never materialised. Instead Jock was telling us how well we were playing. 'You've been the better team in the first half,' he said to the hushed dressing room. 'You've played better football, you've passed the ball better and you've created the better chances. All we've done wrong is lose two stupid goals – I can't believe we're losing the game. If you keep playing the way you're playing in the second half, your fitness will come through and we'll win this game.'

And that's exactly what we did. I got the first goal, Derek Johnstone got the second and I scored the third and winning goal. A superb start to my Old Firm career.

That was the first Old firm game I had been at, never mind taken part in, and before the kick-off we were warming up in the area underneath the main stand at Ibrox. In those days, you didn't go out on to the park to warm up. As I was going through my stretching exercises the Rangers trainer, Tommy Craig, came up to me and asked, 'Have you been to an Old Firm game before?'

I replied, 'Actually, I'm scared to admit this but I haven't.'

'Then go down to the end of the tunnel a few minutes before we're due to go out and soak up the atmosphere.'

That's what I did and I let the noise, the excitement and the atmosphere soak right through me. What a fantastic feeling. You couldn't get a better stage to perform on as a footballer. After a few minutes I couldn't wait to get out there.

I learned another valuable lesson from Jock Wallace a few games after our Old Firm victory when we were playing St Mirren at Love Street. I had been on a good scoring run and playing well but, during his half-time team talk, I felt the full force of his wrath. We were 1–0 down at half-time but I thought I had put in a good performance. Jock was telling everyone they would have to do better, that the performance wasn't up to his usual high standards.

Before I knew what was happening Jock grabbed the front of my shirt and pulled me up out of my seat. His face was only inches from mine and he said, 'By the way, when I'm talking about how we're not doing well, I'm talking to everybody in this dressing room and that includes you.' At that he put me back down.

He had obviously seen something in my face that told him I didn't think he was referring to me when he was talking about having to buck up our ideas. It was a reminder to me that we do well as a team and we do badly as a team. When I look back I think it was a great leap up the learning curve for me as I then realised it was about everybody and not individuals. I might be thinking I'm doing well but, at all times, it's about the team doing well, not an individual. When Jock had a yard or two of my shirt cloth in his giant fist, I wonder if he knew he was teaching me a lesson for life.

This idea of the team being the be-all and end-all of everything meant that I changed the way I played when I was with Rangers. Undoubtedly, the Kilmarnock fans saw the best of my skills as a dribbler and running with the ball. With Rangers, my role was different as Jock Wallace had us playing a 4–5–1 formation with two wingers – Tommy McLean and Davie Cooper. I was to make runs from midfield, supporting the striker by running into space to take a pass from the wing or from the centre forward – normally Derek Johnstone – after he had held the ball up or flicked it on.

In another wonderful piece of man management, Jock Wallace called me up to his office when I was in the middle of my scoring run. 'You're playing well,' he said. 'I just want you to know I'm happy with your performances. It's not just the goals – the goals are fantastic – but your performances are what matter and your work rate is fantastic.'

He continued, 'If you keep working as hard as you have been, you'll stay in the team because – you know something? – the goals will dry up. That happens to everybody. You can't keep scoring at this rate. I don't want you to think that, when the goals dry up, you are going out the team because it isn't about that. It's about how much work you do. If you keep working at that level, then you'll stay in the team.'

A lot of people don't give Jock Wallace credit for being clever like that. He was preparing me for the future and his words of wisdom were a great way to keep a player's confidence up and make him work hard at the same time.

Jock was also a great one for getting the players to go to Rangers supporters' club functions. Every other Saturday, you would be a guest at some function or other. One night, I was at a supporters' club function in Kirkcaldy and, as was the custom on these occasions, the crowd asked the player who was the guest for the evening to go up on stage and give everyone a song.

Sure enough, the fans were pestering me to get on the stage, assuring me that the band hired to provide the music for the dancing were ready and willing to accompany me in my chosen song. The band that night were called Flash Gordon and, having played at Rangers supporters' nights on many occasions, they knew exactly what the fans wanted from me – a rendition of an Orange song like 'The Sash My Father Wore' or 'Derry's Walls'.

I stepped on to the stage and the lead singer and guitarist with the band, Paul Ritchie from Paisley, asked what song I was going to do and if I had any idea what key I was going to sing it in.

He did a double take when I said, "Mull of Kintyre".'

'Are you sure?' he asked.

'Yes. Paul McCartney's "Mull of Kintyre" – I know it quite well,' I assured him. 'And can you play it in the key of D?'

He turned to the rest of the band, shrugged his shoulders and said, 'He wants to do "Mull of Kintyre".'

You should have seen the look on the faces of the fans there that night when the band started the intro to the song and I grabbed the mike and started singing, 'Mull of Kintyre, oh, mist rolling in from the sea . . .'

A rousing rendition of 'The Sash' it most certainly was not. They were scratching their heads wondering what kind of player Jock Wallace was sending them who didn't know the songs they wanted to hear. I've been told that the band leader that night, Paul Ritchie, is still getting laughs telling people of the night Gordon Smith sang 'Mull of Kintyre' instead of 'The Sash'.

Of course, I was well aware of the Protestant traditions at Ibrox but I was only interested in the football side of things. When you went to these supporters' functions there were always people who wanted the players to sing party songs. But I didn't even know the words of 'The Sash'.

I'm not saying this to please Celtic fans but my love for Rangers has nothing to do with religion – it's all down to football. Jim Baxter made me a Rangers supporter because he was a fabulous player and it had nothing to do with which church he went to on a Sunday.

I was brought up on the basis that we were a Protestant family and regularly went to church but my parents were very much non-sectarian and against bigotry from both sides. Rivalry in football between fans of different teams is natural but let's keep that rivalry to football and nothing else.

I wish other people in Scotland would take that attitude because, from time to time, I have been subjected to the actions of bigoted fans who have given me abuse in the street and have even gone to the extremes of phoning the BBC to say that I should be dropped from covering Celtic matches because I am a Protestant and not just because I am an ex-Rangers player. The bigots only demean themselves, and not their chosen targets, when they do these things.

As season 1977–78 went on, we were doing well in the league and it looked like we would be there or thereabouts by the end of the season. Our first trophy that season, however, was the League Cup which had been a good competition for me. I had scored five goals before the final at Hampden, including my one and only Rangers hat-trick in the 6–1 victory over Aberdeen at Ibrox.

It was a strange run-up to the final because our winger, Bobby McKean, had died in strange circumstances and the team had to attend his funeral a few days before the game at Hampden.

Bobby was found dead in his car having been poisoned by carbon monoxide fumes from the exhaust as he had left the engine running. There was a cloud of mystery about poor Bobby's death. Some people said he had committed suicide but there was another theory that he had come home late from a night out and his wife had locked him out of the house. Bobby then went into his car in the garage, switched the engine on to keep warm and fell asleep – sadly never to wake up. It was very sad because I used to pick Bobby up quite a lot and take him into training and he had a very infectious sense of humour.

The League Cup final was an Old Firm encounter and my first final at senior level. I made the first goal with a pass to Davie Cooper in the penalty box and he lashed it into the top corner. In the second half Celtic equalised and it was still 1–1 when the full-time whistle went. On to extra time and with just two minutes to go, Alex Miller crossed the ball and wee Alex McDonald challenged the Celtic keeper, Peter Latchford, who punched the ball out. I was running in from midfield and made a diving header to score the winner. It was my first final and I'd scored the winning goal – what a great feeling!

When the final whistle went, it was pandemonium as we celebrated. Jock Wallace ran on to the park and was hugging everybody. That was when I came closest to being injured that season. Jock grabbed my face in his big rough hands so hard I was in agony – then he gave me a kiss. Strange things happen in football, I can tell you.

With the first trophy in the glass cabinet at Ibrox, our attention turned to the league race, which was between Aberdeen and ourselves. It went to the last game of the season and we had Motherwell at Ibrox and needed to win to make sure the Championship came to Ibrox. We did just that, beating Motherwell 2–0 with me getting the second goal after Colin Jackson had netted the first for us.

That was two down – one to go. And that one meant something very special to me. We were in the Scottish Cup final against Aberdeen at Hampden and it meant I had the chance to emulate my grandpa, Mattha Smith by winning a Scottish Cup medal just as he had done. I was really looking forward to that game as it meant so much to my whole family.

Aberdeen had a great team that year and were tough opponents. It wasn't a foregone conclusion that I would have that medal in my pocket after the final. But, sitting in the dressing room as we were about to get stripped for the game, a strange feeling of calm came over me. I looked at my team mates spread around the dressing room and I just knew we were going to win. I had never felt as confident of winning a game before.

We went out that day and absolutely out-played Aberdeen. We were 2–0 up until we lost a daft goal when Peter McCloy thought the ball was going over the top and he was swinging on the crossbar as the ball dropped into the net.

Up until that point, we had been cruising but, for the last five minutes, Aberdeen put a bit of pressure on us. However, we held out and I had done it – both my grandpa, Mattha Smith, and his grandson, Gordon Smith, had Scottish Cup medals. That was definitely the best feeling I had all season.

My dad was being his usual cool self. 'Well done, that was great,' he said. I was trying to tell him, 'That's us got another Scottish Cup medal in the family.' He was never one for expressing how he felt outwardly. But I've no doubt that inside he was delighted I had done it.

What a fantastic first season I'd had, going from being part-time with a newly-relegated Kilmarnock to winning the treble with Rangers.

At that time there was a great team spirit at Ibrox and that always leads to high jinks in the dressing room. Some of the jokes, pranks and wind-ups were incredible. More than once I came into the dressing room to find my clothes floating in the bath. It got to the stage where I kept a spare set of clothes in my car to change into, especially when I was going in to work at Edward McNeil's in the afternoon.

Normally no one would dare go near the bath or the showers if they were dressed because it guaranteed you would get a soaking. I've even seen guys going past the bath knowing their clothes would get water thrown all over them and sure enough they would end up soaked. But they were the ones laughing because they had put on somebody else's jacket. And more than likely it belonged to someone in the bath throwing the water.

I hadn't long signed on at Ibrox when, in September 1977, Victor the giraffe's picture was all over the papers after it had collapsed and did the splits at Marwell Zoo in Hampshire. Every day for about a week the newspapers had photographs of people trying to rescue this poor giraffe who tragically died of heart failure after five days.

I turned up for training one day and some wag had cut out the picture story from the paper and pinned it to the notice board. In the newspaper headline the name Victor was scored out and replaced with the name Peter – referring to big Peter McCloy who was six-feet-four-inches tall. It was just a bit of gentle ribbing about how tall he was and that he was just like Victor the giraffe but, rather that see it as a joke, Peter took exception to what was on the notice board.

Peter suspected Sandy Jardine was behind the newspaper cutting and he decided he would get his revenge. Peter went into the boot room where there were always sets of boxing gloves lying around for the boys to use to punch a speed ball. He put on one pair of boxing gloves and handed the other pair to Sandy.

'Put these on,' Peter told Sandy.

'No thanks,' replied Sandy.

'Put these boxing gloves on,' insisted Peter. When Sandy refused a second time Peter walloped him in the face.

'Put them on,' Peter told Sandy for a third time. And when Sandy said no again, Peter gave him another right hook.

I was victim to a prank which left me walking around Glasgow city centre with a rather rude message on my shoes. I had come into Ibrox wearing a pair of trendy beige-coloured canvas shoes. After training, I was getting dressed and noticed that someone had written all over both shoes in thick ink – 'Smith's a poof'. I didn't have a spare pair of shoes with me so I had to go into town wearing the shoes. I could see people looking at my feet and wondering if I was trying to announce something. No matter how hard I scrubbed them the ink wouldn't come off so they ended up in the bin.

There was always a lot of banter going on and players giving each other stick. Quiet guys like Davie Cooper and Bobby Russell found it hard to take until they adjusted and started to fire back the barbed comments. I had been in and around a football dressing room since I was fourteen so I knew what to expect and how to look after myself when it came to verbal volleys – but you had to be quick.

I was still a relative newcomer to Ibrox when Peter McCloy said in front of everybody, 'Call yourself a midfield player? Tell you what, Smithy. If I had been a midfield player I would have had fifty caps for Scotland by now.'

Everyone was looking at me to see how I was going to react so I fired back, 'Peter, if you had been a goalkeeper you would have fifty caps for Scotland.' Everyone laughed and that was the way you had to handle it. The more you were able to give as good as you got, the less people were likely to have a go at you.

One incident that happened before I came to Ibrox was legendary. Rangers centre half Ronnie McKinnon took to wearing those Scholl clog-like shoes with no backs to them. He would place them on the floor in front of his place and, after he was dressed, he would step into them, stand up and walk away. One day, the dressing room pranksters decided to nail the shoes to the wooden floor on the exact spot Ronnie had left them. Sure enough, the usual routine – Ronnie got dressed, slipped his feet into his shoes, stood up to walk out the door and fell flat on his face. Apparently, the players were still laughing an hour later as Ronnie had to try for ages to get his shoes free because the nails were so long.

Managers, while maybe tut-tutting at such antics, recognise that this kind of thing is part and parcel of a good team spirit. It's better that players are getting up to nonsense like this together than if they are in cliques and not talking to each other.

I don't know why but, when I was at Rangers, everyone liked to do things with water – whether it was shoving you into the bath fully-clothed or throwing water over you. But, when I think back to an escapade involving Derek Parlane and me, it makes me shudder to think what might have happened if it had all gone wrong.

We were room mates for an away trip to Valencia and in those days the players never flew home the same night as the game – we stayed in a hotel and flew back the next morning. After every European tie, you couldn't sleep because your mind and your body were still very active. Most of the guys would have a few beers and that would help them relax and eventually get some sleep.

I was still teetotal at the time and both Derek and I were still buzzing with the adrenaline from playing. It was late at night and we couldn't sleep, so we decided to have a bit of fun. Our room was on the twelfth floor of the hotel and we decided we would jump the six-foot gap from balcony to balcony to see who was staying in the rooms on the same floor as us. It was a crazy stunt because we were more than 100 feet off the ground and we had to climb over the balcony railing and on to a ledge and then jump across to the next ledge grabbing on to the next balcony's railing.

We did this four or five times until we found a room that had someone in it. It turned out to be three Scottish sports journalists fast asleep. One of them was lying on top of the bedclothes with his hands behind his head snoring away. Derek whispered to me, 'Fancy getting some water and throwing it over him?'

So we did our Spider-Man impersonations, jumping from balcony to balcony back to our room, filled a waste bin with water and, this time passing the bucket of water to each other between the balconies, made our way to where the press guys were sleeping.

When we got to their room, I held the curtain back and Derek threw the bucket of water over the guy who was lying on top of the bedclothes. It was like a big lump of water flying through the air and I can still see it smacking down on top of the sleeping journalist. Before anyone could react to the guy's gasps and shouts, we were out of the room and leaping from balcony to balcony to safety.

In hindsight, it was a crazy thing to do. One slip and we would have fallen to certain death on the ground below.

The press guys made an official complaint to Rangers about the incident and an investigation was launched to find the culprits. All the players were called to a meeting and asked who was responsible but we didn't dare own up. We were told that, if the journalist who was soaked found out who had done it, they would finish their football career through the media. Derek and I hadn't even told the other players we were responsible and it was a long time before we admitted it was us.

But the most outrageous prank I ever witnessed was played on the Rangers coach Joe Mason. We were due to play a European tie and the team were staying in a hotel in Largs before the game. At night, some of the players got hold of the key to Joe's room and they took his suit out the wardrobe – still on its hanger – and climbed on to the hotel roof. Then they tied the suit on to the TV aerial.

The next morning, Joe noticed his suit had disappeared and when he got on the bus to go to the training session he was pleading, 'C'mon boys – where's the suit?' Nobody said a word until we were driving down the road and Colin Jackson – I'm sure he was involved in the escapade – pointed out the bus window at the hotel roof. And there was Joe's suit blowing in the wind like a flag from the TV aerial high above the ground.

Joe couldn't believe it and he told us that someone would have to go back up on to the roof and get his suit down. 'OK, OK, calm down, Joe,' we told him. 'We'll get your suit after training.' But, by the time we got back to the hotel, the rain was pouring down and there was a gale blowing, so no one was going to volunteer to climb on to the roof.

The next day, we were checking out of the hotel and still no one was willing to go up on the roof and get the suit because of the bad weather – and neither would Joe for that matter. As we left Largs, we all looked out of the back window of the bus and waved a fond farewell to Joe's suit – still billowing away nicely.

The games children play . . .

6

LIKE A DEATH IN THE FAMILY

Somewhere in the distance I could feel someone shaking me and saying, 'Gordon! Wake up. You'll have to wake up.' I wasn't sure if it was a dream or if someone really was trying to wake me from my slumbers. I turned over and pulled a pillow over my head but still the voice wouldn't go away. 'Wake up, Gordon. Wake up.'

I sat up on my bed and blinked a few times before rubbing my eyes. 'What is it, Mum?' I asked as I began to focus on my mother as she stood at the side of my bed.

'There's bad news,' she said in a grave voice. 'Jock Wallace has resigned as the Rangers manager.'

If I wasn't fully awake by then, that piece of news jolted me right into full consciousness. I couldn't believe it. This was devastating news. My most successful season ever had just finished having won the treble with Rangers and I was looking forward to getting married to Marlene later that month. Nothing could go wrong – or so I thought.

The news that Jock Wallace had quit as Rangers manager was like a death in the family for me. He had plucked me from part-time football and catapulted me into a Rangers team taking on the best outfits in Europe. I knew he liked me and the way I played the game and, because of Jock, my football career had just taken off.

Years after I'd left Rangers, Jock was being interviewed for an article in the *Evening Times* and was quoted as saying I was the best signing he had ever made. I felt very proud when I read that. He went on to say in the story, 'If I'd stayed at Ibrox, Gordon Smith would have been a legend.' Jock realised that him leaving Rangers was a blow to my career and that's certainly true.

I was living at my parents' house at the time and my mother thought I should be told the news straight away. I couldn't believe it. It was the second time a manager who had signed me, encouraged me and played me in their first team had left after my first season. It happened with Walter McCrae at Kilmarnock and now the same thing with Jock Wallace at Rangers.

I quickly realised that, when I came back from my honeymoon, I was going into pre-season training with a new manager. And new managers always bring with them new ideas, new opinions on players and new favourites. How was it going to affect my career?

For days the papers were full of rumour and counter rumour about why Jock Wallace had sensationally quit the club he loved, but he wouldn't say why he was leaving. We'll never know for sure because he took that secret to his grave. I think there had been some spectacular fall-out with another Rangers legend, Willie Waddell, who had been a player and then manager and held the position of general manager at Ibrox at that time.

Jock was the coach, assisting Willie who was the manager, when Rangers won the European Cup Winners Cup in Barcelona in 1972, so they'd had a good relationship for many years. But the talk among the players was that Jock's fall-out with Willie Waddell was something to do with money or signing players. In the aftermath of his resignation, Jock vowed he would never reveal why he had left Rangers and, as you would expect, he was as good as his word.

Even years later, when I bumped into him on holiday in Spain and we spent an evening chatting, he wouldn't tell my why he left. He was very forthcoming and open about everything but, when it came to that one question, 'Why did you leave, Jock?', all he would say was, 'Ach, there were a few problems that I can't really go into.'

People outside Rangers had a particular perception of Jock Wallace – as someone who would bawl and shout and throw cups around the dressing room. Not true. I never saw Jock make a piece of china fly through the air, nor did I ever see him physically threaten a player when he was angry. He was a big, big man who had served his time in the army and could certainly look after himself. But his weapon wasn't his fists – it was psychology. He was a master at getting you to do the things he wanted you to do and making you believe what he was telling you. And most of the time he was telling his players how good they were, how they were fitter and better footballers than the opposition.

Take the annual visits to Gullane Sands, near North Berwick, in East Lothian, which was much loved by the press every pre-season. Reading the papers ,you would think Jock had the players there every other day of the week, turning them into mighty athletes. The reality was that we only ever went there once a season, which was never going to be enough to make a real difference to our fitness. The difference it did make was psychological and we continued to do it after Jock left.

Don't get me wrong, it was a hard shift – the hardest training session I have ever done. We were running on sand, building up to the dreaded moment when we had to tackle Murder Hill. It was 60 yards of a vertical climb and when you were running up and down, your legs just sank further and further into the sand and it took a fantastic effort to make any progress. You started at the top, ran down to the halfway mark, back up to the top, right down to the bottom and the worst bit was making the uphill run to the top again. Everyone was on their knees for the last few yards. But I don't care what anybody says, going to Gullane was not a fitness day – it was a psychology day.

For the rest of the season, if Jock said it once he would have told his players a hundred times, 'You've done Gullane Sands. You're the fittest team in Scotland.' We'd get to matches and be sitting in the dressing room when Jock would address us, saying,

'It's going to be a tough game today. All you need to do is use your superior fitness and keep going. You've done Gullane, so you'll be fitter than anyone. Your superior fitness will win you this game.' We believed every word he said and we'd go out on to the pitch thinking every one of us was Superman.

Jock would also perpetuate the myth about him being a really scary character. He used this to his advantage and usually all he had to do was ask you to do something and you did it without question. He didn't run the ultra-tough regime that people imagined. He always gave the players two days off every mid-week and told us, 'Rest and then work hard when you are here at training.'

Jock always made sure the players reached the high standards he would set for being part of the club. You had to turn up for training and games wearing a collar and tie, you weren't allowed to grow a beard or come to Ibrox unshaven and your hair couldn't be too long. Being manager of Rangers meant a lot to him and he believed it should mean a lot to the players as well. He took the view that how we appeared and how we behaved outside the club would ultimately reflect on the club itself.

We were sitting in the dressing room one day when Jock came in and threw a copy of a newspaper in front of Bobby Russell. The paper was open at a picture and story about Bobby Russell travelling to Ibrox by bus every day. The photograph was of a smiling Bobby sitting on the bus with his feet up on the seat in front.

'You're a Rangers player,' said Jock. 'You don't have your feet up on the seats when you're on a bus – it's not allowed.'

Jock pulled me up one day after training because I was wearing a green and white shirt and a green tie, which I thought was quite fashionable at the time. 'Don't wear that shirt and tie again,' he said. 'I don't want any of my players wearing green.' I shrugged my shoulders and said, 'OK, boss. Not a problem.' Looking back I think he was probably protecting me because it wouldn't go down well with some of our supporters if they saw a Rangers player wearing a green and white shirt.

I would say the same about the time I gave a post-match interview after we'd beaten Celtic in an Old Firm game. I said that, although I was glad we had won, I thought Celtic were the better team on the day. Jock heard what I'd said and he pulled me aside later and told me never to say that Celtic were the better team. He thought it was wrong for a Rangers player to praise Celtic. He loved Rangers and, because they were the club's greatest rivals, he hated Celtic. I don't think he was a religious bigot – he just loved Rangers so much that he had to be anti-Celtic. It was a football issue with Jock, not a religious one.

When it came to discussing tactics, Jock used another psychological ploy to get across his idea that we were a team not a group of individuals. He would be talking about the way he wanted winger Tommy McLean to play and saying to him, 'When you get the ball, Tommy, just you play it down that line, 'cos Smithy here, he'll run all day in that space.' And when he spoke to me, he'd say, 'Don't be scared to make those runs, 'cos that's where wee Tommy's pass will go or big Derek will lay the ball off to you in that area.'

When he was talking to you, he didn't just involve you, he involved your team mates and he was constantly getting into your subconscious that we all needed each other to play their part before anyone, as an individual, could do something. What he was doing was fantastic management. Instead of saying, 'You do this' or 'You do that', he was letting you know that you were important but only because you were part of something bigger involving other people.

Jock was a great football enthusiast. He would talk to us every day and he'd rave about how we performed in a training session or how we'd played in a daft five-a-side game. But there was always psychology behind it. 'See that kick-about you had yesterday? It was fantastic. The ability you boys have got always amazes me.' Then it would be, 'What a workout you guys had today. The fitness and the pace we've got here is brilliant.' Once again, he was drumming into us that we were better, fitter and more skilful than anyone else so we'd take that belief on to the park on a Saturday.

Jock was from the east coast and sometimes if he was talking particularly fast I couldn't understand what he was saying. He phoned me at home one day and the only word I could make out was 'Majorca'. To be honest, I was scared to ask him to repeat everything he had said so I just said, 'Right, OK. No problems, boss.'

I gave it ten minutes and then I phoned Derek Parlane. 'Did Big Jock just phone you?' I asked.

'Yes, he's just off the phone,' said Derek.

'Well, what did he say? He called me but I couldn't make out a word he said apart from "Majorca". What's that all about?' I asked.

'We're going to Majorca on Saturday after the game for four days before the Scottish Cup tie. We've to remember to bring our passports.'

Jock's shock departure from his beloved Rangers was the end of an era – not only for Jock but for the club as well. However, I put all this to the back of my mind as I eagerly awaited my big day – getting married to Marlene at St Kentigern's Church in Kilmarnock, on 23 June 1978. And, by this time, it had been announced that John Greig would take over from Jock Wallace as manager of Rangers.

I was back from honeymoon and, on the first day of pre-season training, there was a pensive atmosphere as we waited for John Greig to come in to tell us how he was going to run the club. The first thing he said was that he had decided to hang up his boots, stop playing and devote all his time to the manager's role.

Some of the older players were in groups muttering to each other – it's always a bit strange when one of your team mates suddenly becomes the gaffer and he's no longer one of the boys. There was also the feeling that Greigy was too well in with the management at Ibrox and hadn't been fighting the players' corner when it came to conditions and players' bonuses.

Greigy and Willie Waddell were very close and some of the

guys were even suggesting his appointment was proof of that suspicion.

Greigy didn't change much about pre-season training and we had the annual Rangers seaside outing to Gullane. I hadn't missed a game since I made my starting debut at the beginning of the previous season and that carried on at the start of the 1978–79 season – I was always in the starting eleven.

We were a few games into the season and one day before training Greigy came into the dressing room and asked everyone to sit down. He had a cardboard box under his arm and he laid it in front of him on the treatment table. I had no idea what was happening until he put his hand in the box, pulled out a medal, shouted someone's name and threw the medal in their direction for them to catch.

I soon realised this was the League Championship medal presentation – Ibrox style. 'Gordon Smith,' said Greigy and the medal flew through the air into my hands. I was really taken aback and couldn't believe this was the culmination of our heroic efforts in winning the league the previous season.

I said to one of the boys, 'Is this normal?' and I was told that was how it always happened. I thought there would some kind of presentation from the Rangers management, with maybe a wee drink in celebration. But no, at Rangers when you won the League Championship, your medal was thrown at you. It was as if it was no big deal – we'd won the league, but we'd been expected to win the league, so just get on with the new season. It was just one of the idiosyncrasies of the place.

At the start of the season, we had the European Cup to look forward to and the excitement really started to mount when we were drawn against Italian giants, Juventus. We couldn't have been handed a more difficult tie as Juventus had won the UEFA Cup a few months earlier and nine of their team were in the Italian World Cup squad in Argentina that summer. That Juventus side boasted Dino Zoff, Claudio Gentile, Gaetano Scirea, Marco Tardelli, Roberto Bettega, Franco Causio, Romeo Benetti;

and they were managed by the legendary Giovanni Trapattoni.

The first leg was in Turin and there were upwards of 90,000 fans – obviously, mostly Italian – packed into the stadium. What an atmosphere. As we walked on to the pitch, there was a fence around and above us which was just as well because, as soon as we appeared, the fans started throwing missiles on top of us. Although the fence was going to protect us, the noise of these bottles, cans and coins bouncing off the fence was quite frightening.

I was playing up front with Derek Parlane, which was a tactic John Greig employed in European away games because I had the stamina to run throughout the ninety minutes. I had arguably one of the toughest defenders in the world marking me that night – Claudio Gentile – but I still played quite well and made the most of our breakaways. It was a torrid night for our defenders – it was circle the wagons, as we used to call it in those days. We only lost 1–0, but it could have been five or six if it wasn't for Peter McCloy who was in outstanding form.

Near the end of the game, one of the hard men of Italian football almost broke my leg with an outrageous tackle. If I hadn't been sliding in for the ball at an angle the power Romeo Benetti used to go over the ball with both feet to hit my shins would have snapped my leg in two. Fortunately, his boot slid up my leg instead of straight into it and I survived. He should have been sent off for that tackle but the referee only gave him a yellow card. Juventus subbed him right away and, as he was going off the park past our dugout, he motioned with his hands as if he was snapping something and said, 'In Glasgow . . .'

The UEFA official who was at the game had said in his report that Benetti should have been given a red card and suggested that Juventus shouldn't play Benetti in the return leg because he should have been suspended. As it turned out, Juventus didn't play him in the game at Ibrox, despite the fact he was club captain.

A fortnight later in a packed Ibrox stadium, I played one of my best games ever for Rangers. I was back in my usual midfield berth and I hit top form just at the right time. I should have scored the first goal but Dino Zoff saved my shot and Alex McDonald netted the rebound. I did get the second goal, however – after a free kick came into the box and I headed it in from around the penalty spot. We won 2–0 and it was a real shock result because Juventus had been favourites to lift the trophy.

The whole place was on a high after that result but it led to my first big confrontation with John Greig over the bonus of just £200 we got for beating Juventus. There was a lot of unrest in the dressing room when we discovered that was all we would be getting and we asked to see Greigy and he came down trackside to talk to us.

Colin Jackson, Alex McDonald and Peter McCloy were the most vocal of he players arguing for more money. 'A two hundred quid bonus for beating Juventus? They were favourites to win this trophy and it's ridiculous if that's all we're getting.'

Greigy replied, 'The reason it's £200 is nothing to do with the opposition. It's the bonus you get for getting past the first round. The bonus money is determined by what round you are in. Remember we won the Cup Winners Cup in 1972 and it was a £200 bonus we all got when we got through the first round in 1971.'

I just couldn't agree with the logic of his argument, so I joined in. 'Can I just point something out to you, boss? That's the same bonus as 1971. It's now 1978 and we had hyperinflation in 1973, 1974 and 1975. So the £200 bonus is nowhere near the same value now as it was in 1971. And anyway, this is a much superior competition, so I think the bonus should be a lot more.'

Greigy gave me a withering look and snarled, 'What's it got to do with you?'

'What's it got to do with me?' I replied. 'I don't know if you noticed but I was playing in the game and I scored the second goal.'

Greigy's parting shot as he turned and walked away from the group of players was, 'You're hardly in the door. It's got nothing to do with you.' We just shrugged our shoulders, realising there was nothing else we could do.

That was the start of the downward spiral in my relationship with John Greig. He'd marked my card after that – Smithy had too much to say for himself.

In the next round, we drew PSV Eindhoven and the first leg at Ibrox ended 0–0. That was a bad result for us because PSV had never lost a European game at home. In the dressing room over in Holland, Greigy was saying that, if we could stop them scoring in the first twenty minutes, we would be in with a chance of going through to the next round.

We hadn't even had the chance to get our boots dirty when PSV scored. I looked up at the clock and it showed they had scored in only twenty-three seconds – so much for us holding out for the first twenty minutes. When we were trooping up the park for the kick-off after they had scored, we were looking at each other and saying, 'What are we going to do now? That's the masterplan out the window.' Then I heard somebody say, 'F*** it! Let's just go for it. There's no point in holding back and defending now.'

By the end of the ninety minutes, we had pulled off another shock result. We had beaten them 3–2 and we were through. That was a fantastic performance by any standards. I was involved in the winning goal when I played a long cross-field ball to Tommy McLean who played it into the centre for Bobby Russell to run on to the pass and slot it past the keeper. That was us in the quarter-finals of the European Cup and the next round wasn't being played until March of the following year.

We were going well in the league and it looked as if it would either be us or Celtic to lift the title. But there was a terrible winter that year and a lot of games were being cancelled, which meant a backlog of matches. After the New Year, we ended up playing too many matches in a short space of time, which cost us dearly through players getting injured and not having enough time to recover.

We played Cologne in the quarter-finals of the European Cup

and disappointingly went out of the tournament after losing 1–0 in Germany and only drawing 1–1 at Ibrox. Over in Cologne, I had a chance to score after playing a one-two with Tommy McLean and was in on the keeper, Toni Schumacher, and beat him but my shot came off the post. Going out of the tournament was a major blow for me – I felt we could have won the European Cup that year.

We won the League Cup by beating Aberdeen 2–1 in the final and were still challenging for the league title, so all was not lost. The league was going to the wire and we were due to play a postponed game against Celtic at Parkhead which would decide who would win the championship honours.

We went into the game quite confident and were leading 2–1 when Celtic winger Johnny Doyle was sent off about fifteen minutes into the second half. That seemed to be that and it looked as if the title was heading to Ibrox. But, whether we became over-confident and complacent or we switched off, Celtic took on a ferocious spirit and eventually won the game 4–2 to win the league.

We sat stunned in the dressing room after the game that night. There was an amazing din going on outside with Celtic fans staying behind to cheer their heroes. But in that away dressing room there was a stony silence. That could have been a fantastic season for us but we were in the depths of despair because we'd lost to Cologne and then been beaten to the title by ten-man Celtic.

The newspapers were being very critical of the team – having won the treble the previous season and beaten Juventus earlier that season, now we had blown what could have been a historic season for the club. We were also getting stick from fans on both sides of the Old Firm. Our own fans were having a go at us saying that we were a disgrace to Rangers and every window cleaner or building worker in the street seemed to be a Celtic supporter shouting about ten men winning the league.

I don't think that Rangers team ever recovered from the 4–2 defeat at Parkhead. It was a watershed for both John Greig and the players who had been together for so long. No, we never really recovered from that night.

While the dark clouds of depression were rolling over Ibrox, there was just one little chink of sunshine for me. We were playing Hibs in the Scottish Cup final and I had the chance to emulate my grandfather, Mattha Smith, by winning two Scottish Cup medals. I was desperate to do this and I kept myself going with the thought of it.

The final was one of the worst games I had ever played in, never mind for the fans watching from the terraces. It ended in a 0–0 draw and both teams played so badly it could've got football stopped. The replay was slightly better as a spectacle but, again, it ended evens at 0–0. There was no doubt about it – this was a Rangers team shot through. Players were drained and off form from playing too many games in a short space of time.

Greigy was already making it clear to us that he wasn't happy with our performances and I was a particular target. He never mentioned my name but he began to refer to 'somebody not doing enough in midfield' and 'the midfield were poor'. It was a sign of things to come – but I didn't see the sign.

We had arrived at Hampden for the second replay with Hibs and we were sitting in the dressing room waiting for the manager to read out the team. I was still very much up for the game because of another piece of football history that could be made for the Smith family.

Greigy came in and said, 'Right, sit down, here's the team.' He began, 'In goals, Big Peter. Back four of Sandy, Tam, Bomber and Ally Dawson. Midfield – McDonald, Russell and Watson.' At that point, I raised my eyebrows and thought he must be playing me up front, just like the away European games. 'Forward line is McLean, Parlane and Cooper,' Greigy continued. I couldn't believe it. For the first time since I had joined Rangers two years before, I was being dropped. A wave of shock and disappointment flowed through my body – I was totally stunned. I couldn't believe it. I was top scorer for the club that season with twenty-three goals and I was being relegated to the bench. What a sickener. We'd had two 0–0 draws and it appeared that I was getting the blame. There was no explanation from Greigy about why I was dropped although I managed to console myself with the thought that at least I was a substitute and I could still get on the park at some point.

What a difference from the last time I sat in that dressing room waiting to play in a Scottish Cup final. There was a supreme confidence about us the previous season. But all of a sudden we were thinking that, if we lost this one, it was going to turn out a really disastrous season for us.

I was brought on for Kenny Watson during the second half and late in the game the score was 2–2. I moved the ball out to Davie Cooper on the wing and followed up by continuing my run into their box. Coop got past a defender and chipped the ball into the box. The ball was perfectly flighted into the box and I was positioning myself to head it with just the goalkeeper to beat. Just as I was about to connect with the ball, Hibs' Arthur Duncan barged me in the back and the ball came off his head and floated into his own net.

I was so angry with Arthur Duncan for fouling me like that and putting the ball in his own net when I had a clear-cut scoring chance that I was still shouting at him as the rest of the Rangers team were celebrating. I was raging. 'All you'll be remembered for is that own goal, you f****** idiot!' I told him.

He had robbed me of scoring the winning goal in the Scottish Cup Final and not just any final. It was the final in which I was emulating my grandfather by winning a second Scottish Cup winner's medal.

That Scottish Cup victory meant I had been in a Rangers team which had won five trophies in two years but, because we hadn't won the league that year, the criticism we were getting from all sides was unbelievable. The atmosphere created after season 1978–79 meant that Rangers was going to be a different club after that and a rebuilding process was looming. And some of the old guard were going to be losing their place in the team.

This became more apparent all through the following season 1979–80 as some of the older players like Peter McCloy, Sandy Jardine, Tom Forsyth, Tommy McLean and Alex McDonald were being dropped for games. Although I was still only twenty-four and couldn't be counted among the old guard, I found myself being dropped to the bench for big games – especially against Celtic. This surprised me and it seemed like I was being blamed for the horrendous defeat at Parkhead which had given ten-man Celtic the league title. I know I didn't play particularly well that game – but nobody did. It was a below-par performance from the whole team.

Before the start of that season the Tennent Caledonian Tournament was held at Ibrox with four teams – Rangers, Brighton, West Ham and Kilmarnock – competing. I was still in the team at that point and on a Friday night we beat West Ham 3–1 and I scored two of the goals.

The following day we beat Celtic to win the Dryburgh Cup final at Hampden. That was the day Davie Cooper scored his amazing individual goal when he played keepie-up in the Celtic penalty box over their defenders' heads and scored a magnificent goal.

On the Sunday, we were due to play Kilmarnock in the Tennant Caledonian Cup as they had beaten Brighton. We were beating Kilmarnock 2–0 – I'd got one of the goals – and were cruising with only five minutes to go and Greigy decided to take off a couple of experienced defenders and give two youngsters a run out. We lost two late goals, the match went to penalties and we lost after the spot kicks. It was bad start to the season. Little did I know that Alan Mullery, the Brighton manager, had been keeping an eye on me during that tournament, but that fact wouldn't come to my attention until the following year.

We were in the European Cup Winners Cup and negotiated ourselves through the first couple of rounds beating Lillestrom 1–0 at home, with me getting the goal, and 2–0 over in Norway.

We then beat Fortuna Dusseldorf 2–1 at Ibrox and drew 0–0 in Germany. The disappointment of not winning the league the previous season was beginning to fade as we looked as if we would put a decent run together in Europe. But, in the next round, Valencia beat us 3–1 at Ibrox after we had drawn the first leg in Spain 1–1. More disappointment.

And it got worse – we were put out of the League Cup and began to slide back in the league, which wasn't the usual two-horse race between Rangers and Celtic as Aberdeen and Dundee United had strong teams and were challenging the Old Firm.

As the season wore on, I wasn't getting a guaranteed starting place in the team and an incident during our trip to Dusseldorf, which ended in a verbal spat between John Greig and me, certainly didn't help matters on that front.

It was the night before the game and all the team were at dinner in the hotel. Greigy was sitting at one end of a long table and I was at the other. He was talking about economics and taxation but what he was saying just wasn't correct. I hadn't told anyone at Ibrox that I had a degree in Business Studies but, when he finished talking, I corrected what Greigy had said.

There was a stunned silence among the players and Greigy looked down the table at me and said, 'Do you know something Smithy? The smart ones are always the first ones out the door.'

Before I could think of the consequences, I countered, 'Is that why you've been here nineteen years, then?'

The players couldn't believe I'd said that and the looks on their faces told me I had really made a mistake by bringing down the manager in front of everyone. What made it worse was that Greigy never came back at me with a funny comment that would have given everyone a laugh and eased the tension. My barbed comment was left hanging in the air and I quickly realised it had been a stupid thing to say.

After Valencia put us out of the Cup Winners Cup, Greigy dropped a lot of the regulars – including Davie Cooper and me – and put us in the reserves. Some of the boys resented this and didn't try too hard playing for the second string, but I was still giving my all.

I was given a temporary reprieve and put back in the first team after a reserve game against St Mirren, which we lost 3–1. The next morning the manager called everyone together and had a real go at those who had been playing the night before. Then he singled me out as the only one who had been trying. The next week, I was back in the first team.

Give Greigy his due, he didn't have a total down on me and he recognised that I was doing my best, even in the reserves. But being in and out of the team wasn't where I wanted to be. I had another confrontation with Greigy when I was dropped after playing in a Scottish Cup tie against Hearts when we beat them 5–1. The next midweek, we were due to play Dundee, who were bottom of the league, and I was put on the bench.

I went to see Greigy and asked why he was putting Gregor Stevens – a centre half – in the central midfield position I played. Greigy said he wanted to be more defensive in the centre of the park. I argued that we had just beaten a team higher up the league than Dundee 5–1 and we didn't need more defensive cover then. But it was to no avail and I didn't even get on the park. That was one of the times I thought to myself that things weren't going the way I would like at Ibrox.

As the season drew to a close it was obvious we weren't going to win the league and all that was left of the silverware was the Scottish Cup. But at least we were in the final against Celtic.

And, to my great surprise, about a week before the final, I was called up to the manager's office to be told by Greigy that he wanted to extend my contract at the club. It appeared to me that I was back in favour because he told me he wanted to build a new team around younger players like Bobby Russell, Davie Cooper, Ally Dawson, Derek Johnstone and me. To my even bigger surprise, Greigy offered me a five-year deal and a wage rise from my present £150 a week to £250 a week. He said we would be the highest-paid players at the club and I was delighted to stay at Ibrox with the new contract.

This was fantastic news and I was on a high particularly as on 5 May – the Monday before the cup final my son, Grant, was born. However, I had a niggling ankle strain that I couldn't shake off and, as the final got closer, I became more and more concerned that I wouldn't be fully fit.

We were staying at The Marine Hotel in Troon and I had a fitness test the day before the game. I knew I wasn't 100 per cent, but I was desperate to play and I passed myself fit. The facts that we hadn't won anything that year, that I had just signed a new contract, that I wanted to win a third Scottish Cup medal and that my son had just been born all combined to make me all the more desperate to play that day.

Although I wasn't fully fit, I thought I could get away with it because I could cope with playing in the centre of midfield carrying the injury. I could time my runs and be more of a playmaker than having to run about from one end of Hampden to the other. But I got a real feeling of dread in my stomach when Greigy read out the team. I wasn't playing in the centre of midfield, I was playing on the left of midfield.

That meant I was up against the running power of both Celtic's winger Davie Provan and their right back, Danny McGrain. I knew then I was going to struggle during the game because I was going to have to do a lot more running and turning which would put more strain on my ankle.

Celtic's right-hand flank with McGrain and Provan was where the main threat would come from. Greigy thought that, with my running power and stamina, I would be able to counter this threat. Playing in the centre of midfield, I would say I would have been about 90 per cent fit but, out wide, I was only 70 per cent fit which, frankly, wasn't good enough and, after we had been defeated 1–0, I felt I had let Rangers down because I played while not fully fit.

Before the match, I had asked for a light strapping instead of a heavy strapping – which would have been better – to be put on my ankle, as I didn't want to arouse any suspicion about the extent of my ankle injury. It wasn't the worst performance of my life and I must have done reasonably well because I wasn't substituted, although my ankle was really painful all through the game. I know, if I had been 100 per cent fit or I had been in central midfield, I could have contributed a lot more.

As soon as the final whistle went the Celtic fans ran on to the park as we trooped disconsolately to the dressing room. While we were in the dressing room waiting to be called back on to the park to be presented with our runners-up medals, a full-scale riot had erupted with hordes of Rangers and Celtic fans battling it out on the pitch.

All this was going on as I went up to collect my medal, but I never noticed a thing. I was so disappointed, my head was literally down and I didn't see one of the worst football riots going on just a few yards from where I was walking up to get my medal. It was only later when people started talking about those shameful scenes and I saw the pictures on television that I realised how bad it had been.

The end of that season was a real emotional rollercoaster for me. On a personal level, I couldn't have been happier with Grant being born but, professionally, we had won nothing and major surgery was being predicted on the Rangers team.

And I was really cut up when I discovered just how much that was going to affect me.

7

TRICKED INTO TRANSFER TALKS

I'm in a hotel lobby more than 450 miles from home at the other end of the country. I stare at the public phone I've just been speaking on and have laid it back on its cradle. I can't believe what I've just been told by the Rangers manager, John Greig, who, seconds before, has been on the other end of the line speaking to me. I'm numb with shock and finding it hard to think straight.

I lean against the phone booth and take a minute to compose myself. The reception area is busy with people going back and forward, but everything is just a blur – my emotions are in turmoil and no wonder. My football career, my life and my family's life have just been turned upside down by what I can only describe as an act of betrayal.

My anguish at what has just happened turns to anger and then frustration as I began to realise there is nothing I can do about it.

I was leaving Rangers against my will.

It all started twenty-four hours earlier when the phone rang in my home in Kilmarnock on the morning of Wednesday 4 June, during the close season in 1980. We hadn't gone on holiday that summer because Grant had just been born and Marlene was recovering. When I answered the phone, it was John Greig on the other end of the line. 'Smithy, can you come in to Ibrox and see me today? I need you to do me a wee favour.'

'Sure, no problem,' I replied. 'I'm due to go up to Glasgow today anyway.'

At the time I thought the call was a bit unusual but I wasn't suspicious in any way and thought to myself that I'd find out what it was all about soon enough when I got to Ibrox.

A few hours later, I was sitting in Greigy's office in Ibrox and he said, 'Listen, I'll tell what I'd like you to do for me. I'm very friendly with the Brighton manager Alan Mullery – he's a big pal of mine – and, if you don't mind, could you go down there and talk to him? He's seen you play three or four times and he's been trying to sign you all season. Obviously you've just signed a new deal here so you're not going anywhere. But you'll be doing me a favour by going down to Brighton and talking to Alan just to keep him happy.'

Greigy continued, 'Just go through the motions and pretend you're there to look over the place, but obviously you're not going. If you can fly down tomorrow morning, we'll book your flights, you'll get picked up at the airport down there and you'll be back home at night.'

I had no idea that Brighton played in the English First Division or that they had come up through the leagues to the top flight in the previous few years. I didn't even know where Brighton was exactly – I just knew it was in the south of England somewhere. When I told Marlene later that night I was going to visit Brighton to do Greigy a favour, I had to look at the map to find out where I was going. When I saw it I said, 'My God, that's a long way down.'

The next morning, I got to Glasgow Airport and, as I was checking in, who should appear but one of Rangers' coaching staff and former left back, Davie Provan? I hadn't known Davie was coming to Brighton with me and, even by that point, I hadn't smelt a rat. On the flight down, we spoke about Rangers, football in general and the fact that I had no intention of signing for Brighton.

'You're right, Smithy,' said Davie. 'There's no way you'd want to go all the way down there.'

At Gatwick, Brighton chairman Mike Bamber's chauffeur was

waiting to pick us up and drive us to the Goldstone ground to meet with Alan Mullery, who started to tell me how he was impressed with me and that he'd seen me score two goals against West Ham during the Tennent Caledonian Tournament at the start of the previous season.

'You're the type of player we are looking for. Someone who can pop up from midfield and score half a dozen goals a season for us.'

I didn't think that was a lot of goals and I told him I had scored twenty-seven goals from midfield in my first season at Ibrox. Mullery said, 'You'll not score that many goals in the English First Division, but we're looking for someone to play an Ossie Ardiles role, like he does at Tottenham. We see you as that kind of player. Someone who can play behind the strikers from midfield and get forward into the box. We definitely want you.'

He then offered me a £30,000 signing-on fee and £350 a week. Now, that would have been a huge jump in pay for me as I was still on £150 a week at Rangers and wasn't going to move on to £250 a week until the start of the new season. But even at that money I wasn't interested in going to Brighton and I told Alan Mullery I was staying at Rangers.

He chatted a bit more about the club and their ambitions and then said, 'Right – we'll give you a £40,000 signing-on fee paid over a five-year contract and £400 a week wages.'

'Sorry,' I told him. 'But I'm not interested in signing for Brighton. I'm happy at Rangers and I'm staying there.'

He said, 'That's fine but I've arranged a bite of lunch for you and you can meet our chairman, Mike Bamber.'

All this time, Davie Provan was sitting there saying nothing and, as we were about to go out the door, Alan Mullery said, 'Before you go I want to make you a final offer. It's £450 a week basic wage and a £50,000 signing-on fee. That's £10,000 a year over five seasons.'

Again I said I wasn't interested but he insisted I think about it over lunch and he'd see me in the afternoon. On the way out, we met Mike Bamber who said he hoped I would sign for Brighton and, when I said I wasn't going to, he replied, 'That's right. We're negotiating. That's what it's all about.'

I was sitting there thinking, 'No, I'm not signing for Brighton because I want to stay at Rangers and they think I'm negotiating with them to get the money higher. The money Brighton were offering is now at £450 a week and a £50,000 signing-on fee but I'm still not interested in signing for them.'

Davie and I were driven to a hotel for lunch and the two of us sat down to talk about the meeting with Alan Mullery. 'That's some offer, isn't it?' Davie said.

'Yeah, it's amazing,' I replied. 'It's unbelievable that a small club like Brighton can pay three times the wages I'm getting at Ibrox and look at the size of Rangers.'

Then Davie said, 'Do you not think you should just come here, then?'

'You know I've no intention of leaving Rangers,' I told him.

'But it would be a great move for you getting that kind of money and playing down here,' said Davie.

'No. I'm not going to go to Brighton.'

'I think you should.'

'Look, Davie, there's no way I'm coming here and that's it. You know I'm not leaving Rangers. Even the boss says I'm not to come here. I've just signed a five-year deal . . .'

Davie interrupted me and said, 'Right, I might as well tell you. The deal's done – we've sold you.'

I looked at him and said, 'Tell me you're kidding.'

'No,' said Davie. 'They've accepted the £440,000 transfer fee. The reason I'm down here with you is that you've to sign for Brighton.'

'I don't believe this,' I said.

'Well, that's the situation,' Davie replied.

I headed for the hotel reception and from the public phone booth I called Ibrox asking to speak to Greigy. He came on the line and the first thing he said to me was, 'Is that you, Smithy? Have you signed?'

'You know I'm not signing. What are you talking about and what's going on?' I asked.

But Greigy said, 'Aye, you are signing. Look, I've done the deal and I've already spent the money we're getting for you on two players I'm bringing in. The money is spent and as far as I'm concerned it's done, you're going, you're leaving.'

'Well, I'm not leaving. For me to leave Rangers, I'd have to sign the forms and I'm not signing,' I said.

Greigy replied, 'If you don't sign, I'll make your life hell here. You'll never kick a ball in the first team again. I won't even let you kick a ball in the reserves either. I'll have you in training morning, noon and night. Do you want to put up with that? Do you want that kind of life for the next five years?'

I asked Greigy how long his contract was at Rangers and he said three years. 'Maybe, if I wait, I'll see you out the door since I've got a five-year contract,' I told him.

He replied, 'If you want to take that chance, that's fine. But things might go well for me and maybe I'll be at Ibrox a lot longer. In any case, you'll have three years of hell. You want to take a chance on all that?'

At that, I put the phone down, stunned at the turn of events in such a short space of time. This time yesterday John Greig was asking me to do him a wee favour – to go down to Brighton and speak to Alan Mullery, kid on I was looking round the place and just humour them. Now he was telling me he'd already negotiated my transfer fee to sign for Brighton and the whole deal was done behind my back.

I went back to the restaurant and sat down at the table again and said to Davie, 'I can't believe this is happening.'

'I couldn't say why I was down here with you. We thought that Alan Mullery would talk you into signing for Brighton. It's a good deal – three times the money you are on just now – that's unbelievable.'

'It is unbelievable,' I said, 'but I don't want to leave Rangers. I love being at Ibrox.'

I sat for a few moments and thought about what I was going to do. I was angry, really angry, at how John Greig had done a deal behind my back and tricked me into coming down to Brighton to speak to Alan Mullery on the basis that I was only doing him a favour. I thought that I deserved better from John Greig. I was his top scorer with twenty-three goals in the first season he was in charge. I loved the club and I would always have given my all for Rangers. I was disgusted by the way I had been treated and sick at how I had been railroaded out of Ibrox and there was really nothing I could do about it.

If I went back to Ibrox, I was going to be frozen out and sent training with the youngsters every day and, in those days, managers really could make your life hell. The other side of the coin was that the money I was being offered at Brighton was fantastic.

I went back out to reception and called home but Marlene wasn't in. I decided there and then that I had no real alternative but to sign with Brighton. So, without having been able to talk to my wife, I decided I would reluctantly sign with Brighton.

When I got back to he ground I met Mike Bamber and Alan Mullery again and told them I would sign for the money they were offering but I wanted a four-year deal instead of five. I had this thing in my mind that after four years I would only be twenty-nine and there would be a better chance of getting another club at that age rather than thirty. I was devastated at how the day's events had unfolded and, on the flight back up to Glasgow, I was very quiet and didn't say much to Davie.

When I arrived back at my house in Kilmarnock, I got the usual cheery greeting from Marlene, 'Hi, darling. How was your day?'

I told her she'd better sit down. 'I've signed for Brighton,' I said.

'No way,' she replied.

''Fraid so,' I said and began to tell her the full story of what had happened. Marlene was very angry by the time I had finished. She said, 'That means we have to take Grant away from

114

his grandparents – we're leaving our family and everybody we know.'

It was a terrible blow to us. Neither of us had ever lived outside Ayrshire, I was happy playing for Rangers, she was happy with a new baby and we were both happy with our lifestyle in Kilmarnock. Then it was time to break the news to our parents and they couldn't believe I was having to move to the south coast of England.

When the news broke in the papers, it was portrayed as if Brighton wanted to sign me and I was happy to go. The phone calls started coming in from my Rangers team mates who said they were shocked and couldn't believe I was going to Brighton. I don't know why but I never told them what happened and just let them think it was a straightforward transfer with everybody happy. There were also some barbed comments from Rangers fans who accused me of wanting to leave Ibrox because we'd just had a bad season. All I said to them was that they didn't know all the circumstances. Now they do.

I never saw John Greig before I left Scotland and I never spoke to him again until I came back to Rangers on loan from Brighton in December 1982. Even then, we didn't have much of a conversation because the initial phone call to me came from Tommy McLean who was then Greigy's assistant at Ibrox. The players were going on a pre-season tour of Canada and I went to Ibrox to collect my boots and say cheerio to them just before they left. When I did speak to Greigy during my loan period at Ibrox, it was very congenial and neither of us made any mention of how my transfer to Brighton had come about.

I often wonder if John Greig knew I was going to be sold before he offered me that five-year contract before the 1980 Scottish Cup final. He said he knew that Alan Mullery had tried to buy me three or four times that season. By giving me a longer contract, it would have increased my value in any transfer fee.

If I had seen John Greig soon after I'd had to sign for Brighton, I would have told him in no uncertain terms what I thought of him for doing that transfer deal behind my back and tricking me into going down south to speak to Alan Mullery.

If Greigy had been up front about wanting to transfer me, I could have probably gone to a bigger club than Brighton – and I don't mean any disrespect to them because I enjoyed my time there. When I moved to Brighton I was dubbed the Scottish Trevor Brooking and, years later, when I played for Manchester City, they told me they would have bought me from Rangers if they had known I was up for transfer.

If I'd known what was going on between Rangers and Brighton, I might have been better prepared and not so naive about the transfer. For example, my £50,000 signing-on fee was only really worth £20,000 because, at the time, the higher rate of income tax was 60 per cent.

And it was only when another of Brighton's signings that season, Roy McHale, asked if I had got my ex gratia payment from Rangers, that I realised just how naive I had been. Unknown to me at the time, it was common for the selling club to give the player a tax-free ex gratia payment in lieu of a signing-on fee from the buying club. This money was then added on to the transfer fee and the player got the full benefit of the signing-on cash. Rangers never offered me a penny to leave and, at the time, it was a record transfer fee for someone leaving Ibrox.

But my anger at how I was treated by Greigy soon mellowed as I began enjoying life with Brighton. I was on three times the money I was getting at Ibrox, it was a great place to live and bring up my young son, the weather was lovely, we made some very good friends down there and I had very little to complain about. On the few occasions I have spoken to Greigy about my transfer, he told that the money being offered by Brighton was too much to turn down and he was able to bring in Jim Bett and Colin McAdam with the cash he got from me.

But it was more than ten years before the subject ever came up between Greigy and me. I was doing some media work for the BBC, Greigy was now working as Rangers' public relations man and we were trackside with a few other people. He shouted over to me, 'You alright, Smithy?'

'Yeah, I'm fine,' I replied.

Then he said to the assembled media guys, 'I made that boy a lot of money.'

I interrupted and said, 'No, you actually broke my heart making me go to Brighton.'

'No,' said Greigy, 'it was the best thing that ever happened to you.'

'Only because it got really bad here after I left,' I replied.

After all those years, I see Greigy on a regular basis through my media and football agency work and I don't bear him any grudges – although undoubtedly, at the time, I was raging over what he did to me.

Why did he sell me? I think it was probably a combination of the amount of money he was being offered by Brighton for me and the fact that he probably didn't like me that much when I was a player. Perhaps I was a bit too mouthy for him when you consider the run-ins I had had with him over the Juventus bonus and me bringing him down in front of the other players over his economic theories. Yes, I believe he had a wee personal thing about me.

There was one incident when I brought in a video tape of a game we had played. All the players and coaches were watching it and Greigy was saying things like, 'That was a great pass, Smithy' and 'What a ball you gave wee Tommy', as he watched the game on the television. It was as if he was surprised I was doing all those good things in the match. I thought to myself, 'Was Greigy not at the game on Saturday? Why did he not see all those great passes then and say something after the game?'

I think he had a blind spot with me and never appreciated just how much I did for the team. He probably thought I was a player that could get the odd goal from midfield but I wasn't his type of player. To be a John Greig favourite, first and foremost, it would be, 'Are you a hard tackler?' Then it would be, 'Now what else can you do?'

I get on fine with Greigy and, when we are in company, he has a wee go at me and I have a wee go back. He'll say to people, 'You won't believe how I managed to get so much money for such a bad player like Smithy.' I'll come back at him by asking, 'How many league championships did you win after I left?' – which was none. And, 'Are there any other Rangers managers, apart from yourself, Greigy, who never won a league title?' We can have a laugh with each other and our relationship is absolutely fine.

Inadvertently, John Greig did do me a favour by transferring me to Brighton, but his reasons for doing what he did and the way he did it were completely wrong. Greigy ended up losing his job and I had a great time at Brighton, played in an FA Cup final at Wembley, went on to Manchester City and then played abroad for a spell. I reckon I had a more productive career after I left Rangers than if I had stayed under John Greig. I certainly made a lot more money and had a great experience of life after I left Ibrox.

When I played in England I discovered just how mean the people running Scottish football clubs really are when it comes to wages and conditions for players, compared to our counterparts down south. And, even although Rangers was one of the two biggest clubs in Scotland in terms of support and money-making potential, they were just as tight-fisted as anyone else.

When I first went to Brighton, I was stunned by the difference and how well the players were treated compared to up in Scotland. When the Brighton players were travelling to away games on the coach, we had stewards serving us food like on an aeroplane. At Rangers, if the bus stopped on the way back from somewhere like Aberdeen, the players would have to buy their own fish suppers. And, if Willie Waddell decided that the bus wasn't stopping, then we wouldn't even get a fish supper!

When we were training at the Albion ground and one of the players accidentally kicked the ball over the high wall that surrounded the pitches, we were sent to find the ball from the street outside.

Once, just before a big European game, I kicked the ball over the wall and was despatched to recover it. I ran round to the gate and looked in the street outside but couldn't see the ball anywhere. I walked down the road a bit, next to some houses, but still couldn't find the ball. Suddenly I heard a window opening and a woman shouted me over. 'The boy from the bottom left at number four has got your ball,' I was told and window banged shut. I went to number four and knocked on the door of the bottom left flat. There I was, a Rangers player, standing in my football gear and boots, asking the man who had answered the door if I could get my ball back, please.

He said he didn't know what I was talking about and I said I had been told that his son had lifted the ball from the street and taken it into the house. The dad called the boy to the door and asked if he had my ball. The boy denied all knowledge so there was nothing to do but go back to training and confess I had lost the ball.

As I was walking away, I heard shouting coming from inside the house and the boy was getting a real roasting from his father. Their window flew open and the ball I had kicked over the wall was thrown out into the street and it came bouncing towards me. There's no chance of letting big-time football go to your head in Glasgow.

Scotland was also lagging behind when it came to players' lounges. When I was at Ibrox, wives and girlfriends had to wait in the car outside while players got changed. But, in England, it was very common for clubs to have a players' lounge where friends and family could wait for the players from both teams to come out of the dressing rooms.

And, just like when I was Kilmarnock, the football boots Rangers gave the players were well down the Adidas range. As far as I was concerned, we were the top professionals in Scotland, so we should be playing with the best boots available. A lot of players were doing what I did by taking the cheap pair of boots Rangers gave you and trading them in at Greaves sports shop in

119

Glasgow for a top-of-the-range pair and paying the difference in the price out of our own pockets.

Rangers also saved money by not washing our training kit every day – the gear got washed at the end of the week. You would get a clean set of gear on a Monday and, instead of it being washed after the training session, we would have to hang our kit in a cupboard that had heaters inside to dry it for the next day. I was amazed that the senior players at Ibrox put up with that because at Kilmarnock we had our kit washed for us at the end of each day.

The other incredible story about the meanness of Rangers was that we were never allowed to swap shirts with our opponents after a European game. That rule caused me great embarrassment with one of the world's best players who asked to swap shirts with me. And it was only years later that I got the chance to apologise and explain the situation to him.

Mario Kempes had enthralled everyone with his performances in the 1978 World Cup finals. He was outstanding for Argentina as, with his long hair flowing, he glided gracefully through defences and finished as the tournament's top scorer with six goals. Two of his goals were in the World Cup final when Argentina beat Holland 3–1 to lift the trophy.

You can imagine the thrill when I discovered I would be playing against him when Rangers were drawn against Valencia in the European Cup Winners Cup only a few months after that World Cup. Kempes was superb against us that night and was brought down in our box about eight times but, luckily for us, the referee waved away every penalty claim.

We played the first leg over in Spain and I played well in a 1–1 draw. When the final whistle blew, I felt a tap on my shoulder and there was Kempes wanting to shake my hand and gesturing to exchange shirts. I tried to explain that we weren't allowed to change shirts but he didn't speak English and hadn't a clue what I was saying. I even started waving my hands and shaking my head but that probably made matters worse.

When he saw that I wasn't going to give him my shirt, he just shrugged his shoulders, waved me away and walked off. I was raging that I couldn't swap shirts with him but I knew that, if I had, then John Greig would have sent me into the Valencia dressing room to ask for it back.

I was really embarrassed about the whole thing and I decided on a plan that would mean I could swap shirts with Kempes after the return leg at Ibrox a fortnight later. Before the game, I went into Greaves sports shop in Glasgow and bought a replica Rangers top. I asked the women who handled the kit if they would do me a wee favour on the quiet and sew a number ten on the back as that was my number. I then put the replica strip into a plain brown paper bag and sneaked it into the Ibrox dressing room and hid it under the seat at my place. The plan was that I would change shirts at half-time and wear the replica shirt for the second half. And when the whistle went I would swap my top with Kempes and I would get his shirt. When I went back to the dressing room I would pull out the original top I was wearing and there would still be a full set of strips when they were counted.

Everything was in place until John Greig came in and read out the team and instead of me being number ten, he had me down as playing number eight. I couldn't believe it. The first time I wasn't number ten and it was the night I've set everything up to swap my shirt with Kempes.

I went up to Greigy and said, 'Boss, you've got me down as number eight and I'm usually number ten.'

'What's the big deal?' said Greigy. 'You're number eight tonight.'

'I'm dead superstitious,' I said. 'I need to wear my number ten shirt. It brings me luck.'

'It's too late to change things now,' said Greigy. 'The teams lines are already in. You'll just have to wear number eight.'

That was my shirt-swap plan up in the air, as I couldn't suddenly appear in the second half wearing a number ten shirt when another Rangers player was wearing that number as well. I ended up giving the replica shirt away as a raffle prize and the draw organisers couldn't quite understand what I meant by saying they should announce the prize as the shirt Gordon Smith almost swapped with World Cup winner Mario Kempes.

Seven years later, when I was playing with Admira Wacker, Mario Kempes was also playing in Austria with Vienna. We hadn't yet played them when our goalkeeper Harald Baumgarten – whose wife was Spanish – told me they were having a drink with Mario Kempes and I asked if I could come with them.

Harald had good English and he asked me why I wanted to come along and I told him there was something I needed to explain to Kempes. When we met up, I was introduced to Kempes and I got Harald to explain to him I wasn't allowed to swap shirts with him when I had played against him with Rangers.

Kempes had a laugh when Harald translated what I said into Spanish. Kempes then said something and Harald told me, 'Mario says you're the only player in his career who has ever refused to swap shirts with him.'

Well, at least Rangers got to keep their number ten shirt.

8

UP BRIGHTON EARLY!

The players look at each other and wonder if they should believe what they have just heard. Standing on the training ground, they look askance at the Brighton youth team coach, Brian Eastick, who is taking the first-team training for the first time.

'Right, lads,' he has just told us 'we're going to have a game of football, so pick two sides. But what's different about this game – and if you take this seriously it will be a great help to you – is that we'll be playing with an imaginary ball.'

'It's twenty minutes each way – a practice game with a pretend ball.'

He senses a reluctance from the players and nobody moves. 'Look,' says Brian, 'the boss is watching and it's either this or he'll have you running all morning – what's it to be?'

Since anything's better than running round a track for a couple of hours, we decide to go along with this rather unconventional training method. We're at the start of the 1982–83 season and this is undoubtedly the weirdest training session I have ever taken part in and that would go for the rest of the Brighton players as well.

We get ourselves into teams and line up to kick off. The former Arsenal star, Charlie George, has joined Brighton on a month's loan and he's in my team. I kick off by touching the imaginary ball to Charlie who makes an imaginary pass to our winger, ex-Manchester United player, Mickey Thomas. Mickey then makes a 20-yard run at full pace, slides along the touchline and jumps up to shout, 'For f***'s sake, Charlie, play it to my feet, will you?'

The players can hardly stand up for laughing and that's the

end of the game. Brian Eastick is not happy and, since we're not taking his game with the imaginary football seriously, it's back to running round the track.

Brian had been on the continent looking at how the European teams train and noting their coaching methods. He must have seen some foreign team trying out this practice match with no football and decided to introduce it to the British game. Brian had persuaded Brighton's then manager, Mike Bailey, to let him take the first-team training for a morning and try out these new methods. Unfortunately, the British footballers weren't quite ready for such progress and diversity of coaching methods.

Although I had never wanted to leave Rangers in the summer of 1980, I was now in my second year at Brighton – or The Seagulls, as they were known locally – and everything had turned out fine. We were living in a smashing big house, the Brighton players and their families had a great social life and the south coast of England was lovely place to stay. Best of all, Marlene had given birth to our second child, Leigh-Anne, in November 1981 so everything was hunky-dory.

But, when I'd had to move down to Brighton two years earlier, there were more than a few tears shed among the extended family at us having to leave our home in Kilmarnock. But we did get a smile when I thought I was the victim of a wind-up after I'd put our house in Ayrshire on the market. It had only been advertised for a couple of days when I got a call at night and a very polite voice said, 'My name is Mr Brighton and I'm interested in buying your house.'

'Very good,' I said to myself. 'I'm going to Brighton and somebody called Mr Brighton phones me saying he wants to buy my house. This must be one of the Rangers boys having a laugh at my expense.'

I was very offhand with the guy on the other end of the line because I thought it was just a wind up. 'Can I come and view the property?' Mr Brighton asked.

'Sure,' I said. 'Any time you like.'

'Would tomorrow night be convenient?'

'Not a problem,' I said. 'Look forward to seeing you then.'

When I came off the phone I said to Marlene, 'That's one of the boys taking the Mickey. I thought at first it was big Peter McCloy but maybe not. It's bound to be one of them.'

I never thought any more of it until the following night when the doorbell rang and standing there was a well-dressed middle-aged man wearing a trilby hat. 'Can I help you?' I said.

'I'm Mr Brighton. I called you last night,' he said.

I apologised for the way I had spoken to him on the phone and explained I thought it was some friends playing a joke on me. It didn't seem to put him off because he bought the house. How's that for a coincidence? I'm moving from Kilmarnock to Brighton and a Mr Brighton buys my house in Kilmarnock.

Before pre-season started, I travelled down to Brighton to look for a new house and bring some brochures and schedules back up to Scotland for Marlene to look at. About a month later, I arrived at Brighton for my first day's training and manager Alan Mullery called me into his office.

He welcomed me to the club then placed a hotel bill on the desk in front of me and said, 'Look Gordon, I know you've been down here looking for a house but you can't really expect the club to pay this. You'll have to pay the hotel bill yourself.'

I looked at the bill and it was from a hotel in Eastbourne. 'I've never been to Eastbourne,' I said. 'This has got nothing to do with me.'

'But this is your bill.'

'No it's not. Honestly, I've never been to Eastbourne.'

The club then began an investigation into how they had ended up getting a hotel bill for a Gordon Smith who had stayed at a hotel that Gordon Smith was saying he had never visited. And what a can of worms that investigation opened.

It turned out that a complete chancer was having an affair with a woman and they decided to spend the night in a hotel.

He had seen my picture in the local paper and thought he looked a bit like me. When he was booking in to the hotel at Eastbourne, he told reception he was the footballer Gordon Smith, who had just signed for Brighton. He did the lot – the room, champagne and dinner – and told the hotel Brighton FC were picking up the tab and they were to send the bill to the club.

But worse was to come for the amorous duo. When the club phoned the hotel, they asked if any calls had been made from the room their phoney Gordon Smith had stayed in with his lover. It turned out that the woman had phoned her husband to say she was staying over with one of her friends and she wouldn't be home that night, so don't worry darling, love you, blah, blah blah.

When the hotel phoned the number, they got the husband and told him he had been caught impersonating me and sending the hotel bill to Brighton FC. Naturally, the guy hadn't a clue what was going on until he twigged that, on that night, his wife had phoned to tell him she wouldn't be home because she was staying with a pal. The cat was well and truly out of the bag and the cheating wife had been caught. You can only imagine the conversation that took place when she got home that particular night.

I had always been proud of my fitness and made sure it was one of my main attributes as a footballer but, when the Brighton players acted as a bunch of cheating b*******, Alan Mullery must have thought I was well out of condition. This happened early in the pre-season training when we were taken on a cross-country run. For the final part of the course, we had to do a U-turn at the end of a road and run back about half a mile to the finishing line.

I was in third place behind John Gregory and Giles Stille and, when we got to the point where were to make the U-turn, I looked back and saw that the rest of the squad were taking a shortcut through some trees well behind me. Now they were well in front of me and I came in last. I couldn't believe it, nor could I believe that Brighton's assistant manager, Ken Craggs, who saw the whole thing, didn't do anything about it. Back at the training ground, Alan Mullery spoke to the players and said, 'Good run.' Then he turned to me and said, 'I know you have come down from Scotland and the fitness levels are maybe not the same as down here but you're obviously going to have to work a lot more on your fitness.'

I looked at Ken Craggs, waiting for him to say something, but he never let on that the rest of the squad had cheated. I never found out if I was being set up and they were waiting for me to protest about being done out of first place or whether there was a cheating culture at Brighton that needed to be exposed. In any case, having just arrived at the club, I wasn't in a position to make a song and dance about what had happened.

We did a pre-season tour of Holland and I played well in those games, particularly against Twente Enschede. Their manager approached Alan Mullery and asked if I was available for transfer as they wanted to buy me. But, when they were told how much I had cost Brighton a few weeks earlier, their interest suddenly waned. Obviously, the big money transfer fees being paid in the UK hadn't reached across the North Sea to Holland yet.

I was being played in central midfield in exactly the same role I had had with Rangers and being encouraged to break forward from midfield to support the strikers. At the time, Brighton played with two strikers up front – Peter Ward and Mike Robinson. I was Brighton's biggest signing for all of two weeks until they signed Mike Robinson from Manchester City. I had cost £440,000 and they paid £500,000 for Mike.

We had quite a good side with players like Brian Horton, fellow-Scot Neil McNab, John Gregory and centre backs Steve Foster and Mark Lawrenson who went on to play with Liverpool.

I scored for Brighton on my debut, which was the first league game of the season against Wolves. We won 2–0. I had a good start to the season and scored only the second hat-trick in my professional career against Coventry away from home. I was all the more delighted to score the hat-trick because we were 3–0 down at the time.

They were all good goals, scored from shots outside the box. I almost got a fourth when I beat the keeper with a header and one of their defenders popped up on the line to clear. Alan Mullery was delighted with me that day and was very appreciative of my efforts. He was very good with me all the time he was manager at Brighton.

As the season wore on, we did start to struggle in the league, which was not surprising when you consider the standard of football being played in the English First Division. We were playing against giants like Liverpool, Manchester United, Tottenham Hotspur – who were a force at that time – and Aston Villa who won the league that year.

With only four games to go, we were well and truly entrenched in the relegation zone and, to guarantee we stayed in the First Division, we would have to win our last four games. That was when I had the most amazing pep talk of my career.

The players were called into the boardroom for a meeting with the manager, Alan Mullery, and the chairman, Mike Bamber. The manager began by saying that we had been struggling and that we would have to win our last four games. Alan Mullery looked round the table and said, 'If we get relegated this season, I will probably lose my job and, if I lose my job, it will all be down to you players. Let me tell you, I will get you all one by one if I lose my job here and I'm not joking. I just want you to know that I have got some heavy friends and that is all I'm telling you right now.'

It was the weirdest thing I have ever heard a manager tell me but nobody was taking him seriously. I was sitting beside Neil McNab and the two of us were shaking, trying not to burst out laughing. What made it even funnier was that Alan Mullery said, 'You will be crossing the road one day and I will knock you down with my car.' I almost fell off my chair when Neil leant over and whispered, 'If he loses his job, he'll no' have a f****** car!'

I thought Brighton's chairman Mike Bamber was going to calm things down when he interrupted the manager and said, 'Let me come in here.' But he went on to say, 'I just want you boys to know, I've got some heavy friends as well.'

There were a few seconds of silence until the team captain, Brian Haughton, said, 'Look, boss, this should be all about the football. You've changed the team about of late and at the beginning of the season it was going really well with Gordon playing centre midfield and having a free role to go and attack. But you changed it and had Gordon playing more as a sitting midfield player. Why don't we go back to the way we were playing earlier in the season?'

Alan Mullery replied, 'That's what we'll do. We'll go back to playing the system we started with at the beginning of the season.'

With that, the meeting broke up and the players were laughing about what they had just heard. It was really weird and I can only assume that Alan Mullery and Mike Bamber were just winding us up. It really would be a stretch of the imagination to believe gangsters were waiting to do us all in if the team got relegated. None of the players took it seriously, we were just laughing our heads off.

However, the system we had been playing was indeed changed and we reverted to the tactics employed at the start of the season. The main change was that I was given a free role behind the strikers. That was what was happening at the start of the season but, when a few results started going against us, I was put in a more defensive role. Now I was back in that free role again and playing in front of midfield just behind the strikers. It was a 4–3–1–2 formation and it worked well for us. There's no question that has always been my best position.

The next game we played was a big game against Crystal Palace in which I scored one and made the other two goals in a 3–1 victory. The following week it was a chance to meet up with my old manager Jock Wallace who was then in charge of Leicester City. We were at home that day and, although I didn't score, we won 2–0.

Next up was Sunderland who were also in deep relegation

trouble. We beat them 2–1 with a goal in the ninety-second minute. I crossed to our fullback Gary Williams who volleyed home. For the final game of the season – and the one that could keep us in the First Division – we had to beat Leeds United at home. We won 2–0 and that meant we had won the final four games of the season and survived in the top flight. We had beaten the odds because we were a small team and favourites to go down.

I had scored ten goals from midfield that season, which was quite a good return for a midfielder at that level. For me, it had been a good season – we had stayed up, I felt I had made a significant contribution to the cause and I was getting on well with the manager. Then another bombshell dropped. Two weeks into the close season, I was on holiday and it was announced that Alan Mullery was leaving Brighton.

So, another manager who had brought me to the club was quitting after just one season. I liked Mullers and I was genuinely sorry to see him go. The story doing the rounds was that he'd had a fall-out with the chairman, Mike Bamber, about how the previous season had gone. We often wondered if him leaving had anything to do with that strange team meeting in the boardroom when it was one of the players and not the manager who suggested we should change our tactics and that was what had kept the club in the First Division.

Another blow that close season was Brian Horton, the club captain, leaving to play with Luton and Mark Lawrenson being transferred to Liverpool. There were four clubs chasing Mark's signature – Arsenal, Tottenham, Manchester United and Liverpool – so he was in a great position and his future was set.

Mike Bailey, the then Charlton manager, was brought in to replace Alan Mullery who, ironically, then went on to Charlton to replace Mike Bailey. The new Brighton boss brought in a guy called John Collins to be his assistant and made Steve Foster captain.

It was an entirely different regime from the one that Alan

Mullery had in place. The new manager and his assistant were much more intense and were much more into playing to a well-organised and strict formula than free-flowing football. We were all told where we had to be on the park when the ball was in a certain position. It was almost like playing football by numbers. At the start of that season 1981–82 I was moved from central midfield out to the left wing. We were playing a strict 4–4–2 formation with no room for a free player. But, in fairness, Mike had brought in two excellent central midfield players in Jimmy Case from Liverpool and Ireland's captain Tony Grealish.

I was being told that, when the opposition had the ball on my side of the park, I had to force play to the inside and the next midfield player in from me had to be ten yards away from me. I used to joke that we should all be tied together with a giant piece of string so that no matter what happened we would always be in the right position. Whatever the players' feelings, we were well organised and difficult to play against.

Having said that, it was becoming obvious to everyone that we were becoming a really boring team – boring to watch and boring to play in. The last thing Mike Bailey would say to us before we left the dressing room for a game was, 'Nil–nil will do me.'

Boring we might have been, but our organisation on the park ensured we were picking up points in the early part of the season. Instead of a club that had been battling relegation, we were now in the top six in the First Division. And that was good for the wage packet.

The bonus structure changed and we were now on a £500 bonus if we won and we were in the top six, £400 for a win if we were in the top half of the league and a £200 bonus if we were in the bottom half. That was really good money and we stayed in the top six until about November and in the top half of the league for most of the rest of the season. It was only until the last three or four games that we fell into the bottom half of the league.

In January of 1982, my penchant for being outspoken got me

into trouble – again. We were in the dressing room and John Collins said all the players should have a bet on ourselves to win the FA Cup because we would get odds of 25–1. I was trying to have a joke with him and said, 'I'll give you 50–1 if you want to put a bet on.' He asked what I meant and I replied, 'The way we play is great for the league, but you have to go out and try to win games in the cup and we don't do that.'

One word was about to lead to another and he said, 'What do you know about winning the cup?'

I replied, 'Well, I've got four cup medals.'

'Yes but that's in Mickey Mouse football.'

'It got us into Europe. Have you ever been with a team that's played in Europe?'

'Nobody bothers about Scottish football – anybody can win a cup up there.'

The spat finished there and it was obvious, from that point on, that there was going to be a bit of animosity between us. I don't know if that incident had any bearing on me being left out of the team on a few occasions before the end of that season. And, by the way, we were put out of the FA Cup in the first round, at home to Oxford.

I had a big row with Mike Bailey around that time. We were playing a friendly against the Nigerian national side at Brighton and it turned into a real roughhouse. I was playing up front and we were winning 3–0 when their six-feet-four centre half came up to me and said, 'You are shit.'

'What do you mean?' I asked.

'I said you are shit. You are a bad team. Liverpool are a good team but you are shit.'

'Well, if we're beating you 3–0 and we're shit, what does that make you?'

And the giant centre half answered menacingly, 'I am going to get you. I'll kill you.'

After that, some really bad tackles were going in and Tony Grealish got such a bad tackle you could see the bone and the ligaments in his leg through the gash. The whole Nigerian team were acting like maniacs and, at the final whistle after we had won 5–0, I said to the big centre half, 'So who's shit now?'

'But we're amateurs,' he said.

'Yes, we can tell,' I replied.

That's when he went off his head and came chasing after me. There was a huge scuffle in the tunnel and he had to be held back while I headed for the dressing room.

About ten days later, I walked into the club and was told to go to the treatment room to get an injection from the club doctor. When I asked what it was for, I was told we were going to play a return match against Nigeria, in their capital city, Lagos. I immediately said I wasn't going. 'It's one of the worst places in the world,' I said. 'The land that time forgot.'

I was sent to see Mike Bailey and told him I was refusing to go to Nigeria. 'Lagos is a horrible place and you saw what they were like playing us. They're maniacs and one guy said he was going to kill me.'

Mike Bailey said that, if I didn't go, he would fine me two weeks' wages.

'Do you want to take it out of my wages or do you want a cheque right now?' I asked him.

I got back to the dressing room and the boys were wondering what was going on. I told them about Nigeria and why I wasn't going. One by one, the rest of the team agreed they wouldn't go either. A team meeting was held and we told the management we weren't prepared to go to Lagos to play the Nigerians. The following day the doctor was back in, giving the reserves their injections for going to Nigeria. Mike Bailey didn't even go and no one was fined. The incredible thing was that, although the reserve boys didn't enjoy the trip, they played in front of 90,000 people in Lagos – the biggest crowd most of us would ever have experienced at that stage in our careers. The reserves were used to playing in front of 200–300 fans.

At the beginning of pre-season training in 1982–83, I got a

phone call from Ken Craggs, our former assistant manager, who was now at Charlton along with my old manager, Alan Mullery. He said they knew I was out of favour with Mike Bailey, but they wanted to buy me and they had already offered Brighton £200,000 plus two of their young players in the deal. The two youngsters were Paul Elliot and Paul Walsh, who turned out to be top-class players. Ken said it would take another week or two to finalise the deal but, when I came back from the Brighton pre-season trip to Holland, they would get the deal tied up.

Two days later, the players met up at Brighton's Goldstone ground at 7.30 a.m. to get on the team bus for Dover and cross the Channel to our training camp in the south of Holland. I was on the bus, which was just about to leave, and Mike Bailey asked if everyone has their passports. 'Hold on,' I said. 'I've forgotten mine. But I live only a few minutes from here and if you drive the bus to my house it won't take me a minute to find it.'

The bus driver headed to my house, I jumped off and rushed inside. I shouted to Marlene, 'Where's my passport?'

'I've no idea,' she replied.

'What do you mean you've no idea? You know where all that kind of stuff is kept.'

For the next fifteen minutes, Marlene and I were like robbers ransacking a house. We were emptying drawers and just throwing the contents everywhere and pulling things out of cupboards. The place was an absolute mess by the time we stopped and we still hadn't found my passport.

Embarrassed to say the least, I went back out to the bus and told Mike Bailey I couldn't find my passport and he said there was no alternative but for me to get off and get my bag out of the hold at the back of the bus. The rest of the team had heard that Charlton were interested in me and they thought I had pulled a stunt so I wouldn't have to go to Holland with them. As I walked to the back of the bus to get a carrier bag I had left there, they were saying things like, 'You're well out of order' and 'You're some man, we know what you're up to.'

I went back into the house, Marlene made some breakfast and we were discussing what I could do next. Marlene suggested I had better go back to the stadium and try to get the club to organise something for me because everyone would think I deliberately couldn't find my passport. So I saw the club secretary and explained what had happened. He sent me to get a passport picture taken at a photo booth, while he organised the forms. By the time I got back, everything was in order and I took the forms and my photograph to the Post Office to get a one-year passport. Meanwhile, the club were booking me on a flight to Amsterdam.

I flew to Amsterdam, got a train, changed to another train and then another before getting a taxi to the hotel at our training camp. It was just after 4 p.m. and I was standing in reception when the team bus drew up outside. You should have seen the look of disbelief when they walked into reception. I was the last person in the world they expected to see standing there.

I explained to Mike Bailey how I'd got myself a new passport, got a plane, three trains and a taxi to get here and I could see his attitude towards me was changing. I'm sure he thought I was at it when I said I couldn't find my passport but, when he discovered I had made such an effort, he realised I had been genuine.

That was me at the training camp and we were to play three games in the PSV Eindhoven tournament, as part of the trip. I came on as sub in the first game and started the next two.

Back in Brighton after the Holland trip, the phone rang and it was Ken Craggs. 'What have you been doing?' he asked me.

'What do you mean?'

'The deal's off. Mike Bailey was delighted with you in the games over in Holland. He thought you were great and he was impressed with your attitude. He says he's not selling you – he wants to keep you.'

I was astounded – I'd blown the whole transfer. I was happy to be going to Charlton and I was happy with the wages they were willing to pay me. I was even getting the old ex gratia payment from Brighton, which was worth £25,000 to me. It was a real blow as I thought everything was set up and ready to go when I got back from Holland.

I didn't want to go in and say to Mike Bailey I wanted to leave because he could have said no and kept me out the team for being disloyal. So I started off the next season thinking I had better make the best of it and be part of the team at Brighton. I loved being at Brighton but I wanted first-team football.

In the early part of the season, I was getting a regular game but the results weren't going our way. By November, Mike Bailey and John Collins were being heavily criticised for their boring style of play by everyone from the chairman to the fans. There is no doubt we were a boring team to watch. Every game was played like an away European tie, stopping the opposition playing and only getting up their end of the park on the counter-attack. It was not nice to watch and the fans were becoming restless.

A few years earlier, when Brighton were working their way up the leagues from the Third to the First Division, the fans were used to exciting attacking football played with a bit of flair. Now, although they were in the top flight, they were seeing their team not even trying to win – just playing not to get defeated, even in the home games.

I was dropped from the first team in mid November and was left kicking my heels for a fortnight when, out of the blue, I got a phone call from Tommy McLean who was now assistant manager to John Greig at Rangers. He wanted me to come back on a month's loan to Rangers.

I spoke to him on the Wednesday before Rangers were due to play a League Cup final against Celtic, at Hampden. I told Tommy I would need to think about it but, if I was coming on loan, I would see him the following Monday after the cup final.

'No,' said Tommy. 'We want you to play in the cup final.'

I still wasn't convinced about going back for the cup final because, if Rangers didn't win, I was going to be the one getting the blame. I told Tommy I would get back to him.

I went to see Jimmy Melia, who was Brighton's chief scout at the time, and told him about the loan offer. 'I'm not sure about this, Jimmy,' I said. 'Going back up the road and straight into a cup final in my first game. What do you think?'

'Why don't you go back to Scotland for a month. You'll be home over Christmas and New Year, play in your cup final and another few games and, when you come back after your month, I'll be manager here.'

I was shocked at what Jimmy had told me as there hadn't been any talk of Mike Bailey's position being under threat.

'Don't say anything to anybody,' said Jimmy.

That made me feel a lot easier, so I agreed to go to Rangers for the month's loan. As it turned out, Celtic beat Rangers 2–1 in the final. I played another league game and was dropped for the remaining two games of my loan period.

There was one good thing about my month at Ibrox and that was meeting up with the Rangers sprint coach, Stuart Hogg. When he saw me in training at the start of my month's loan, he pulled me aside and said he thought my fitness had suffered since I had gone down south. I had to agree because the conditioning training I was getting at Brighton was nowhere near as tough as what I had been used to at Kilmarnock and Rangers.

For the remaining fortnight of my loan period Stuart worked with me and gave me back the fitness and sharpness I had been missing. I was very grateful for what he did for me and I gave him my League Cup runners-up medal as a thank you.

Only a week after I had left Brighton to go on loan to Rangers, Jimmy Melia's prediction came true. Mike Bailey and John Collins were shown the door and Jimmy was made Brighton manager. When I got back to Brighton in January, Jimmy noticed right away that I was a lot quicker and sharper so he put me straight back into the Brighton team.

Although Jimmy Melia was manager in name, the real power at Brighton was the club captain Steve Foster. Fossie had a huge amount of influence at the club. So much so, you could almost describe him as the chairman/manager/social convener – the lot. But, credit to him, he was good at it. He was a huge character about the place and kept a great atmosphere going.

Although everyone in Brighton was caught up in FA Cup final fever in the early part of 1983, we were struggling to pick up points in the league. We were playing quite well and getting the breaks in the cup games and that's what helped us get all the way to final – and there's more about that in the next chapter.

Our form was good but we were still struggling to get out of the bottom end of the table. I always say that, if you are playing well and not winning, that's when you are in real trouble. That was what we were doing so we were classic relegation material – and that's exactly what happened. Amidst all the hype and euphoria about getting to the FA Cup final, hardly anyone noticed we had been relegated.

After the FA Cup final, the team went on an end-of-season trip to America. It turned out to be a bit of a farce because the manager and all the directors could take their partners and they stayed in a swanky hotel in Beverly Hills, Los Angeles. The players were dropped off at a hotel in Inglewood, which was a very rough area of Los Angeles. There was a bit of resentment amongst the players about this and, since we were left to our own devices, we got our own back by going out on the town at night and the early hours of the morning. We had three games to play there and we were in a terrible state. The players would get back to their hotel about 7 a.m., after being out partying, have about three hours' sleep and then get on the bus to be taken to a stadium to play our game. There was no discipline among the players because all the club officials were in Beverly Hills hobnobbing with the rich and famous.

I was drinking by this time but nothing like as much as some of the boys. I had been teetotal until my second season at Brighton. I would go out with the boys and they would refuse to buy me a drink because they said they wouldn't embarrass themselves by buying a soft drink. So I was buying my own.

Eventually I got fed up with this and they started ordering me beer shandies. The night I got my first shandy with them in a club, they gave me a round of applause. From shandies I progressed to pints of lager and lime but, apart from wine with a meal, I never took anything stronger.

There was a real drinking culture among the players at Brighton. Normally, our day off was a Wednesday and that was when the boys would meet up for a game of golf, a meal and then drinking until three or four in the morning. I discovered that even if I'd had quite a few pints, after a few hours' sleep, I'd be as right as rain. The other ritual, which I found strange for professional footballers, who were supposed to perform at their peak on a Saturday afternoon, was the Friday afternoon Italian meal with a good few glasses of Lambrusco to wash it down.

I can't remember the first time I was drunk – well, if I was that bad I wouldn't remember, would I? But it would definitely have been on one of the Wednesday golf and drinking sessions. We would normally head to a well-known Brighton nightspot called the King's Club. There was a private bar there where all the boys would congregate and practise being apprentice sponges. They were that good at soaking up the drink. There's no doubt when I was learning to drink I had excellent tuition. When it came to drinking, the boys were brilliant. If they had been in a league for drinking, they would have been in the Champions League.

At the start of season 1983–84, Jimmy Melia found himself with an assistant manager. Chairman Mike Bamber had brought in former Brighton player, Chris Cattlin to work alongside Jimmy. Up until that point, Chris Cattlin had been running a shop that sold sticks of Brighton rock. When he arrived at the club, I noticed he began to take a lot more to do with the training sessions and, almost from the start, he undermined Jimmy Melia with the players. He was talking behind Jimmy's back all the time, slagging him off and telling us to ignore things that Jimmy had said.

There was one incident which summed up the difference in

attitude between Chris Cattlin and Jimmy Melia. Normally, Jimmy Melia would make sure there wasn't a very hard training session on a Thursday because he knew we would all have been out clubbing it the night before. This message obviously hadn't been passed on to Chris Cattlin who took a Thursday morning session and proceeded to run us ragged. Some of the boys were still drunk from the night before and their exertions were really causing havoc. Some were falling over when they went to shoot and were kicking their own legs and tripping themselves up. Chris Cattlin abandoned the session and ordered everyone into the dressing room where he started to read the Riot Act. At that point, Jimmy Melia came in to ask what was going on and Chris Cattlin went on a rant about our disgraceful attitude and lack of professionalism.

He turned to Jimmy and said, 'You can see the state of them. They were out drinking all last night.'

Jimmy looked at the players and said, 'Were you lot out drinking last night?'

'Yes, boss.'

'Well, I was in the King's Club last night looking for you all. Where were you?'

We knew that something was going on and Jimmy was being set up for a fall. Sure enough, the season was only about two months gone and Jimmy was sacked with Chris Cattlin taking over as manager.

We weren't doing well in the league. The FA Cup final was history and we were playing against teams who were willing to fight like fury and were desperate to beat us. We were languishing mid table when Jimmy was shown the door. The first game after Jimmy was sacked was at home and, all of a sudden during the game, there was a great commotion on the terraces. The players looked up and there was Jimmy being carried along on the shoulders of the supporters. The fans loved Jimmy and taking us to the FA Cup final will always have him in the club's folklore.

A month or so after Jimmy Melia left, I was called in to see the manager, Chris Cattlin. 'What's the problem with you?' he asked. 'You don't seem to be enjoying your football.'

I told him I wasn't really happy about the way we were being asked to play. Suddenly he said, 'Do you know your problem? You don't have any passion for the game. You don't hate losing enough.'

Now, that just lit my fuse. 'What do you mean I don't have any passion for the game? You run a rock shop. You didn't even used to come to watch us play, you were so busy selling sticks of rock on a Saturday afternoon,' I said.

Continuing my onslaught I said, 'You'd never seen us play and all of a sudden you're the manager. I've got more passion for football than you'll ever have.' Conversation over, I walked out of his office.

The following Saturday I wasn't even listed in the first-team squad. There was a reserve game the following midweek and I wasn't even in the squad for that either. I went to see the reserve team coach George Petchey and told him I really needed to get a game to keep my fitness levels up but he said I wasn't allowed to play.

I decided that, even although I wasn't getting a game for the reserves, I would go and watch them play in their away game that Wednesday. When I turned up at the stadium to get the reserve team bus, I was told that I wasn't being allowed on. Not only was I being banned from playing, I wasn't even being allowed to travel on the reserve team bus.

The following day I went to see the club secretary, Ron Pavey, and he informed me that I was banned from travelling with the first team or the reserves. By the time I was back downstairs, George Petchey was there with some of the youngsters and he told me I was to train with him and the kids.

I had about five months of this treatment – training with young teenagers, not getting a game and having to sit at home watching television when the first team was playing away from home. I sat in the stand at home games and a lot of the fans were telling me they couldn't believe I was being frozen out. Chris Cattlin had made it very clear to everyone that he wasn't happy with me and he thought my attitude was bad. But I still trained hard, did a lot of running and kept myself fit. George Petchey was a good coach and I didn't cause him a moment's problem.

Then at the beginning of March in 1984 I got a call from Billy McNeill – the ex-Celtic captain and now manager of Manchester City. Billy asked me how I was doing and I told him I was being frozen out at Brighton. He said City had a chance of being promoted from the Second Division and he wanted to bring me in to boost their chances.

That call was on the Monday and, the following Thursday, I was about to start my training with the youngsters when Sammy Nelson, the assistant manager who was taking the first-team training, shouted, 'Smudger, you're with this group.' As I walked towards the group of players they gave me a round of applause to welcome me back.

I was back in the first-team squad and we had an away game against Derby County on the Saturday and to my surprise, I was in the team. We won 3–0 and I scored the third – a 25-yard screamer into the top corner after taking a nice pass from Danny Wilson. I played well, considering I hadn't played for five months, and I was delighted. I wondered if the sudden interest from Manchester City had meant I was back in the first team. You always get more money for a player getting a game in the first team compared to someone who isn't even playing in the reserves. Chris Cattlin hadn't said a word to me for months but, after the Derby game, he told me I had done well.

The day after the Derby game, Billy McNeill called me and said he was definitely interested in signing me and he had already been in touch with Brighton about a transfer fee. They were asking for £45,000 and he said he hoped everything would be sorted by the end of the following week. On the Monday, Chris Cattlin called me into his office again to tell me that Manchester City wanted to sign me but I was surprised, to say the least, when he said he didn't want to sell me.

'I've got to be honest with you. Your attitude over the past few months has been fantastic. You've been bombed out but George Petchey says you're a great trainer, a first-class professional and you haven't caused him one bit of bother. I brought you in on Saturday and you were absolutely outstanding and I've made a mistake by leaving you out of the team. But you're back in – I want you playing for my team.'

'Let me tell you this right now,' I said, 'I want to leave this club this week. The way you have treated me over the past few months doesn't change anything after only one game back. I know I'm a good professional, I know I train well and I know I'm a good player. I want to go to Manchester City.'

He pleaded with me to stay but I told him I had made up my mind. Manchester City was a team I wanted to play for at that stage and I wanted them on my CV. The manager said, if that was the way I felt about it, I'd better go home.

For the bus journey to Derby for the game the previous Saturday, I had brought a cassette tape I had recorded of different songs and the boys had asked me to play it over the bus sound system. As I was going out the door of Chris Cattlin's office, he said a strange thing to me. 'See that compilation tape you played on the bus on Saturday? It was good. Any chance you would make one up for me?' I told him I would give him the tape I had with me on the bus and he said, 'That would be great.'

Later on that day, I got a call at home to go back in to the club. In Chris Cattlin's office he told me, 'The deal's done. You can go to Manchester City.'

'What about the £5,000 Brighton owe me in signing-on fees?' I asked.

'No, you won't get that,' he said.

'I'm owed that money and I want it before I leave.' I replied.

He left the room to talk to the chairman about my demand and when he came back he said, 'We'll give you £3,000.'

I said, 'No, I'm owed £5,000 and that's what I want.'

'Go away and think about it,' he said. 'That's the most I can offer you.'

As I was going out the door, he asked if I'd brought the compilation cassette tape he had asked me for. I said I had and was about to hand it to him when I pulled it back from his outstretched hand.

'I'll give you the tape if I can get the full £5,000 you owe me,' I said.

'Alright then,' he said. 'You can have your money.'

So I got the other £2,000 they owed me for making up a compilation cassette tape. That must have been the dearest piece of music Brighton ever paid for. I suppose you could call it Brighton Rock 'n' Roll!

9

LIFE IN THE CITY

The pain is excruciating as I lie in a hospital bed wondering if I'm ever going to walk properly again. The nurse has just left my bedside after giving me yet another injection of antibiotics in my backside but neither those jabs nor the painkillers I've been getting have any effect on the agony in my groin.

Memories of the games I have played in, goals that I've scored and trophies I've lifted go through my mind but it always comes back to the horrible, fearful feeling that I'll never be able to play football again.

I can't even begin to explain how much pain I was in and I wouldn't have wished what I was going through on my worst enemy. A specialist, Mr Markham, had just diagnosed me as suffering from osteomyelitis – bone marrow inflammation due to infection – in my pelvic bone. And, instead of celebrating winning promotion with my Manchester City team mates, I was in the Royal Alexandria Hospital, in Manchester.

The doctors suspected I caught the infection from a chilblain in my foot, which appeared after the penultimate game of season 1984–85 when we had beaten our promotion rivals Portsmouth 2–1. That had set us up for the final game of the season against Charlton, which we needed to win to clinch third place and a move to the First Division.

The night after the Portsmouth game, players and club officials were at a function in Cheadle Hulme, outside Manchester. I was with Marlene and as the night went on I began to feel a bit of discomfort in my groin. I thought nothing of it and put it down

145

to a strain from playing the game the previous day. But by the end of the meal I was in such pain I decided I needed to see someone about it.

The team physio, Roy Bailey, was also at the function and he came over to see me. Right away, I said I wanted to go to hospital, but he suggested we go to the team doctor's house for him to have a look at my groin.

Marlene and I got into Roy Bailey's car and, by the time we arrived at the doctor's house, I was in agony and could hardly walk from the car to his front door. I was in so much pain I had to lie on the floor while we were waiting for him to come into the room. Roy Bailey's wife was also there and while we were waiting she said, 'Maybe it's indigestion.' If I could have moved, I would have got up and given her a slap.

He checked me over and said, 'I don't know what the problem is but it looks quite serious and we should get Gordon to hospital.'

I was admitted to the hospital and had several X-rays of my groin but the doctors there couldn't find what was causing the pain and the high temperature I was now experiencing. They plied me with painkilling tablets and injections, which didn't do anything to ease the agony.

After two days, I asked them to call Mr Markham who was a specialist Manchester City used. He came to see me and, after checking me over, he told me I was suffering from osteomyelitis. 'This is pretty serious,' he said. 'You'll need major antibiotics to stop this from getting any worse.'

I have to admit I was frightened lying in that hospital. I'd been told that, if the infection gets into a joint, it can destroy that joint and you would need a stick to walk with for the rest of your life. I was very lucky – the infection stayed in my pelvic bone and didn't spread to any of my joints. The needles they were using to inject me were huge but I was in so much pain with my pelvis I couldn't feel a thing when they japed it into me. After several days the antibiotics were obviously starting to work because I could start to feel the injections in my backside.

I was in hospital for two weeks and, when I was discharged, I was taken home in an ambulance. At that point, I couldn't walk and was in bed at home for another two weeks. After a few days, I tried to take a few tentative steps. It was like learning to walk again. My legs had stiffened up so much I could only take tiny steps and, at first, I could only manage three or four steps a day. I was getting out of my bed but, within a minute, I had collapsed back into it again.

After being almost bedridden for a month, my walking began to get stronger but I knew there was going to be a long and lonely road back to being fit enough to play professional football.

When I was convalescing at home, Marlene asked me if, at any point in hospital, I thought I was going to die. I told her in all seriousness, 'No but there were times, when the pain was so bad, I wished I would die.'

That was at the end of season 1984–85, just over a year after I'd joined Manchester City from Brighton. I was delighted with the move and especially with getting to work with a legend of Scottish football, Billy McNeill. I had the utmost respect for Billy and what he had achieved in the game and, earlier in my career, he had shown in interest in signing me when he was Aberdeen manager. He was so magnanimous in defeat that he even congratulated me for scoring a hat-trick against Aberdeen when Rangers beat them 6–1.

Although I was taking a drop in wages from £650 a week at Brighton to £450 a week, I knew I had been offered a two-year contract and was going to get a regular game in the first team. That was the most important thing for me.

It was also a reunion with my old team mate at Ibrox, Derek Parlane, who was already playing for Manchester City when I arrived there. Derek even found me a new house in the same street where he was living in Wilmslow, a posh suburb. We were good pals at Rangers so the way things had panned out was brilliant.

When I joined the club in March 1984, City had an outside chance of promotion to the First Division and I was being brought in as a last-minute boost to try and make it to the top flight. However, despite a big effort on the part of the team, we were fourth in the league, just missing out on third place which would have seen us go up.

Just before the end of that season, I got a call from my old pal from Brighton, John Gregory. He had been talking to his manager at Queen's Park Rangers, Terry Venables. He had seen me play in a televised game against Chelsea – yes, believe it or not, they were in the Second Division that season – and was asking if I would fancy signing for him. Although QPR were in the First Division, I told John that I was happy at Manchester City and wasn't sure if they would agree to the transfer.

Nothing more happened and the next thing I heard was that Terry Venables had become manager of Barcelona. It did cross my mind that he might come in for me and I would be heading for Spain but that never happened.

I was having a great time at City. There was a real buzz about being at a big club, which Brighton didn't really have, and there was more of a family atmosphere there. I felt I was back in the big time and, even though our rivals, Manchester United, were always the bigger club, City were still pulling in more than 30,000 fans for home games.

City had a fanatical support. They were brilliant and one thing I noticed was that they rarely gave you a hard time. If things weren't going well, they'd always encourage you – really great supporters.

When I signed on for City I never asked what position Billy McNeill was going to play me in and it was a bit of a surprise when he read out the team sheet for my first game to discover I was wide on the right. I hadn't played in that position since my Kilmarnock days when I was used out there on the odd occasion.

I thought it was a bit strange but I was so happy to be getting a game after my months in exile at Brighton. I was keen to play there but I thought I would give it a few games and then try to influence Billy to play me in the centre of midfield or on the left. Eventually I was moved to play on the left.

We never got on the winning streak that was needed to get promotion but I was in there and the next season was going to be the big one.

I found pre-season hard-going and it was a sign my body was getting older. I was able to keep up with the other players but I noticed it took a lot more effort on my part to do that. I was twenty-nine and that was when I realised that I needed do some training myself during the summer break. Billy McNeill and the coaches – Glyn Pardoe and legendary City player Tony Book – put us all through the mill but I survived and felt better for it by the start of the season.

Before a run of pre-season friendlies, Billy McNeill was giving me a bit of stick about only scoring one goal since I'd signed in March. But that acted as a spur and I scored in all those games. It was also the first time I saw another side of Billy.

When I arrived at City, there were a few moans from the players about how he was treating the players. They didn't like the way he spoke to them and they said he was a Jekyll-and-Hyde character. One day, he would be your best pal, laughing and joking and, the next, he would be in a bad mood and giving you a hard time.

I would defend Billy in the dressing room when the other players started to moan about him. I told them he just wanted success because he had played at the highest level and wanted the same for City. I told them I had the greatest respect for the manager. But, a few months after signing, I witnessed a couple of incidents and I began to wonder if the players had a point.

The club provided the players with similar tracksuits to wear on the way to matches. On the way to one game, our centre half, the Republic of Ireland internationalist Mick McCarthy, suggested to Billy that it would be good idea if the club got Adidas to give us the same training shoes, so they matched as well. Billy told him he thought it was a good idea.

At half-time that day, we were getting beaten 1–0 and Billy was none too happy with our performance. He turned to Mick

McCarthy and said, 'As for you, all you're interested in is what trainers we're wearing.' Mick wasn't best pleased that something they'd had a conversation about six hours before was being brought up as a way of having a go at him.

Billy would also have a wee dig at me and the fact I stayed in what he thought was a posh area. 'That'll be you and your wine-drinking set,' he would say when he was supposed to be talking about something I'd done on the football park.

The players used to have a laugh at Billy and say he could trace the reason for a goal against us halfway through a match all the way back to the kick-off if he wanted to put the blame on a particular player.

But I soon got wise to Billy's mood swings. He would have a go at me for making a mistake during a game and I would say, 'Yes, boss. You're right – I shouldn't have given the ball away.'

Billy would reply, 'Are you just going to agree with me?'

'I'm just agreeing with you because you're right,' I'd say.

'You're just agreeing with me so I'll shut up!' and Billy would storm off.

I don't know why but Billy was always looking for an argument – he liked confrontation. It might have been that he thought confrontation would make us more determined and we were too soft for his liking. He didn't even like the fact that I was agreeing with him when he was criticising me.

There was one particular incident which made me think the other players were right to complain about Billy. It happened during that first pre-season I had with City and the squad had been split in half to play two games over the weekend. I was in the team to play Crewe on the Saturday and we beat them 5–1 with me getting two goals. Billy was delighted and said we could have Monday off because of the good performance.

On the Sunday night, I got a phone call from one of the coaches who said I was to be at the ground the following morning for training. 'I've made plans,' I said. 'I was told I'd be off until Tuesday.'

'Doesn't matter,' I was told, 'everybody's to be in.'

What had happened was that the other half of the squad had been beaten 2–1 by Chester and Billy was raging at their performance. He had ordered everyone in for training because of the defeat. When we got on the park the next morning, Billy said, 'That lot's a disgrace losing 2–1 to Chester. You're all going to be running this morning.'

As always, I was the one to speak up. 'Hang on a minute,' I said. 'We played on Saturday and you told us that if we did well we could have Monday off. We won the game 5–1 so why am I here? Why is any of that team here?'

'Because you're all a team together,' said Billy.

'You're only a team when you can actually influence what happens,' I replied. 'The team I was in won our game and we shouldn't be here.'

But Billy was having none of it. 'I don't care if you agree with this or not – start running.'

The players were angry at the way they were being treated and there was a lot of muttering under the breath as we did lap after lap for half an hour. We had stopped for a breather and everyone had their heads down, not wanting to look at Billy when he said to me, 'You enjoying this, Smudger?'

I looked at him and said, 'It's the most fun I've had without laughing.'

Billy then started laughing and said, 'That's a great line – I like that.'

And, to everyone's amazement, he added, 'On you go – that'll do you.'

As we trooped off to the dressing room, the boys were slapping my back in congratulations for managing to get the training session cut short. Because I had made Billy laugh, he decided everything was OK again and we were given the rest of the day off.

Every time Billy did something to annoy you, you'd be gritting your teeth. But, the next time he saw you and was nice and friendly, you couldn't help but like him. That's the way I was with him. When he was in a good mood, he endeared himself to me. He was such a football legend, we were always looking for his approval and, if you didn't get it, you got annoyed with him.

By midway through season 1984–85, we were going well and always in the hunt for a promotion spot but I was heading for what I believed was a watershed in my life – my thirtieth birthday. We had a game against Wolves at Maine Road on my birthday and I scored my 100th league goal in a 4–1 win. I was given the man-of-the-match award and took the presentation bottle of champagne home with me for the party that had been organised with all my family coming down from Scotland.

But the bubbles had gone flat for me. I was strangely down about the whole thing. Depression is too serious and strong a word to describe how I felt but turning thirty definitely had a strange, melancholy effect on me. I was on a downer because I believed being thirty meant I was coming to the closing stages of my football career and I didn't want that. At that time, when you reached thirty, people started to write you off as a has-been – and that worried me.

You'll have already read about the Manchester City trip to Malaysia in the January of 1985 when the wee boy had a go at me for missing the goal in the last minute of extra time in the FA Cup final at Wembley. Well, that trip was a bit of shocker in other ways. And it was another example of how Billy's change of mood and attitude could upset players.

Before we left for Malaysia, Billy had told us that we were going for ten days. We'd be playing one game over there and we were just to relax and enjoy ourselves. That was great and everyone was looking forward to the trip. When we got to the airport, the boys piled into the bar for a few beers. Billy came into the bar and announced, 'Put your drinks down and get out the bar.'

'What are you talking about?' we asked.

'You're not drinking on this trip – this is a serious trip.'

'But you said we were to relax and wind down.'

'No, you're not having a drink.'

So that was the players hauled out the bar and we were also told there would be no drinking alcohol on the flight out either.

We got to Kuala Lumpur and were on an internal flight to play what we thought was our one and only game of the trip. I had bought an English-language local paper and was reading it on the flight. As I was flicking through the pages, I saw this advert – 'Dunhill presents Manchester City on tour'. There were four matches listed and it gave the teams we were playing. I showed it to the other players and they said it must be a mistake. I showed the paper to one of the stewards who said, 'Yes, Dunhill are sponsoring you.'

I said, 'No, it's not the Dunhill bit I'm talking about – it's the games.'

'That's right, you're playing four games over here. Did you not know that?'

We certainly did not and would have had something to say about having to play four games in ten days in the sweltering heat. Our captain, Paul Power, spoke to one of the club officials and he confirmed that, instead of just the one game, we were going to play four.

The players were angry because playing in that heat and humidity was strength sapping. The sweat was pouring out of us – and that was us just getting changed in the dressing room.

We had left Britain on the Sunday after a league game, didn't have a game the following Saturday because we had been put out of the FA Cup and arrived back home the Thursday before our next league game. We were shattered and the youngster, Clive Wilson, went down with a virus he had picked up over there.

We went into an important game with Crystal Palace away from home on the Saturday and struggled. We managed to squeeze a 2–1 victory, thanks to a goal in the final minutes of the game. Back in the dressing room after the final whistle, Billy was in a rage and shouting in people's faces about bad we were.

If Billy was angry, the players were even angrier. We were in the middle of a promotion race and the club had flown us to the other side of the world to play four matches in stifling heat. And we only had one full day to recover from the trip home before being harangued for only winning 2–1.

Billy's style when he was angry was to tower over you and be in your face as he launched into his tirade. But there was one player in the team who would always stand up to Billy. Mick McCarthy wouldn't put up with Billy's shouting displays. There was one occasion in the dressing room at half time when Billy and Mick faced up to each other and were going at it hammer and tongs. The decibel levels would have broken any noise meter. Billy finished off by saying, 'Know your problem, mate? This is your big problem – you've always got to get the last word.'

'I don't always have to get the last word,' replied Mick.

'Yes, you do.'

'No, I don't.'

'Yes, you do,'

'No, I don't.'

It was like a pantomime script and the curtain only came down on the performance when one of the coaches, Jimmy Frizell, got between them and quietened them down before it came to blows.

Although the team were doing well and we were getting the results, Billy had, to a degree, lost the dressing room. We were playing for the club, the fans and ourselves and that's what kept up a good team spirit.

We were well in the running for a promotion place when I hurt my ankle quite badly. It was the week of the penultimate game against Portsmouth and I was desperate to play. I told the physio, Roy Bailey, I wanted an injection of cortisone to reduce the inflammation and pain so I could play on the Saturday. I was sent to see the specialist, Mr Markham, who agreed to inject my ankle but he wanted to do an X-ray first.

He came back with the X-ray and asked me, 'When did you break your ankle?'

'I've never broken my ankle,' I replied.

He assured me I had broken my ankle and showed me the X-

It's in the blood – my grandad, Mattha Smith
(front row, second from left), in a Kilmarnock team photo from the 1920s

Winning ways – the 1st Stevenston Boys' Brigade league-
and cup-winning team – I'm in the front row on the far left

At home – here are my dad, Bill, my mum, Edith, my sister, Elaine, and me. I was twenty when this picture was taken in 1975

The graduate – in June 1977, I graduated with a degree in Business Studies

The Kilmarnock team pictured in 1974 – back row, from left to right: Ian McCulloch, George Maxwell, Alan Robertson, Jim Stewart, Derek McDicken, Ronnie Sheed and Jim Whyte; front row, from left to right: Jim Cook, Eddie Morrison, Brian Rodman, Jim McSherry, Ian Fleming and me

Who's the star? – when I took the job developing the marketing strategy for a firm called Edward McNeil, I was very proud to have the use of this company car, a Datsun 120Y. We were snapped on my first day at Ibrox in 1977

My wedding day in June 1978 – Marlene and I had arranged the wedding for this time but, if the call had come from Ally McLeod to join the Scotland squad for the World Cup in Argentina, I would have postponed it

Proud parents – our first child, Grant, was born in May 1980

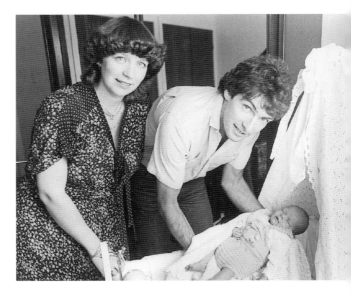

A happy family – Grant was followed by our first daughter, Leigh-Anne, in November 1981 and, in May 1988, our family was complete with the arrival of baby Libby

Three generations of Smiths – me with my son, Grant, and my dad, Bill. We're in the Scottish Football Museum at Hampden Park, looking at the Rangers shirt I wore when I won a Scottish Cup medal in 1979. This was fifty years after my grandad, Mattha Smith, won his second Scottish Cup medal with Kilmarnock and, next to my top, is the strip he wore that day

A dream come true – here I am signing for Rangers in August 1977 with, to the left, the Kilmarnock manager, Willie Fernie and, to the right, the Rangers manager, Jock Wallace, looking on

Early success – Rangers have just won the League Cup in 1978 and here I am celebrating with, from left to right, Derek Johnstone, Davie Cooper and Alex Miller

A Brighton boy – I may not have been keen on a transfer from Rangers but, in 1982, I joined Brighton. I ended up loving it there – especially when we got to the final of the FA Cup in 1983

A City boy – in 1985, I was playing with Manchester City under manager, Billy McNeill, who, I later found out, had long been an admirer, having tried to sign me for both Celtic and Aberdeen

© Simon Dack – *The Argus*, Brighton

And Smith must score . . . it's 2–2 in the closing minutes of the FA Cup final against Manchester United and the ball falls to me. All I have to do to win the cup for Brighton is put the ball in the back of the net but what do I do? I miss! No, of course, I don't – goalie Gary Bailey makes a fantastic save

Golfing mates – from left to right: Paul Lambert, a Celtic hero, now managing Livingston; me; Dutch midfielder, Ronald de Boer, who played for Rangers between 2000 and 2004; and the Celtic goal-scoring legend, Henrik Larssen, who played for the club from 1997 to 2004 before moving to Barcelona

Happy birthday to you – Leigh-Anne, left, Grant and Libby celebrate Grant's twenty-fifth birthday in May 2005

ray and pointed to where the bone had broken off. 'It looks like you broke it a few months ago, probably at the beginning of the season,' he said.

I hadn't missed a game all season but I remembered early on complaining about having a sore ankle, which was put down to a bad sprain. It didn't stop me playing because, before every game, I would put on a heavy stirrup strapping. I went on like this for weeks and the ankle was never X-rayed.

Mr Markham said, 'You've definitely broken your ankle at some point and it's healed itself to an extent but you'll probably have an arthritic problem later on in life.'

'Something nice to look forward to,' I thought but the more pressing problem was to be able to play on the Saturday, so I got my cortisone injection.

Within a week my ankle was the least of my problems as, by then, I was in hospital with osteomyelitis. I missed the celebrations when they beat Charlton 4–0 to win promotion, but I got a call from Billy McNeill the following day to ask how I was and to thank me for the part I'd played in their success by being top scorer with fourteen goals. And that was the first and last I heard from the club in all the time I was in hospital. The players were being advised not to visit me in case I had the same virus Clive Wilson caught while he was in Malaysia.

By the time I was back on my feet and well on the way to recovery, I weighed only ten stone instead of my normal playing weight of twelve stone. I was determined to get back playing and I did a lot of weight-training on my own to build up my muscles again. But, when pre-season training started for the rest of the team, I was nowhere near ready to join them and I had my own training regime to work my way back to fitness. Then I started training with the reserves but the club wouldn't give me a game with them. By September, I was desperate to play and I had to ask the coaches to play me in a reserve match but they kept asking if I was sure I was ready to make a comeback.

I felt like a leper – the forgotten man. I wasn't being allowed to train with the first team and I wasn't getting a game with the reserves. When players asked how I was getting on and I said I would soon be back playing, their reaction was as if they didn't believe me. The word had got out that nobody can come back from something as serious as osteomyelitis.

I pestered everyone for a game in the reserves and eventually they relented. I was playing quite well and getting among the goals. The next step was that I was allowed to train with the first team although I wasn't getting anywhere near a game with the first team.

By this time, it was December 1985 and, just before Christmas, I got a call from Billy McNeill to tell me Wolves were interested in signing me. On Christmas Eve, I went to Molyneux to see their manager, Sammy Chapman. He seemed very keen to get me and told me he knew about my health problem but knew by this point I was over it. He offered me the same wages I was on at Manchester City and, because I knew I was being bombed out at Maine Road, I decided to take up his offer. I did also warn him that I was still owed signing-on money from Manchester City and I would have to get that sorted first.

Early the following day – Christmas Day – I got a phone call from Billy McNeill who said, 'What's happening? Are you going to sign for Wolves?' He was delighted when I said I had decided to go there.

'But first I need to get the money Manchester City owe me – it's £8000,' I told him.

But Billy said there was no way I was getting the money and we argued about it for a few minutes before he put the phone down on me.

A couple of days later, I got another morning phone call from Billy before I had left the house to go to training. 'What's happening with the Wolves thing?' he asked.

'I'm not going until I get my money,' I replied.

'I'll give you £1000.'

'I'm not taking £1000.'

'Well, that's all your f****** getting.'

I went into training that morning and nothing more was said.

The next morning, I hadn't even got up out my bed when the phone went. It was Billy saying, 'What are you doing?'

'I'm still in my bed and I'm coming into training,' I told him.

'We'll give you £2000 and that's our last offer.'

'I'm not taking it,' I said. 'I know you want me out, but I'm not leaving until I get my £8000.' I put the phone down and went into training.

A few days later, Billy and Jimmy Frizell were in the referee's room where they got changed and I was called in to see them.

'What are doing?' asked Billy.

'You know I'm not going unless I get my money,' I told him.

'Right, I'll give you £3000. That's our last offer – three grand to go.'

But I said, 'I'm owed £8000 and I want £8000, so I'm not going for three grand.'

Jimmy Frizell then said, 'Gordon, let me say something – I don't think you realise how much money £3000 is.'

I looked at him and replied, 'Jimmy, I do know what £3000 is worth. I've got a degree in Business Studies and I know as much as anybody what it's worth.'

Jimmy had a startled look on his face when he turned to Billy and said, 'Has he got a business degree?'

And Billy replied, 'Yes, he has. And he's a smart-arsed bastard.' Billy then turned to me and said, 'The deal's off. Get out of here.'

I never heard another word from Wolves so that was me still at Maine Road and it looked like I was destined for an existence in the reserves.

A week later, I was playing for the reserves at Old Trafford against Manchester United's second string. I thought I was having not a bad game until I was subbed with half an hour to go. By the time the game finished and the team came into the dressing room, I was showered and changed into my suit. When I came off, it had been 0–0 but then United scored to win 1–0.

157

Tony Book was taking the team and he was having a go at some of the players about their performance. Suddenly he turned to me and said, 'You're keeping a young player out of this team and you're hopeless. You shouldn't even be here at this club. You're doing nothing for any of the young players here with your attitude.'

For the first time in many years, someone had said something that had shaken my confidence and self-belief. I was beginning to wonder if I was kidding myself on and I wasn't such a good a player any more.

The following week I was in training and Billy McNeill said, 'You've to go back to the ground and phone Joe Royle. He wants you to go to Oldham on a month's loan.'

I phoned Joe Royle and he said he was interested in getting me in on loan to give a bit of experience to the team as they were struggling near the bottom of the Second Division at the time.

'Can I ask you something?' he said. 'I know you had an illness at the beginning of the season and I was wondering if you had fully recovered. We had you watched against Manchester United reserves and our scout said you were different class but you were taken off with half an hour to go.'

'You scout said what?' I asked.

'He said you were different class but because you were taken off we wondered if you still had a problem.'

I told him I was fully fit, I'd be more than happy to sign on loan and I'd see him at Oldham the following morning for training. I was stunned by what the scout had said. I now realised that the whole thing at City was to undermine me – that was their ploy. What Tony Book had said was all part of it. They were trying to make me believe I was finished and I couldn't play at the top level any more. It was all to make me leave the club. Since the start of the season, I only had one game in the first team in the English League Cup at outside right. They were making it perfectly clear I wasn't wanted at Maine Road.

There were two reasons for this. Firstly, I believe they must have thought I was finished after my illness. I was bedridden for a month, I was well off the pace for pre-season training and it took me a good couple of months to catch up with the rest of the team fitness-wise.

Secondly, I think they wanted me out to make way for some of the younger talent they had at the club. Young Paul Simpson was brought in to replace me and, to be fair, did well. There's no doubt Manchester City had a superb bunch of youngsters during my time there. When I was in the first team we used to play practice matches against the youth team instead of the reserves because we were given a better game of it.

I feel I could have been treated better at Manchester City. I'd been top goal scorer the season they were promoted yet, months later, the campaign was on to get me out by sickening me and making my life uncomfortable.

While at City, I became a part-time male model and one of the photo shoots I did was for Kangol rear seatbelts. For years after that, people would tell me there was a guy who was my double, pictured on the seatbelt box. There was no way I was admitting it really was me. I also modelled for Umbro and lots of pictures of me were in their football-gear catalogue. After moving to Austria, I thought no one would know about my modelling – until the catalogue was sent to Admira Wacker, the club I was playing for there. What a ribbing I took when the players got to see the pictures of me posing for the camera.

When I joined Oldham, it was like a new lease of life for me and I was desperate to prove to people that there were no ill-effects from my illness. There were four games during my loan period and we won all of them, which took the team halfway up the league table and away from relegation danger. Joe Royle asked me if I wanted to extend my stay at Oldham and sign on until the end of the season and then we could talk about a longer contract. I told him, if I could get the money I was owed from Manchester City, I'd be happy to sign on.

Wondering if the £8000 was still going to be a major hurdle, I spoke to City's club secretary, Bernard Halford. I told him Oldham wanted to sign me until the end of the season but I was still concerned about getting the £8000 signing-on money I was owed by the club.

'Not a problem,' said Bernard. And the next day I had a cheque for £8000 in my hand.

But, just like the John Greig situation, I don't bear any grudges against Billy McNeill. You've got to move on and I don't have any animosity towards him. Years later, in 1989, I was a guest at my former Kilmarnock team mate Davie Provan's wedding and Billy came up to me and said, 'I hear you've been bad-mouthing me.'

'No I haven't,' I replied. 'I've been telling people how you treated me in the latter days at City. If you think that's bad-mouthing you – that's up to you. I'm only telling the truth.'

'I had a lot of decisions to make,' said Billy. 'You'll find out one day, if you are a manager, that you've got to make difficult decisions and I had to make these decisions about you.'

'Well, I found them to be a bit personal and that's why I've told people,' I said.

At that we shook hands and that was the matter cleared up. I certainly don't have a problem with Billy McNeill.

I had a great few months at Oldham and the spirit at the club was fantastic – great fun to play at a place like that. We continued the good run that started when I joined them on loan and we ended not far off a play-off place. The ironic thing was that I was playing well but not scoring any goals from my favoured position of centre midfield. I went eighteen games without scoring and that was the longest I had ever gone without hitting the back of the net.

In the end, I didn't stay with Oldham for another season. A chance conversation with the former Liverpool star, David Fairclough, would see me heading off on my travels abroad.

160

10

SOCK IT TO ME, BOSS!

As each minute ticks by our chances of playing in the UEFA Cup are getting slimmer and there's nothing I can do about it. I'm stuck on the bench as one of the substitutes in the most important game of the season for the Austrian team, Admira Wacker, and it doesn't look like I'm getting on the park. We're down 1–0 and what should have been a historic season for the club is about to turn into a disaster. We only need a point to qualify for Europe, but the team is about to snatch defeat from the jaws of victory.

As the second half enters its final stage and there's no sign of us scoring that vital equalising goal against Linz Athletic Sports Club, I become more and more frustrated. Suddenly, I look at the stadium clock and I see there's only fifteen minutes to go so I decide to take matters into my own hands. I get off the bench and jog around the track to behind one of the goals and go through a warm-up routine. That done, I come back to our dugout and stand in front of the manager, Gustl Starek, blocking his view of the game.

'What is it, Gordon?' he asks.

'Are you going to put me on?' I reply.

The manager looks at me for a few seconds and says, 'Are you going to score a goal?'

'Yes,' I tell him.

'OK then. I'll put you on.'

Right there and then, with about seven minutes to go, he calls to the linesman and puts me on the park. It takes me a few minutes to get my first touch of the ball and nothing seems to be happening for us but, then, with five minutes to go, we get a corner. I'm being man-marked by a defender but, as the ball is swung into the box, I step back from him to give myself some space. The defender jumps for the ball and I'm thinking to myself, 'If this guy misses the header, I'm in with a chance here.' Sure enough, just as I'd hoped, the ball sails over the defender's head and I volley a shot low and hard into the bottom corner of the goals. My team mates jump on top of me, delighted I've scored, and it takes a minute or two to disentangle us before the game can be restarted with just a few minutes to go.

At the final whistle there are even more celebrations that, for the first time in the club's history, they have qualified for Europe and I've scored the goal that has got them there. About a thousand of our fans have travelled to the game and they are singing and chanting in the stands. I'm lifted on to the shoulders of my team mates who carry me round the ground to where our fans are. Much cheering and punching the air ensues from both players and supporters. I'm still on the players' shoulders when they eventually carry me up the tunnel and into the dressing room.

It is a great, triumphant moment for me and I'm so pleased I scored the goal that means so much to the club, the fans and the other players. We're still chanting and singing in the dressing room and everyone wants to shake my hand and congratulate me. It's incredible. I told Gustl Starek I was going to score and I'm glad to say I delivered the goods in fine style.

Everyone is still buzzing with excitement as we get on the team bus to make our way back to Vienna. The seats of the bus are on two raised platforms along both sides so we're sitting higher than someone walking up the central passageway. The manager walks up the bus to where I'm sitting and begins talking to me. 'That was brilliant,' he says. 'That was a fantastic goal you scored.' As he's talking to me, I can feel his hand rustling something at my sock. When the manager goes back to his seat, I lean down and feel my sock and discover he has stuffed a bundle of notes inside my sock. It is the equivalent of £200! I've no idea why he has done this instead of just handing it to me. Nevertheless, I'm very grateful for the unexpected bonus from the manager of a club that, several weeks previously, told me they couldn't afford my wages, along with those of the other two foreign players in the team.

I had signed with Admira Wacker in June 1986 after I had finished my short stint at Oldham. But I could have been there more than six months earlier if only I hadn't been told their offer of a signing-on fee was so low. At the beginning of December the previous year, when I was still at Manchester City, manager Billy McNeill called me into his office and said a football agent from London had phoned him to ask if he thought I'd be interested in playing in Austria. I told Billy I had never thought about it and asked what the money would be like.

Billy said, 'There's £5,000 in it for you – a five grand signing-on fee.'

'I'm definitely not interested in going all the way to Austria for that kind of money,' I said. 'I could get a £5,000 signing-on fee with an English non-League side.'

Billy shrugged his shoulders and said, 'That's up to you. I'm just asking.'

I had forgotten about the idea of going abroad until I was reminded on my second day at Oldham a month later. David Fairclough was chatting to me and said, 'I hear you didn't want to go to Austria.'

'How do you know that?' I asked.

'The agent who took me to Switzerland – a guy called Helmut Epp – told me you knocked it back.' David explained.

I had never heard the name Helmut Epp before so I asked David for his telephone number in Switzerland. I called him and he said, 'I was trying to find out if you were interested in going to Austria.'

'I would have been,' I replied. 'But the signing-on fee was only £5000 . . .'

He interrupted me. 'No, that's not right – it's a £30,000 signing-on fee.'

'Oh, really?' I said. 'That changes things. I might be interested then.'

Helmut told me the club was Admira Wacker and we would try to sort something out for the start of their new season in the summer. And he was as good as his word.

So there I was in June of that year flying out to Austria having been told all I needed to do was put pen to paper and that was me on my foreign travels. It had been five weeks since my last game or any serious training but I wasn't too worried as I knew I could get fit enough in their pre-season training. After all, it doesn't take much energy to sign a bit of paper.

I met Helmut in the hotel I was staying at in Vienna the night I arrived and he told me I was to go to the Admira Wacker ground for a training session the next morning.

'What training session?' I asked. 'Surely I'm getting a medical?'

'You'll get a medical, but they just want to see you in training.'

So much for me flying over just to sign a form but I duly turned up the next morning with no training gear and had to borrow boots and other kit. When I arrived at the training ground I discovered no one spoke English – everybody was speaking in German. It wasn't a very heavy session, mostly ball work. I struggled a bit as I hadn't kicked a ball in five weeks and, when I got back into the dressing room, my feet were very sore and almost blistered because of the borrowed boots.

After the morning's training, Epp picked me up and we were having lunch when he asked how I felt the session went. I told him about my feet being sore because the boots didn't fit me properly and he said, 'Hopefully they will be OK for tonight.'

'What's on tonight?' I asked.

'The match.'

'What? Are we going to see a game tonight?'

'No, the club management want you to play in it.'

'Wait a minute,' I said. 'I've come here to sign a contract not play in a football match I don't know anything about.' I had been totally conned and, when Helmut said they had arranged the friendly with a team from a lower division, I realised I was actually here on trial and not just to sign on.

I had no option but to go along with this and played in central midfield. I was given the same boots as in the morning and it wasn't before long that my feet were in agony. In the first half, I hardly got a kick of the ball – I was so off the pace I couldn't get involved at all.

At half time, the teams didn't go into the dressing rooms – they just had a rest on the park. I was sitting on the grass with aching feet, having a stinker of a game and thinking that I would chuck it there and then. I was having a debate with myself about what I should do and eventually I decided I would just tough it out and play the second half. As the game went on, I got more touches and started to hit a few long passes from midfield – not because I wanted to show off my accuracy but because I couldn't run properly in the ill-fitting boots. From one of my passes, the young Andreas Ogris – who went on to become a well-known international player for Austria – scored.

I was finding my form, getting better all the time and I scored two of the best goals in my career in that second half. The first was a header from outside the box. The cross came in from the left and I got in front of the defender and met the ball perfectly on my forehead. To even my amazement, the ball ended up in the top corner of the net and the other players were patting me on the back. Late on in the game, when I was really tired, I was outside the box when someone knocked a ball towards me. Normally, I would have taken a touch and run forward with it, but I decided to let fly with a volley and, for the second time that night, I watched in amazement as the ball flew over the goalkeeper and dipped under the crossbar and nestled in the back of the net. Again, I was crowded by team mates telling me in German what a good goal it was. Well, I assume that was what they were telling me.

We won 4–2 and, when I got back into the dressing room, I went to see the doctor to ask him to do something for my blistered and bleeding feet. When I took my socks off everyone was looking and pointing at my feet. They told me later they were shocked I had played on. After getting changed, Helmut told me that at half time the management had decided they weren't going to sign because my performance was so bad. But after my second half efforts, two wonder goals and a pair of bleeding feet, they couldn't get me upstairs quick enough to sign on. It was a two-year deal that included a car and a house that was big enough for Marlene, Grant and Leigh-Anne. I was amazed how the whole thing had panned out but also angry that I had been conned into going to Austria on a trial without being told about it. However, back home in England I realised how much I needed that contract. Apart from Oldham in the Second Division, no one else was interested in signing me. So, after a two-week break, I was back on the plane heading for Vienna and a new career on the continent.

I scored on my debut with Admira Wacker against Hungarian team Ujpest Doza in the Intertoto Cup. We won 2–0 and I also made our other goal with a long pass to Andy Ogris who was as quick as lightning. They thought my long passes were great because normally football is played very short in Austria and no one was playing the long ball. The strange thing about our home games in the Intertoto Cup was that they weren't played in the club's own stadium. We were turning out in what I can only describe as the equivalent of one of Scotland's junior football stadiums – a pitch and one small pavilion.

It was good to get a goal on my debut but I knew I was struggling with my fitness and that wasn't helped by how hot it was during the summer in Austria. I hadn't realised it would be like that – it was like being in Spain – and that really took it out of me during games.

We didn't qualify out of our group in the Intertoto – which included Ujpest Doza, Grasshoppers Zurich and the Danish team, Århus – and when our involvement in that tournament ended, Marlene and the kids came over to stay in Vienna. Our flat was near the ground and I could walk to training every day. The club's facilities were fantastic with a running track and fifteen football pitches to practise on.

I was dropped to the bench by the manager, Ernst Dokupil, for the final Intertoto Cup game and the team doctor spoke to me about my fitness. He said my conditioning wasn't very good and I told him I was struggling to come to terms with playing in such scorching hot weather. His solution was to get me on a drip putting the plasma from bull's blood into my system.

Twice a week, I had to sit in the treatment room getting this bull's blood plasma pumped into my veins. As far as I could make out, it didn't make one bit of difference to my standard of fitness.

When the league season started, I was on the bench and getting on for the last twenty minutes in most of the matches. The other problem I had was that the club had signed two Yugoslav players and, in Austria, you were only allowed two foreign players on the field at one time. They were first-team picks so, if I was to get a game, one of them had to come off.

The two Yugoslavs – Zoran Stojatinovic and Vatro Petrovic – were good lads and I got on well with them. I began to wonder what was going on between them when I used to invite them over to our flat. If I invited Zoran over, he would ask if Vatro was going to be there as well and vice versa. If one had already agreed to come over, the other didn't want to come. Then I discovered Zoran was a Serbian and Vatro was a Croat and they didn't like each other.

While Vatro was a centre back, Zoran was a fantastic striker and scored lots of goals for us. He was the most talented individual I had played alongside since Davie Cooper but he was so arrogant it was unbelievable. When the manager tried to talk to him, Zoran would shrug his shoulders and wave him away. On the surface, you would think these guys came from the same country but, in reality, they would have been as well coming from countries on the other side of the world from each other. It's sad to think that, a few years later, the Serbs and the

Croats were at war with each other. But their attitude towards each other obviously reflected what was happening in Yugoslavia at the time.

Results weren't going our way and Ernst Dokupil was sacked, to be replaced by former Bayern Munich star, Gustl Starek. He had only been there for a couple of days when he pulled me aside and spoke to me through an interpreter. 'Why are you not playing in the team?' he asked. 'I saw you come on as substitute in the last game and you did very well. I just wondered why you weren't in the team.'

I told him I had no idea why I wasn't getting a place in the starting line-up and that it was down to the previous manager who wasn't picking me. Then he said, 'OK – you will be in my team. You will start the game on Saturday.'

I was quite shocked – but also very relieved – by what he said, particularly as he was saying I would be in his team and not that he'd give me a game on Saturday to see how I'd do.

Gustl changed the formation of the team and while I was still playing central midfield, he had given me more of a defensive holding role – very similar to how Paul Lambert played when he went to Borussia Dortmund. The manager's change of tactics worked and we began to pick up points and move up the league from the bottom three where we had been when he took over.

I was learning German from a cassette language course and I was picking up the language quicker than I thought I would. And a lot quicker than the players and manager thought as well.

We were sitting in the dressing room at half time during a game and the manager was speaking in German to the players. 'Help the foreigner,' he told them referring to me. 'He has not got the ability you boys have but he tries really hard.'

When he had finished speaking, I said, 'Danke schön.'

He immediately looked over and asked me in German if I had understood what he had said. When I nodded to him that I had, I could see the other players looking at each other as if to say, 'We'd better watch what we're saying from now on.'

For the first time in my life, I was being described as a tryer. Although I wasn't playing the best football of my career and the new role I had didn't allow me to get up and down the park like I used to, I would have thought I had shown enough to let people see I had a reasonable amount of skill.

Perhaps he was trying to endear me to the rest of the team by saying I wasn't as good as them but I was trying hard. And he was probably right in doing that as it became apparent later on that the players did have a problem with me because they thought I was just a football mercenary, only interested in the money. When they saw I had been struggling with my fitness, they probably thought I wasn't trying too hard for the team, without realising how much the heat was affecting me.

You could see it in the training routines where one player would be in the middle of a circle of players trying to win the ball as they passed to each other. They always wanted me to be in the middle and would try to make a fool out of me when I was trying to win the ball.

But, as we got into autumn and the temperatures cooled down, I came on to a much better game and could work a lot harder during matches. The turning point in my relationship with the other players came after a game when one of them gave me the thumbs-up and had an expression on his face that said he now appreciated that I was a decent player and doing my best for the team. Up until then, he would hardly look the road I was on.

Their attitude definitely changed after that and they became friendlier towards me. Before I had started speaking to them in German, they would give me a curt answer and then ignore me but, by November that year, I was being invited out to lunch by the players and joining in with their social events.

Being able to speak German was a big boost and the manager would chat to me about football in general. One day, he asked if I had seen the English football on satellite television the previous night. When I said I had, he asked, 'What drugs do the players take in England?'

I told him they weren't on any drugs but he insisted, saying, 'They must be on drugs. When they are tackled they get so angry and they jump up and want to fight everybody.'

I told him it was nothing to do with drugs and pointed to my chest and told him it was that they played with their heart and soul and are very determined to win. And, talking about determination, my former managers, coaches and team mates in Scotland would have been amazed that I became the toughest tackler in the team. Once again, I had changed my game because I wanted to play in the team. I became a defensive player, won headers and won tackles because I was desperate to play.

In one of my conversations with Gustl Starek, he asked me if I'd ever heard of a player called Jim Baxter. I was shocked by his question and asked him why he wanted to know that. Gustl – who had played alongside Gerd Müller and Franz Beckenbauer with Bayern Munich – said Baxter had put on the finest performance of any player he'd seen when Rangers played Rapid Vienna in a European Cup tie in December 1964. Baxter broke his leg in that game as the Rapid Vienna players were putting in some really vicious tackles trying to stop him playing. It was amazing that here was an Austrian football manager asking me if I knew the player that had inspired me to want to be a footballer ever since I was a youngster and first saw him at Rugby Park in Kilmarnock.

The Austrian football season starts in July with a twelve-team league, in which all the teams play each other twice. In December, the season stops for a winter break before resuming in March and continuing until the end of May. During the second part of the season, the top eight teams play each other to see who wins the title and the bottom four join the top four of the lower division in a series of play-offs. Admira Wacker were in the top eight of the league by December which meant we would still be facing the better-known teams from Austria.

The weather was still quite mild when we had our last game in December and we hadn't bought any winter clothes for the kids or ourselves. People kept saying to me to get a set of winter tyres for my car but, since the weather was so good, I couldn't see the point.

There were a few days before we were due to go home to Scotland for a six-week break at Christmas and, when I woke up one morning and looked out the window of my flat, I couldn't believe that the whole place was covered in snow – and I mean covered. A snowplough had been up our street, pushing the snow from the centre to the side of the road and completely covering the cars parked there. I couldn't remember exactly where I had left the car so I had to dig the snow off several licence plates until I found my car. Overnight, it had turned unbelievably cold – it was minus six and getting even colder.

During my six weeks back in Scotland, I kept myself fit by training with Rangers. I wasn't going to make the same mistake again by turning up and not being in peak physical condition.

I went back to Austria in the latter part of January as the team were beginning their training for the second part of the season. We went to Florence in Italy for a ten-day training camp with a couple of friendly matches thrown in. It was very regimented – every day was the same. We would get up about 7 a.m. and do some running, then we had breakfast at 9 a.m. More training before lunch and then three or four hours' sleep in the afternoon. At 5 p.m., there was another training session until it was time for our evening meal. At 10 p.m., we were sent to bed and that was the routine every day.

After a few days of this, the manager and coaches announced they were going to Milan to watch a game and they wouldn't be back until the following morning. During the evening, the players were lounging around playing cards and pool. At 10 p.m., the team captain, Herbert Obermeyer told us it was ten o'clock and we should get to our beds. I watched in amazement as everyone immediately stopped what they were doing and headed up to their rooms.

I was sharing with our striker Walter Knaller and he saw the look on my face and asked me what the problem was. I told him

I was surprised that everyone stopped what they were doing and went straight to bed. He said, 'Wouldn't you do that in Britain?'

'To be honest,' I told him, 'after the last few days and the manager and coaches leaving the hotel for the night, there would have been six taxis ordered right away to take the players into town for a night out.'

That was the first time I had witnessed such a high level of professionalism in a bunch of footballers. There was no alcohol consumed during that training camp and, with my experience in British football, the idea of not going out on the town when the manager and coaches were gone baffled me.

During February and the early part of March 1987, we continued training in Vienna until the league got under way again. We were driving to a match at Innsbruck one day and I was playing cards with three other players. I looked out the window and saw a signpost for Mauthausen. I remembered from my Sixth Year Studies History at school that there had been a Nazi concentration camp where Jews had been killed in its gas chambers at a place called Mauthausen, in Austria.

I said in German to the other three players I was playing cards with, 'Is that the concentration camp?' But I didn't get an answer. I asked a second time and still didn't get a response.

And again I asked them, 'Is that . . .' And before I could finish my sentence, Herbert Obermeyer curtly said, 'Yes.'

There was a real atmosphere for the rest of that bus journey as I'd obviously touched a raw nerve. I only later found out from other foreigners in Austria that you don't mention Hitler, the Nazis or the Second World War – the subject is taboo.

We were playing well in the second part of the season and, with four games to go, needed only one point to clinch third place and a coveted UEFA Cup spot for the first time in the club's history. Everyone was on a high but, just before we were about to go into the run of those last four games, I was called in to see the Admira Wacker chief executive, Mr Tieselmyer.

I was taken aback when he said, 'We can't afford you any more. We would like to cancel your contract and you can go on and play somewhere else.'

'But we're one point away from qualifying for the UEFA Cup,' I said.

'I know that,' he said, 'but we can't afford you and we want you to leave right away.'

I told him I wasn't prepared to leave as I still had another year on my contract and I would be contacting my agent about this. When I got home to phone my agent I saw Zoran Stojatinovic outside my flat. 'Has the club spoken to you about leaving?' he asked. When I told him they had, he said, 'They have said the same to me so I'm leaving now.'

Sure enough, a couple of hours later Zoran was packing his gear into his car and he drove off. This was incredible considering it was Zoran's twenty-odd goals which put us in with a chance of European qualification. The same had happened to Vatro and he too left the club immediately. It was totally bizarre. The club were on the threshold of doing something they had never done before and here they were getting rid of three of their best players with just a handful of games to go.

I spoke to Helmut Epp and told him what happened and he said he would try to find me another club. But I made it clear to him that I wasn't moving from Admira Wacker unless I had another club to go to.

The following morning, I spoke to Mr Tieselmyer again and told him I wasn't prepared to tear up my contract just because he wanted me to. A few days later, the team was being read out for the next game and I was dropped to the bench. We lost that game. I trained as normal the following week but, when it came to the Saturday, I was on the bench and we lost again. The same happened for the third game. All we needed to qualify for Europe was a point from any of these games but we couldn't do that.

Then came the final game of the season and the stunt I pulled of standing in front of the manager so he couldn't see the game finally got me on the park. Thankfully, that worked and I scored the goal that took Admira Wacker into Europe.

Even although I had scored that goal for them, the club still wanted me to go but I told them I would be back for pre-season training in three weeks' time as normal.

We came home to Scotland during the Austrian close season and, while I was back, I was asked by Tommy McLean, who was now manager of Motherwell, if I fancied coming in to the club for a few training sessions. They were obviously having a look at me. But while I was at Motherwell, Helmut Epp called and said that the Swiss outfit Basle were interested in signing me although nothing would happen for a few weeks.

Because the Basle deal looked a possibility, I went back to Admira Wacker for their pre-season training. As the pre-season friendlies began, I was stuck on the bench and the club were still pushing for me to cancel my contract. They said the Basle move was definitely on the cards but I would have to go to Switzerland to let them see me in action.

I knew I wouldn't be getting a game at Admira Wacker so I agreed to go if they gave me three months' money up front. They gave me the cash and I headed back to Scotland for a few days before getting the call to fly to Basle. During that short time, I even managed to fit in a friendly playing for Airdrie who were being managed by Gordon McQueen. They played me as a striker and it was a position I didn't really fancy as I had been used to playing defensive midfield. I was waiting for the call from Basle so I didn't encourage any further interest from the Lanarkshire club.

Eventually I flew to Basle and took part in a training session before signing a one-year deal at much the same money as I was on in Austria. That seemed fine until I discovered that it's a lot more expensive to live in Switzerland than in Austria.

I was too late signing for Basle to take part in their first game in August 1987 so I watched them playing from the stand as they struggled and were defeated 2–0. It wasn't until I was getting a new car the following week that I discovered that Basle had been having financial problems and had just got rid of all their top players at the end of the previous season.

The salesman at the car showroom was a Basle fan and he told me how the club were going to be relying on youngsters with a couple of experienced players thrown in to help them. They didn't tell me that when I signed on.

The first game I played for Basle was against Lausanne and I scored a cracking goal with a left-foot volley to make it 1–1. But a young Stephan Chapuisat – who went on to win the Champions League with Borussia Dortmund and played many times for Switzerland – scored a late goal against us and we lost the game 2–1. Years later, I met Stephan at Ibrox when he was visiting his former Dortmund team mate Stefan Klos and he told me that game was his debut in professional football.

After the defeat, we were back in the dressing room and the manager, Urs Siegenthaler, turned to me and said, 'I'll give you the benefit of the doubt on how you played considering it was your first game for us and you haven't played for a while.'

Straight away, a wee alarm bell rang in my head and I got the feeling that this guy doesn't really like me. I had scored a great goal and played really well and he was suggesting that my performance still wasn't good enough. I thought to myself, 'Should I say now that that's as good as it's going to get?'

As the season went on, any time there was a bad performance, the manager would turn on me. And every week I was reading quotes from Urs Siegenthaler in the local papers that he was expecting more from 'the foreigner' or that 'the foreigner isn't doing well enough'. No matter how well I played, he would be critical and I was getting fed up with this constant and unmerited sniping at me.

This time round at a foreign club, I got on well with the players right from the start. I could speak German so immediately I struck up some good relationships and I had a lot of respect from them. And, as a more experienced player, I also became their leader in the dressing room.

Marlene and the kids stayed in Scotland while I was with Basle as I wanted both Grant and Leigh-Anne to get a good start to their education. In Switzerland the youngsters don't go to school until they are seven.

The worst defeat I have ever been involved in came when Basle played Swiss cracks Neuchâtel Xamax, who had just won the league and had a lot of international players in their squad at the time. We had been hit by injuries and I was the only experienced player in the team for that game. Into the second half, we were getting beaten 3–2 but the roof caved in on all the youngsters we had playing and the final score was 9–2.

Of course, Urs Siegenthaler pinned the blame for the heavy defeat on me, but I just took it on the chin as most of the players didn't rate him as a manager and, although he was an ex-Basle player, tactically they didn't think he was doing very much.

After that game, the manager decided to play me as sweeper. It was a new experience for me – I found that I enjoyed playing in that position and I was doing well for the team there. We were still losing games but they were a lot closer. Of course, the manager was still slaughtering me in the papers.

When the Swiss season's winter break came, we were in the bottom four in the league, so we would be involved in the play-offs when the season restarted. I was glad to get home for Christmas because I really missed the family. The toughest thing for me was phoning home to talk to the kids and they would start crying because they wanted me at home.

I went back to Switzerland in January and the play-off part of the season began. I was still getting a game at sweeper and the criticism from the manager wasn't bothering me. I had a real bust-up with him one day when he turned on one of the young boys in the team and gave him a real – and unfair – roasting because we were getting beaten.

I told the manager to lay off the boy as the whole team was responsible and he shouldn't just pick one player to vent his anger on. He turned to me and said, 'You're one to talk. The way you've been playing at this club has been a disgrace. I didn't even want you in the first place.'

That was confirmation of what I suspected all along. He didn't want me at the club before I had even kicked a ball for them and he had had a downer on me from the start.

I told him that, if he wanted to pick on anybody, he should pick on me because I was old enough to take it and that I didn't have any respect for him as a manager anyway. I was very angry at that point and it showed as I told him in no uncertain terms that I thought he was a poor manager. The young player who had been at the receiving end of Urs Siegenthaler's tirade later thanked me for sticking up for him and the rest of the young players.

There were only a couple of games to go before the end of the season and Basle were about to be relegated. To my surprise, I was asked to a meeting with the club's board of directors who told me some of the players had spoken to them and blamed Urs Siegenthaler for the bad season they'd had. Then they said that every player they had spoken to had said that I should be the manager.

The directors explained that, after the first few players had complained about Siegenthaler, they had canvassed the other players and they all had asked that I be made manager for the next season. That was very flattering but there was one problem. The present manager still had a year of his contract left and they couldn't afford to pay him off.

They asked if I would work as Siegenthaler's assistant for a year and then I would be given the manager's position. I didn't want to work with him after all that had gone on during the past year. Also, my family were in Scotland and I missed them terribly – so I said no. I turned down the chance to become a manager at thirty-three. I had taken some of the young players on coaching sessions while I was there but, all things considered, I didn't think the job was right for me. Looking back, I do regret not taking that chance because who knows what it might have led to? In retrospect, I should have brought the family to Switzerland and started my managerial career there.

On my final day at Basle, I was sitting in the dressing room saying my goodbyes to the players and I could see the manager sitting in his office down the corridor. I was seconds away from going into his Siegenthaler's office, closing the door and punching his face in. I was just about to head along the corridor and do that when I thought about the consequences. Going to the airport, looking forward to seeing the family again, the police grabbing me before I got on the plane, being arrested and thrown in a cell. He wasn't worth it. At that moment, looking at the young players and thinking about the way he had treated them, I never despised anyone so much as Urs Siegenthaler.

Ironically, one of these young players in the dressing room that day, Massimo Ceccaroni, had a testimonial match at Basle in 2002. He asked if I would play in the game and I was delighted to go back to Switzerland. When I got back to the stadium who was there but Urs Siegenthaler? He gave me a big hug and asked how I was doing as if nothing had happened between us and we were long-lost pals.

I gave him as big a hug as he gave me. I always think that life's too short to bear grudges – and you're a long time dead.

11

I NOSE WHAT A FOUL IS

I steady myself to challenge for the high ball coming towards me. There's an opposing player at my side and he has exactly the same thing in mind. Both of us jump and, before I can connect with the ball, the guy's elbow connects with my nose. I land on my feet and put my hand up to my face. When I look at my hands there's blood everywhere and immediately I know my nose is broken.

I turn to the referee and say, 'What about that for a foul?'

But he says, 'It was a fair challenge.'

'Don't talk rubbish,' I reply. 'That just shows how bad you are.'

I walk across to the physio and tell him that my nose is broken.

'I don't think it is,' he says.

'Do me a favour. My nose is definitely broken. I want to see the doc.'

The club doctor is called down from the stand and the physio says, 'Gordon thinks his nose is broken but I'm not so sure.'

The doctor examines my face and asks, 'Is your nose normally under your eye?'

'No, not normally,' I tell him.

'Well, then, you've definitely broken your nose.'

The doctor says that he is going to reset my nose while we're on the touchline and warns me it will hurt. He's not wrong.

This was my welcome back to Scottish football after my foreign sojourns. Playing for Stirling Albion in a friendly against

Aberdeen and the player who elbowed me in the nose was a guy called Tom Jones. A great headline for the newspapers – Tom Jones broke my nose!

I returned to Scotland from Switzerland in July 1988 and decided I would get my football coaching A Licence since I already had a B Licence from my days at Kilmarnock. I attended the coaching course at Largs and alongside me were people like Jim Leishman, who's now manager at Dunfermline, the former St Mirren boss, Tony Fitzpatrick, the present Patrick Thistle gaffer, Dick Campbell, and the Celtic legend, Danny McGrain.

What surprised me was the disregard people had for Swiss football. When I spoke about the people I had played with, there was such a lack of recognition on their faces you would have thought I had been playing in Outer Mongolia. They obviously thought the standard of Swiss football was pretty low, which was not the case. There were well-known players like the German, Karl-Heinz Rummenigge, Brazil's Paulo César and Italy's World Cup winner, Marco Tardelli playing in Swiss football when I was there.

It must have come as a real shock to them that, a year or so after that, Scotland were beaten home and away by Switzerland. All of sudden, Swiss football wasn't so bad after all.

I passed the course and got my coaching A Licence. After that I sat at home for several weeks waiting for the phone to ring with an offer of either a playing or player-coach job. But the phone never rang with that offer which would take me back into the Scottish game. I was looking to play in the Scottish Premier League – although I knew it wouldn't be Rangers or Celtic – but I was sure I could do a good job for one of the provincial clubs like Kilmarnock or Motherwell.

There were one or two stories in the papers saying I was back and looking for a club but nothing came of them. I heard a few years later that Graham Souness had considered bringing me in as player coach for the Rangers reserves. But, as I understand it, Jimmy Nicholl – now assistant manager at Aberdeen – got that job.

I NOSE WHAT A FOUL IS

The offer of work that did come my way wasn't to play football but to work in financial services for a company called London and Capital who were working with the Professional Footballers Association. They knew I had a business degree, had spent a career as a footballer and had made a lot of contacts during that time. I didn't want to commit myself full-time to working for them because I still had it in my mind that I would get a job in football. Instead I organised a few seminars for them in Scotland.

While I was doing that, I got a call from a former Kilmarnock team mate and pal, Jim McSherry, who was now at Stirling Albion. Jim Fleeting, Frank Coulson and Jim had taken over there and they wanted me to play for them. I agreed to sign on for a month, thinking that, at the very least, the training would keep me ticking over until a bigger club came along. There was very little football being played at that level – it was just a big hoof up the park and I would spend most of the games playing midfield watching the ball sail back and forth over my head.

When I did get a hold of the ball, I would wait for two or three opposition players to come towards me and then pass the ball to one of my team mates. A few of them would complain that I had passed the ball to them and they weren't ready for it and didn't want the ball. I would have thought they would have realised that I'd created some space for them by drawing defenders towards me.

The problem may have been that, when you have been a top player and you move to a lower level, other players seem to think you will do it all yourself. But nothing could be further from the truth. Players at the highest level know that you have to interact with your team mates. That's what stops a lot of players in the lower levels reaching the top – they cannot play with other people. They have individual skills but their ability to play alongside others isn't there.

So, that's how I came to be with Stirling Albion playing against Aberdeen and getting my nose broken for my troubles. I only played two friendlies and two league games for Stirling at the start of season 1988–89 and, when my month's loan was up, I said thanks but no thanks to an extended contract. I just wasn't enjoying my football.

Instead, I took a full-time job with London and Capital working in financial services selling investments, pensions and insurance – mainly to footballers. I was working Monday to Friday in London and flying back home at the weekend. I was staying in the company flat close to their offices and the lifestyle couldn't have been more alien to what I was used to as a footballer. I started work at 7.30 a.m. – that's when everybody started – and didn't finish sometimes until 8 p.m.

A major downside to this was that I stopped training altogether and that meant I piled on the pounds. Within three months of working in London I had put on more than two stone and that came as a shock. It was the heaviest I had ever been.

Two of my clients went on to have distinguished football careers. Teddy Sheringham and Neil Ruddock were just youngsters at Millwall when we signed them up for a pension plan. If only I had thought about becoming an agent at that time and signed these two up. Who knows how much money those boys might have made me?

My third child, Libby, was born on 24 November 1988 and, at that time, I was still flying back and forward to London. But, within a few months, I was back in Scotland on a permanent basis. London and Capital wanted to open a Scottish branch and they asked me to run it for them. Early in 1989, I opened their Scottish office in Park Circus, Glasgow, recruiting staff and running the business in Scotland. I was so used to the early start when I was in London, I carried on that routine.

Libby wasn't a good sleeper so, when she was a baby, I was awake all night and leaving the house before 7 a.m. to get to Glasgow from our house in Kilmarnock. I don't know why I kept on with that early-bird regime. I suppose that was the way London and Capital worked and I was conditioned by that.

Thanks to my football career, I had a healthy savings account of £45,000. I bought my parents' council house in Stevenston for them – which cost £8000 – but lost the rest in a Spanish property deal. All my savings were gone thanks to a company called Howson Homes, which went bust leaving a lot more people worse off than me.

I had seen an advert in the British Airways' *High Life* magazine about an English company, Howson Homes, which was building villas at Las Cancelas Doradas, near Marbella. The deal was that you paid a deposit of just under 40 per cent of the total value of the villa, which was £100,000. Howson Homes then made money by renting the villa to holidaymakers for the next ten years before ownership of the property became yours. We were to be given free use of the villa for six weeks every year – including two weeks in high season. I thought this was a great idea as I was going to be busy for the next ten years and, by then, I would have been able to spend a lot of time over in Spain living in a luxury four-bedroomed detached villa with a jacuzzi and plunge pool on the patio.

We were buying into Phase Three of the project, which we were told was going to take two years to complete. The following summer, we flew out to Las Cancelas Doradas and stayed in one of the Phase Two properties. We liked what we saw and everything appeared to be fine.

Shortly after we returned home, I got a call from the solicitor in London who had handled the deal, asking me to attend a meeting as there was a problem. When I got to London, I was told Howson Homes had gone bust and there were seventy-one other investors in the same boat. The suggestion the lawyer made was that the only way of recouping our money was to build the villas ourselves and then sell them on if we wanted. But to do this we needed to hand over ten per cent of our original investment in the property deal. Even this didn't work as a few weeks later the solicitor called to say that even the land earmarked for my villa to be built on had been mortgaged by Howson Homes and I didn't own it. The money was gone.

To put it mildly, it was a bit of a shock to us all. We had lost everything – every penny saved from my football career was gone on a Spanish villa that would never be built. The only good thing was that I'd been able to buy my parents their house before I got involved in that dodgy Spanish property deal.

The Spanish property scandal made the papers down south, but no one could find the Mr Dawson who was behind Howson Homes.

Although losing all my savings was a terrible blow, after a time I became philosophical about it. There are worse things in life that can happen to you other than losing your money. I still had my family, my health and, as they say in better parts of Stevenston, at least nobody's dead.

I agree with that. You just pick yourself up and get on with it. Falling down isn't the problem – it's not being able to get back up. During my life when things haven't always gone my way, I like to think I've had the resilience to bounce back.

Thinking back, though, if that deal had gone through, I would now have a house in Spain worth about £750,000 and no mortgage to pay on it. If I could only get my hands on the bastard who sold me that dummy!

Because I was running the Glasgow branch of London and Capital, I also had the chance to regain some my physical fitness. And it meant coming full circle and turning up at Ardeer Thistle's ground every second Saturday. My pal Davy Patterson and I used to sneak in to see the junior football club when we were kids but now I was going to play for them.

My younger brother Billy played for Ardeer and he said their manager, John Evans, had asked if I would come out of my premature retirement and play for them. I said I would if I could play sweeper. I played my first game for Ardeer in March 1990 shortly before the season finished and I was still well out of condition. I was also well out of the next four or five games after a rather over-physical welcome to the world of junior football in Ayrshire.

I NOSE WHAT A FOUL IS

During the game the usual long ball was punted up the park and, in those days, you could still pass it back to the goalkeeper for him to pick it up. The opposition forward started chasing it although I knew there was no chance of him getting to the ball because I had it well covered. He carried on running and I decided not to pass back to the keeper until the very last minute. If the striker wanted to waste his energy chasing a no-hope ball, then that was his problem.

I waited until he was three or four yards away before I passed the ball back to our keeper. The forward didn't stop running and he went right through me, taking my ankle, calf and knee in the one tackle.

I was crippled and had to be helped off the park. As I was passing the referee – who hadn't even booked the boy for the tackle – I said, 'Did you not see that or are you completely off your head?'

'It was your own fault,' he said. 'You were messing about and it's your own fault you were fouled.'

So that's junior football for you – it's your own fault when someone fouls you.

I came back from that injury and played the final few games of the season. I was asked back for the following season although I was going to be playing in midfield.

During the summer, I joined a gym to get my fitness back and had a really good pre-season with Ardeer and was raring to go. My brother, Billy, had also moved into midfield and it was great fun. I played with Ardeer until October of 1990 and that's when I got a welcome phone call from someone I had met at the Largs coaching course a couple of years earlier who would bring me back into senior football.

12

SAINTS AND SINNERS

My wee pal at the BBC, sports pundit Chick Young, doesn't know that I know he cost me the manager's job at St Mirren. Now, when you're reading this, Chick, you'll realise that I'm not one to bear a grudge. In all the years I've worked alongside Chick, I've never once mentioned how he had gone behind my back and lobbied for someone else to get the manager's job I'd been told by the club chairman was mine.

I'd been assistant manager at Love Street for two years under two different managers, both of whom had said I should succeed them. Chick's skulduggery began at the end of season 1991–92 when the then Saints boss Davie Hay decided to quit the club and head off to a coaching job in America. Although St Mirren had just been relegated, it was still a shock that the former Celtic manager was leaving Love Street.

Davie had pulled me aside with only a few games of the season left and told me he had been offered a job in America and he was ready to go if we were relegated from the Scottish Premier League to the First Division. He said, 'If I go, you should be the manager here. You're ready for it – the job should be yours.'

After Davie told the board he was leaving, St Mirren chairman, Bob Earlie, told me that I was to be the new manager and former Celtic star, Roy Aitken – who was playing with St Mirren at the time – would be my assistant.

For two weeks after that, nothing was announced to the media about me taking over. I was going into Love Street every day, preparing for the following season. At the end of the fortnight, I asked Bob Earlie for a meeting and told him, 'You need to announce this because I want to get on with my work. I've got to let players go and there are players I want to bring in.'

I was stunned by Bob's reply. He said, 'I've been meaning to tell you the past couple of days that we're making a move to bring Jimmy Bone in as manager. We've been told he's willing to come back from Africa and we're giving Jimmy the manager's job.'

'What's happening to me, then?' I asked.

'You're staying on. We want you as assistant manager and Jimmy has accepted that.'

I asked Bob what was happening to Roy Aitken, who had been told he would be my assistant. Bob said he was being sold to Aberdeen. I thought this was a big mistake because Roy would have been great for St Mirren in the First Division and would be needed to play a major role at the club to get us back into the Premier League.

I felt very let down being told that I was to be the new manager and then not being given the job. I don't necessarily blame the board for what happened because, in 1987, Jimmy Bone had been assistant to Alex Smith when St Mirren won the Scottish Cup. Jimmy had then gone to coach in Africa after leaving St Mirren and obviously he wanted back into the Scottish game.

Chick Young had always been a favourite with the St Mirren directors and managers because of his public declarations of undying support for the club. I was later told by Bob Earlie that, when the word got out that Davie Hay was leaving, Chick had contacted the chairman and told him Jimmy Bone was willing to take the job.

I suspect Chick must have known I had been offered the job but he was very friendly with Jimmy Bone and lobbied for him to get the St Mirren hot seat as he had more allegiance to him than me.

I'd known Chick for a long time, as he was a sports journalist on newspapers before moving on to radio and television while I was playing for Kilmarnock and Rangers. I had also been a regular in Chick's charity football team, Dukla Pumpherston. Ironically, I played in Dukla's first match alongside Chick and Jimmy.

Shortly after Jimmy Bone was installed as manager at Love Street, I was playing in yet another charity match with Dukla Pumpherston and both Chick and Jimmy were also in the team. I was sitting in the changing room behind a door and I could hear Chick and Jimmy talking outside. They obviously had no idea I could hear what they were saying because Chick asked Jimmy, 'How's the job going and what about Gordon?'

Jimmy said, 'Don't worry – I'll sort Gordon out.'

On hearing that comment, I suspected he thought I was a threat to him and that he wouldn't want me around Love Street for very long. But that's life – especially in football – and I don't have a problem with either Chick or Jimmy. In any case, Chick gets a hard enough time from the punters for claiming he is a St Mirren fan – because everyone thinks he really is a closet Rangers supporter.

He also gets stick from his colleagues on BBC _Sportsound_ especially when he goes over the top off on the air celebrating a St Mirren goal. Richard Gordon decided he would end all the speculation about who Chick really supports by giving him a St Mirren test of five questions about the club. When Chick got to the fourth question and had got the first three wrong, I said to Richard, 'I think you have made your point – you should stop now.' It must have been embarrassing for Chick since I – a self-confessed Rangers supporter – had answered the first three correctly.

There aren't many sports reporters and pundits who will own up to supporting either of the Old Firm – they all tend to pick a wee team. I think it is a shame that, because of the environment, people believe they have to do that. However, if Chick insists he's a St Mirren fan, who am I to disagree?

Chick is a good friend and one of the hardest things I have

ever had to do was console him when the news came through that his son, Keith, had been killed in a motorcycle crash. Both of us were in Dubai on a speaking engagement in January 2001 when the terrible news came through on my mobile phone. Chick's phone was turned off and Tom Connor, a producer at the BBC, had called me instead.

It is the worst experience you can imagine and it puts life in perspective when you're with someone and they have to cope with news like that. I will never forget that day and every time I think about it my heart goes out to him.

My arrival at St Mirren came after a phone call from their then manager, Tony Fitzpatrick. I hadn't spoken to Tony since I had completed the A Licence coaching course at Largs with him. But, when he called me, it was with an offer I just couldn't refuse. His assistant manager, Frank McGarvey, had left to become manager of Queen of the South and Tony wanted me to replace him at Love Street.

I was earning £25,000 a year plus bonuses with London and Capital and Tony's initial offer of £15,000 was what Frank McGarvey was getting. I told Tony I couldn't possibly give up my job and come to St Mirren for less than my basic wage. So, when he came back and offered me £25,000 to come to Love Street, I said yes.

My bosses at London and Capital couldn't believe I was giving up such a good job to go back to such a precarious profession as football. But I liked Tony and had a lot of respect for him – and it was something I just wanted to do.

It was great to be back in football and in the Premier League. I got on really well with Tony and he seemed to be happy with the role I was taking at the club – although someone told him not to take me on as his assistant as I would stab him in the back and be after his job. Tony told me this but he never revealed who had given him this warning. As it happens, nothing could be further from the truth as I believe that the manager is the manager and an assistant is there to do just that – assist.

I never pushed my own ideas on how the club should be run, even though Tony regularly let me take first-team training sessions. Tony was always keen to learn new methods so I told him about how the teams on the continent were coaching players and training. He agreed that we should introduce some of these methods at St Mirren.

We had a good bunch of players at Love Street that season – Campbell Money was in goal, Norrie McWhirter, a young Paul Lambert, Kenny McDowell, Paul Kinnaird, George Shaw, Gudmunder Torfason from Iceland and the superbly fast and talented German wide player, Thomas Stickroth.

But I quickly realised that one of the problems we had with the squad was that they weren't fit enough and needed a much tougher training regime to match the other teams in the Premier League. A good example of this was when we were due to play Dunfermline one Saturday and the game was postponed.

Tony asked me to take the squad for a short training session before we let them go for the day. I gave them a fat leg run, which is running around the track continuously for twenty minutes, but varying the pace every minute or so. The 'fat leg run' has been about for years and it's very good for conditioning both your stamina and your speed. I led the pace and, as we were running round the track, I could hear some of the boys moaning that this was too hard a run and it was ridiculous they were being asked to do this level of training.

When I saw two or three of the players dropping out because they couldn't keep up, I stopped the run and gathered them together. I asked them what the problem was and a few said it was just too hard for them.

'Let me put this into perspective for you,' I said. 'You were due to play Premier League football today and you're saying that a twenty-minute run is too hard for you? I'm thirty-five years old, haven't played senior football for two years and I'm leading you all in the running. And another thing – I was at the golf club dinner last night, drinking until four o'clock this morning before

I got home, not realising I would be doing any training, and you're telling me this is too hard. I want you to go home, look yourselves in the mirror and ask some serious questions about how fit you really should be.' I left it at that and told them the training session was over.

Tony and I discussed the problem of the fitness levels but there wasn't much we could do about it as I hadn't come to St Mirren until October and pre-season training was long gone. We didn't have a bad team but the lack of fitness was one of the main reasons we were struggling that season.

However, I was enjoying myself, even though I discovered being in football management means you can never switch off. After a game on a Saturday, I just couldn't let it drop. When you are a player, you ask yourself after a game if you have played well or whether you could have done anything different. After you've answered these questions, you think, 'Right, I'll do something about that next week.' But, in management, you are thinking all the time about what training we'll do next week, if we had the right tactics in the last match, what to do about the young players and the million and one other things a manager has to do. Tony and I would speak on a Sunday and discuss the game played the day before and decide what we were going to do with the players the following week.

Despite our best efforts, the team were at the bottom end of the table by November and something out of the ordinary would have to happen if we were to make any progress in the league. When Tony took a phone call from a sports journalist, we thought that might just have happened.

After talking to the reporter, Tony called me into his office and said he had just been told me that former Aberdeen, Spurs, Barcelona and Scotland striker, Steve Archibald, was looking for a club and he would be willing to come to St Mirren. I thought it would be a great move getting someone who had been a top player and had a season or two left in him to come to Love Street. So Tony went to see the chairman, at the time Louis Kane, and

191

got the go-ahead to make an offer to Steve, although I wasn't told what that offer was.

Steve came in to Love Street and met with Tony and me and agreed to join us until the end of the season. While we were talking, Steve asked if we were looking for other players and when we said yes, he astounded us by saying he could get the former Spanish international midfielder Victor Munoz to come to St Mirren.

At first I couldn't believe someone who had won more than sixty caps for his country and had played for Barcelona and Sampdoria would come to play for St Mirren. But Steve assured us Victor would come to Love Street. Tony said he would have to clear it with the board of directors but we were definitely interested.

When Steve left, I looked at Tony and said, 'That's unbelievable. Imagine a player of that standing coming to play for us. Can we afford him?' That question was soon answered when the board gave the go-ahead and a deal was struck to bring Victor to Love Street along with Steve Archibald.

I was never told what their wages were at the time but, a year later, when Davie Hay was manager, he revealed that the deal to bring both players to St Mirren for less than a season cost the club about £250,000. And on top of that, Victor was put up in arguably one of the swankiest and most exclusive hotels in Glasgow during his time at St Mirren.

When Victor came over to Scotland from Spain I was asked to find rented accommodation for him, which the club would be paying for. Now, in those days, that was quite unusual in Scotland, although it was common on the continent. I got together some brochures and identified about half-a-dozen cracking apartments in Glasgow. I took Victor round to see them all and he rejected every one as not to his liking.

I always have a laugh to myself about how I could have saved St Mirren all the money they were spending on Victor if I hadn't saved his life while he was looking at those flats. We came out of one apartment block and Victor was just about to step on to the road and in front of an oncoming car he hadn't seen, when I grabbed him and pulled him back. He was inches from getting knocked down when I stopped him. Yes, I could have saved the Saints a fortune if I hadn't been so alert and pulled Victor back on to the pavement!

When I got back to the ground, I told the club secretary, George Pratt, that Victor hadn't liked any of the flats we had picked for him. George said, 'I can't believe that. Leave it to me. I'll find him somewhere.' And, sure enough, George did find Victor somewhere he would like to stay. He found him a place in one of the most expensive hotels in Glasgow – One Devonshire Gardens. That's where wee Victor was living it up in the lap of luxury while he was playing with St Mirren and the club were footing the bill.

At first, having two players of that calibre gave the team a boost although that didn't last long. The rest of the team soon cottoned on to the money the pair of them were earning and started to switch off. The move we thought would keep us in the Premier League was starting to backfire on us as the resentment from other players built up and they looked upon Steve and Victor as football mercenaries. It was similar to the problems I faced when I was playing in Austria.

Despite this, the new big-time arrivals were absolute professionals in how they went about their business. Warm-up exercises before training and before games, then warm-down exercises after a match. You couldn't fault their approach to the game. The only problem was that the coaching staff, players and fans all expected Steve to get a barrow-load of goals and that just didn't happen.

We played him up front but he constantly came off defenders and moved deeper towards the midfield. It was the old strikers' syndrome – avoid getting kicked by defenders by coming so deep the centre half won't stay with you and you are always the free player. The problem with that was Steve would get plenty of the ball and link up with our midfield but there wasn't anyone in the opposition's penalty box to do any damage – that's where he should have been. Perhaps we should have used Steve in a different position and played him as the link-up man between midfield and another striker. Steve couldn't do both jobs.

The fans were getting restless with Steve not scoring, which is not surprising because he was billed as the man who would get goals for us. He was doing a good job and playing well but not in the area of the park we wanted him to be – in front of goals.

As for Victor, he was a tremendous player in midfield – winning the ball brilliantly, reading the game – and he was so fit. But he decided he would become a playmaker and started hitting long passes. The problem was he couldn't do that very well as his passing was poor over a longer distance.

I even asked Steve to have a word with Victor in Spanish as his English wasn't that great.

'Do us a favour,' I said to Steve. 'Could you tell Victor not to pass the ball more than ten yards?'

'What are you talking about?' asked Steve.

'His passing is awful,' I replied. 'It's so bad the boys have nicknamed him Scud after a Scud missile because he's explosive but not very accurate.'

But Steve said, 'There's no way I'm telling someone like Victor who's played for Spain all those years not to pass the ball more than ten yards.'

'I suppose you're right,' I said. So Scud kept on playing his long passes.

The lads had called him Scud after the missiles the Iraqis fired at Israel during the first Gulf War. Thankfully those weren't very accurate either.

Later in the season, around about February or March 1991, we were under a lot of pressure as we weren't picking up the points and relegation loomed. The team were on the park checking the pitch before a game and Victor turned to me, pointed and said in front of all the other players, 'Why don't you play?'

I was taken aback and didn't know what to say. Eventually I blurted out, 'What? Me play?'

Victor, who by now had picked up some English, said, 'Yes. I see you in training and you are a good player. You could play in this team. Why don't you play?'

I was embarrassed because all the players were looking at me and I came away with a stupid statement because I couldn't think of anything else to say. 'I've made my money, Victor – I don't have to play any more.'

But he countered, 'I have more money than you and I'm still playing.'

I pulled Steve Archibald over and said, 'Victor seemed quite confident he had more money that me. How does he know that?'

Steve smiled and said, 'The wee man's worth millions. He's got a stake in a huge health club in Barcelona. He's got lots of money alright.'

If the truth were known, anyone who had £2,000 in the bank would have had more money than me at that time.

What Victor said did get me thinking about playing again. I was still as fit as most of the players and I played in all the training games. But I hadn't been registered as a player and it wasn't until the following season that I did register myself.

We finished the season at the bottom of the league but we were saved from relegation by league reconstruction when the Premier was increased to twelve teams. The strange thing was we were playing good football at times but just not getting the goals that would get us the vital points we needed to move away from the bottom of the table.

We did have one great result in the Scottish Cup when we beat Stranraer 5–1 away from home and Victor scored a superb goal from 30 yards out – a real screamer that crashed into the back of the net.

Hindsight is a great thing and, looking back, maybe it wasn't such a great idea spending so much money on Steve Archibald and Victor. For one thing, St Mirren shouldn't have spent all that money bringing the two of them to Love Street and many people reckon that was the start of the club's financial problems. And secondly, in football terms, the move failed to deliver the success we thought it would.

It was a shame because the pair of them were really committed to doing well for the team. But Steve and Victor's presence in the team gave everyone an excuse for not doing as much as they could. All the attention was on Steve and Victor and the players – along with the fans – expected them to do everything. There was definitely an attitude problem amongst the rest of the players with those two being at St Mirren. A poor season, indeed, but at least we were still in the Premier League.

Pre-season training started for the St Mirren players – minus Steve Archibald and Victor – and I was determined to increase their fitness levels for the start of the 1991–92 campaign. I had the players at a local gym doing weights and the amount of running they were doing was stepped up compared to the previous year.

The new league season started but it wasn't long before we had a crisis on our hands. Early on in August, we played Hibs at Easter Road and lost 4–1. It should never have been that score as we lost three late goals through bad defensive errors.

We were all pretty down and, on the Sunday, Tony phoned me and said he had handed in his resignation to the then chairman Alan Marshall. I couldn't believe he had done that and I did all I could to persuade Tony to change his mind. 'I need to speak to you,' I told him. 'What you're doing is just crazy.' But there was no shifting him and he said he would come into the ground on the Monday morning and I could see him then.

The following morning I got a hold of Tony before the chairman appeared and said, 'I've been thinking about the game. It was three defensive mistakes, it was a big defeat but it wasn't your fault. If it was tactical and you made a wrong decision, sure, you hold your hands up to that. But losing these late goals had nothing to do with you. It's too early in the season to be doing

something like this.' I told him I didn't w
had made up his mind and said he was go.
'I've told the chairman I'm quitting and I've re
as my successor,' he said.   e

When the chairman arrived, he asked me if I wo
as caretaker manager while they found a replacement.
My first game in charge was against Celtic at Love Stree
lost 2–1, despite the team playing quite well. The day befc
second game in charge – against Motherwell at Fir Park –
four candidates for the manager's job were interviewed. The
were my former Rangers team mate, Alex McDonald, the ex-
Celtic boss Davie Hay, Jimmy Bone and me.

Before my interview, I had compiled a business plan for the
club – how it should be structured with regard to the first team,
the reserves, the youth set-up and the scouting system. It was
quite detailed and was several pages long. I presented it to the
board members interviewing me and I thought everything went
well for me. I was up against experienced managers but not many
of them would have thought about compiling a business plan.
I knew I had to do something different and the business plan
was it.

In the week running up to the interviews, our goalkeeper
Campbell Money had also made it known he wanted the job but
he never got an interview. Looking back, I should have replaced
Campbell with Les Fridge because, in the Motherwell game,
Campbell's mistakes cost us two goals. I don't think for a minute
the mistakes were deliberate but maybe he was angry because
he didn't get interviewed for the job and that affected his
performance. Campbell was a fine goalkeeper, but he didn't play
well that day.

The game finished 3–1 to Motherwell and it was my old pal
Davie Cooper who rubbed salt into my wounds. With a bit of
magic to beat his marker, he scored 'Well's third goal and that
was us well and truly beaten.

On the Sunday, the chairman, Alan Marshall called me at home 've got some good news and some bad news for you.'

ne the bad news first,' I replied.

fraid you're not getting the job,' he said.

l, how can there be any good news?' I asked.

ne good news is that your business plan was excellent and been accepted by the board. Davie Hay is going to be the ew manager and he is happy with it as well.'

I didn't take that as good news. I was raging that, while they didn't think I was good enough for the manager's job, they thought my business plan was and were taking that instead. Even being told that I could stay on as Davie Hay's assistant didn't quell my anger.

Before Alan Marshall went off the phone, he said he was seeing Davie Hay later in the day and would I like to come along and meet him as well. 'No thanks,' I said curtly. 'I'm busy and can't make it.'

The following morning, I went into Love Street and Davie Hay was there. I had never met him before and we shook hands. He said, 'I know you will be disappointed not getting the job and that's probably why you never came yesterday. I can understand that – you were the assistant manager and it's only natural you'd want the manager's job.'

He continued, 'I've seen your business plan and I like what's in it. I think we should go ahead with it. I'm happy that you should implement it and take responsibility for putting it into practice. I know we don't know each other but, as long as you don't mess me about or stab me in the back, we'll get on just fine.'

I thought that was a very honest and refreshing approach. He knew that I'd be angry at not getting the job but Davie was prepared to let me get over that and form a good working relationship. And that's exactly what we did.

I got on with putting my business plan into practice and one of the first things I did was start two reserve teams. Up to that point, we had a team in the Premier Reserve League and then an

Under-18 team in the local youth league. It was the first time anyone had been allowed to do that. For the time it was quite a radical plan but, when they were just sixteen, I had young players like Barry Lavety, Jamie Fullarton, Martin Baker, Ricky and Kenny Gillies and Barry McLaughlin playing in the Reserve League West instead of the Under-18 Paisley and District League.

I felt that these players would learn nothing from playing boys' football – I wanted them playing against men, so I could see how they were coping in a better, harder environment. I looked at my own youth football days and, when I was sixteen, I was playing for Kilmarnock reserves and a year later I was in the first team. You learned and improved much faster playing against older players and it gave you the chance to show you could step up to the higher level.

The other move I made was to play myself in the Reserve League West team so I could see close up who could play and who would have a chance of making the next step up. Although I was playing and closely involved with the young players, we also had former Celtic midfielder, Brian McLaughlin, as the reserve team coach.

Davie took control of first-team matters and decided to make some wholesale changes and he brought in a group of players – many of them ex-Celtic – to the club. They included Lex Baillie, Mark Reid, David Elliot, Jim Beattie and the ever-mercurial Chic Charnley.

I didn't have a say on those signings as Davie had taken complete responsibility for the first team. But I thought they were decent signings, even though they cost the club a lot of money in signing-on fees and high wages. St Mirren fans probably wouldn't agree with my view that they were good players because, that season, everything that could go wrong did go wrong. Mark Reid took a bad injury very early on in the season and had to give up football altogether, winger David Elliot showed much promise but he never caught fire as I thought he would and, of course, Chic Charnley got himself into so much bother with referees he was never on the pitch long enough to show what he could do.

If Chic could have controlled himself better, there's no saying how far he could have gone in football. He could have played at the top level because he had fantastic ability as a midfielder. Chic was superb at disguising what he was going to do with a ball and buying himself time before making a pass to one of his team mates.

Chic might have been getting himself into bother on the park but off the park he was a sensible guy. You would tell him not to get involved and he would agree with you but, as soon as he stepped over the touchline, the madness would start and he would get himself booked for stupid things. There was a comment in the *Glasgow Herald* at the time that referees should carry three cards when they were officiating at a St Mirren game – a yellow card, a red card and a card with Goofy on it to show Chic Charnley.

Everyone knew that Chic was Celtic mad and they were his heroes. One Saturday, when Chic was suspended, he came into the dressing room at Love Street about half an hour before kick-off. He wished the boys all the best and was telling them how important it was to win the game.

Later that weekend, I was talking to someone who said, 'I see Chic Charnley was suspended again. I was talking to him at Celtic Park.'

I said, 'No, that can't be right. He was at Love Street.'

'Chic was definitely at Parkhead because I was sitting next to him,' my informant told me.

On the Monday morning, I pulled Chic into the office and asked him what he thought about the St Mirren game on the Saturday. 'I thought we played alright,' said Chic.

Then I asked him how he thought individual players had performed, what he thought about the change of system when we went to a 3–5–2 formation and whether he thought he would fit into the new formation when he got back into the team.

'It seemed to work OK,' said Chic. 'Yeah, I could fit into the system no problem.'

I started laughing and said, 'Chic – we didn't change the system on Saturday. You didn't see the game because you were at Parkhead.'

Chic just smiled and held his hands up, 'OK, I admit it,' he said.

That just summed Chic up – his love of Celtic was greater than his affection for St Mirren.

And when we went to play Rangers at Ibrox, Chic would be running around the park like a dervish, kicking anything that moved and wore a blue jersey. At one game, Davie Hay had to go out on to the park during the warm-up and pull Chic back into the dressing room. When we arrived at Ibrox, Chic got changed in double-quick time and was out on the park. While he was doing his warm-up exercises, Chic started winding up the Rangers fans by making gestures and saying things to them. It got so bad a policeman came into our dressing and asked us to get Chic back inside before there was a riot. He was getting a red card and sent off the park before the game had even started.

Despite all his daftness, Chic is a great lad. Unfortunately, I think he wasted his great talent and I've told him that. If he had been sensible and not got into trouble, he would have been top drawer.

Another great laugh we had at the club that season was at the expense of our physio, Andy Binning – although, I must admit, we let the wind-up go on for too long and I ended up having to apologise to him.

It started during a game at Love Street one Saturday and the referee wasn't giving any decisions our way. At one point, my frustrations got the better of me and I shouted, 'Hey, ref – you're a f****** nightmare.' The official heard this and glared over at our dugout. We all just shrugged our shoulders as if to say we hadn't a clue what he was on about.

On the Monday, Andy was talking to Davie Hay and me about the incident and said, 'I'm sure that referee thought it was me who shouted at him. Did you not see the way he was looking at me?'

When Andy left the room, I hatched a plot to wind Andy up and have a laugh. At the time, Tony Fitzpatrick was back at Love Street working as the SFA's community coach and he had plenty of SFA headed notepaper lying around. I took some of this paper and typed out a spoof letter to Andy telling him he was the one suspected of swearing at the referee.

The letter went on to quote all sorts of rules and subsections that he was alleged to have contravened and that he was being called to a meeting to explain himself. In the interim, the SFA would like him to write to them with his version of events, the letter continued. I signed the letter with SFA chief executive Jim Farry's name.

I typed out Andy's name and the St Mirren address on the envelope, put a stamp on it and even left the ground to post it. The next morning the letter arrived back at Love Street and Andy was starting to panic. He went to Davie Hay – who was in on the joke – and said, 'The referee thought it was me right enough. Look at this letter they've sent me. I'm going to have to tell them it was Gordon.' David told him he couldn't do that to one of his colleagues and eventually Andy agreed but said he was definitely going to have to reply to the letter and plead his case.

I immediately pulled aside Kathleen Steel, who worked at the reception at Love Street, and told her, if Andy handed in a letter to be posted, she was to give it straight to me and not to send it out with the mail. Sure enough, Andy wrote his letter, gave it to reception to post and, when it was handed over to me, I opened it. What he had written was extremely conciliatory and said he was sorry about the incident and assured them that he had the ultimate respect for referees.

This was not quite what Andy had been telling everybody he had written in his reply. He told us that he made it clear in no uncertain terms that the SFA had no right to call him to account for something like that and these things happen all the time in football. 'It was quite a strong reply,' he assured us. However, we all knew different and the wind-up didn't end there.

I wrote Andy another letter on SFA headed notepaper a few days later, this time telling him he was being fined £1000 and banned from the dugout for six months. When it arrived the next morning, Andy was distraught and he asked Davie Hay what he was going to do. How Davie managed to keep a straight face I'll never know but he told Andy he would just have to sit in the stand and, when a player got injured, he would have to run down the stairs to the trackside and then on to the park. Davie warned him that at some grounds, like Ibrox or Parkhead, it was quite a distance from the stand to trackside.

Later that day, I pinned all the letters I had on the dressing room notice board for everybody – including Andy – to see. When he realised it was just a wind-up, I think he felt a mixture of relief and anger.

The joke had been going on for a week and I hadn't realised how seriously Andy was taking it and how worried he was about getting into trouble with the SFA. Andy had never worked at a football club before he came to St Mirren and he wasn't used to the jokes, pranks and wind-ups that go on in dressing rooms. As I've said, I realised we had maybe taken things too far and I apologised to Andy. However, I'm not sure if I would like to be lying on Andy's treatment table with an injury and be at his mercy – just in case he still wants some retribution!

The best signing Davie Hay made during his time at St Mirren was bringing Roy Aitken in from Newcastle. If all the players had the same dedication and enthusiasm as Roy, we wouldn't have had many problems that season.

Potentially, we had a great player with us in the German, Thomas Stickroth. He should have been playing for either Rangers or Celtic because he was tremendously quick and skilful and was, by far, the fittest player at St Mirren. We would have the players running round the track at Love Street to develop their stamina and after a few circuits the players would be hanging over the walls of the terracing getting their breath back and Thomas would be standing talking to me about what had been on television the previous night.

The problem about Thomas was that he couldn't get it into his head that he was playing at a level where he should be destroying defenders with his pace up the wing. He always had to go up to defenders and throw his leg over the ball half a dozen times before trying to go past them. This always gave the opposition time to get more defenders around him and stifle his effectiveness. It was only in every fifth or sixth game that Thomas would revert to the simple game of knocking the ball past a defender and beating the fullback with his blistering pace. If Thomas had played all his games like that, he would have been phenomenal and gone on to play at a much higher level.

The other foreign player we had at that time was the striker and Icelandic internationalist, Gudmunder Torfason. Guni, as he was known to the fans, was a good finisher and would get you goals. But he lacked fitness and one of the most frustrating things about him was that he wouldn't try to win the ball back from the opposition if he lost possession. Players would have the ball two or three yards away from him but he wouldn't make the effort to tackle them.

Guni was the first player I ever reacted to at my time at Love Street. His work rate at defending got so bad that I had a go at him in the dressing room one day. 'Guni – you have to close players down when we don't have the ball,' I told him. 'People are walking past you with the ball at their feet and you're not doing anything about it.'

He looked at me and said, 'Do you have a problem?'

I said, 'I do have a problem and it's watching you every week playing like that.'

At that Guni stormed off into the showers in a major huff. When things cooled down, I had a quiet word with him and explained that, because he was one of our top players, we were expecting more from him. Don't know if it did much good, though.

The only other player who fell out with me was Paul Kinnaird. He had been criticised during a team meeting before training and he was still in a huff when the boys were being put through their paces. When I saw what he was like I said to him, 'Do you want some for ice for your bottom lip? – it looks a bit swollen.'

He didn't like that at all and stormed off the training field, got dressed and went home. He was fined a week's wages for that little outburst, the poor wee soul.

One player who came through the ranks at Love Street and went on to perform at the highest level was Paul Lambert. Even in those early days, you could see that Paul was a bit special and wanted to learn everything he could about the game.

In the afternoons, I used to take the young players and coach them on systems and positional sense. Paul would have been twenty-two by this time and had established himself as a first-team regular, but he still came in for that extra coaching. You couldn't get him to take a day off because he was so enthusiastic about the game and wanted to improve himself. His dedication worked because he went to become a Champions League winner with Borussia Dortmund and a regular in the Scotland team.

He tended to get a bit of stick from the fans about being a square passer at times but the thing that amazed me was that he didn't get more goals playing for St Mirren. Every day in training or in practice matches, Paul would rattle in the goals but, when it came to the real thing on a Saturday, they dried up and we would only get two or three goals a season out of him.

As well as staying in the Premier League in season 1991–92, our aim was to build a new future for the club based on bringing through our own talented young players. Three youngsters who I was able to guide through to the first team were Jamie Fullarton, Barry Lavety and Martin Baker. I was also heavily involved in persuading Ricky Gillies to come to St Mirren as Celtic were chasing his signature as well.

I'm glad I was able to talk Davie Hay out of freeing one youngster we had on our books because he went on to have a good career as a professional footballer. Barry McLaughlin hadn't developed as quickly as other players of his age and hadn't broken through into the first team as quickly as we thought he would. Davie thought he wasn't going to make the grade but I managed to persuade him to give Barry a bit more time. Thankfully I was proved right.

Although Davie picked the first team, he would always discuss it with me before the line-up was announced and tell me why he had decided to go with the team he had chosen. I'd had more of an input in picking the team with Tony but the way Davie played it wasn't a problem for me.

We struggled that season and we were relegated to the First Division – no league reconstruction to save us this time. Then Davie left and Jimmy Bone was appointed manager for the start of season 1992–93. As I've already explained, early on I had my doubts about whether Jimmy really me wanted as his assistant in the first place. But, at the beginning, Jimmy said he wanted to work with me and we did just that.

Jimmy brought in a much harder pre-season training regime, which I thought was needed, and he used a lot of the practices he had picked up in African football and showed me a lot of new training routines. But, as the season wore on, I discovered he was taking away a lot of the things I had previously been responsible for. I used to pick the reserve team but soon Jimmy was interfering and telling me not to pick this boy and I'd better play that one. I was still playing in the reserves and, when I showed him the team I was going to put in for a game, he would change it.

Davie Hay would always call me into his office to discuss the team for the next first-team game but, with Jimmy, I found I would have to make a point of asking. When I realised this, I wondered what would happen if I didn't ask Jimmy – would he tell me voluntarily? I decided one Friday to put this to the test.

All that day when I was speaking to Jimmy I never once mentioned the team for Saturday and neither did Jimmy. The following day, I was just like the rest of the players finding out what the team was for the first time when it was read out in the dressing room – quite an unusual situation for an assistant manager to be in.

From then on, that was the way of it. I wouldn't ask what the team was going to be and Jimmy wouldn't tell me. When Davie Hay was there, I was able to explain to players why they had been left out and what the manager's thinking was. But, because Jimmy wouldn't discuss it with me, I had to tell the players who approached me that I knew just as much about it as they did – which was nothing. As far as I was concerned, that was the confirmation that Jimmy was edging me out and he was trying to sicken me into quitting.

From that point, I was going through turmoil, not knowing what to do for the best. I found Jimmy was a very good football coach who knew the game inside out and a lot of his ideas were similar to mine. He was fine when it came to football but I couldn't understand his attitude towards players and the way he treated them – especially the younger ones.

That was the main area of conflict between Jimmy and me. I believe players deserve respect and the only time I had an issue with young players was if their attitude wasn't right. If their attitude was good I never had a problem with them. But Jimmy was always giving them the rough edge of his tongue, shouting at them and calling them every name under the sun. I don't agree with that style of man management.

It came to a head during a reserve game I wasn't playing in and Jimmy and I were watching it from the stand at Love Street. We had a young lad called Roland Fabiani on the books and he was playing at left back. Seconds after the kick-off, Roland made a pass which was intercepted by the opposition. Jimmy turned to me and said, 'Take him off.'

'What are you talking about, Jimmy?' I said. 'That's the boy's first kick of the ball.'

'Doesn't matter, get him off.'

'No, I don't agree with that. Taking him off is out of order.'

We sat in silence for another few minutes but then the boy made another mistake. 'Right,' said Jimmy 'that's it – get him off.'

'You'll lose that boy if you take him off this early,' I said. 'The next time he plays, he is going to do nothing because he'll be so worried about making a mistake and being taken off.'

But Jimmy persisted and said, 'I'm the manager. Go down there and get him off.'

I went down trackside and had a word with Brian McLaughlin and told him Jimmy wanted to haul Roland Fabiani off the park because he had made a couple of mistakes.

I said to Brian, 'Send one of the subs away to warm up as if you are going to put him on. Let's see if Roland can survive this. A couple of good passes and he might get away with it.'

Within seconds of the sub starting to warm up, Jimmy was standing beside us and ordered that Roland Fabiani be substituted. After the game I had a blazing row with Jimmy and told him that was no way to treat a young player. It wasn't the first time I had said to Jimmy that I thought he was wrong shouting at the boys the way he did. But his answer was that football is a tough game, everyone gets shouted at and they had better learn quickly to get used to it.

By Christmas, I'd had enough. For the first time, I wasn't enjoying being at St Mirren. I was going in every day and getting less and less to do as Jimmy wanted to run everything himself. I knew it wasn't going to change and I was wasting my time hanging around.

I got New Year out of the way and, in January 1993, I told the board I was leaving, although they tried to talk me into staying. But I had made up my mind and, although I was sorry to leave St Mirren, there was no going back. The board were very good with me and I left with three months' money. I was grateful to them for that.

Talking about money, when I was assistant to Davie Hay, I

was being paid £25,000 a year and Davie was on £40,000. When the manager's job came up I expected whoever came in to also get £40,000. But I later discovered that the board hired Jimmy Bone on £25,000 a year – the same money that his assistant was on. And the chairman asked me to keep quiet about this.

Imagine football directors doing something like that to save money – the rascals!

13

THE CAP OBVIOUSLY DIDN'T FIT

It's every Scots footballer's nightmare – being involved in a game against England and getting played off the park. It had been a shambles from start to finish and I was sitting on the bench alongside Scotland manager Willie Ormond, his backroom team and the other subs. We were at St James' Park, Newcastle for an Under-23 international against the Auld Enemy and Scotland were in danger of getting a real doing.

I was still at Kilmarnock at the time and I only found out I was in the squad as I was walking down a Glasgow street reading the *Evening Times* sports pages. I was amazed when I saw my name in the squad alongside guys like Kenny Dalglish, Joe Jordan, Gordon McQueen and Alan Rough. I didn't have a clue I was being considered until I read my name in the paper that day after college.

We were due to play the game on a Tuesday night and we'd met up in a Glasgow hotel on the Saturday before the match. There were a lot of call-offs and, on the Sunday morning, a few of the players sat down with some SFA officials to scour through the match reports in the papers to pick out players they could phone and draft into the squad.

When we got to the airport on the Monday, there were only five players flying to Newcastle. One of the five was Eddie Kelly from Arsenal who had just flown up from London to meet us at Glasgow Airport. When he saw there were just four of us – and he didn't recognise any of the four players – he called off with a mysterious illness there and then. With Eddie heading back home, it meant there were eleven call-offs out of the original sixteen-man squad.

After we arrived at the hotel in Newcastle, the players we had phoned on the Sunday began to turn up. Willie Ormond picked the team from his patched-together squad and I wasn't in it. I was one of the four left from the original squad and, after helping out by phoning around to get stand-in players, I didn't even get a game in the starting eleven!

England had a really good team out that night with guys like Alan Hudson, Trevor Francis, Bob Latchford and Tony Currie playing. I was on the bench and we were getting a good going-over although we managed to keep the score down to 2–0. On the bench with me were the Kilmarnock physio Hugh Allan – who was also the Scotland sponge man – Willie Ormond and our other subs. I was sitting in the middle of all these guys and Willie Ormond leaned across and asked me, 'Can you play left back?'

I said, 'No.'

Willie said, 'Are you sure you don't want a game at left back?'

Again I said, 'I don't play left back.'

Willie then turned to Frank Gray, who was a midfield player, and asked, 'Well, do you want to play left back?'

Frank said, 'Aye, no bother.'

'Right,' said Willie, 'get stripped – you're on.'

Another hilarious moment from that game – if anything can be funny about Scotland getting humped by England – was when Willie Ormond asked Hugh Allan who the number eight was.

Hugh said, 'That's Tony Currie.'

'No,' said Willie, 'not for them – for us. Who's our number eight?'

Hugh had to get the team lines out to discover who Scotland had playing at number eight. So he told Willie it was Alan Lamb of Preston.

Willie looked straight ahead and said, 'Well, he's f******
hopeless!'

211

I couldn't believe what I was hearing. The best line ever from an international manager. Who's our number eight? And he's hopeless, anyway.

I'd already won international honours playing for the Scotland Under-18s. When I was seventeen, I played in a Scotland Under-18 trial game at St Mirren's Love Street ground between the home Scots and the Anglo Scots – the lads who were with English club teams. I played in the centre of midfield for the home Scots and scored two goals in a 3–1 victory.

I was picked for the Under-18 Scotland squad to play in the European Nations Cup, which was quite a prestigious youth tournament. We beat Wales and France to get through to the final stages, which were being played in Italy. France had a really strong team at the time and some of the young players in that French team went on to be household names in football – Michel Platini, Jean Tigana and Dominique Rocheteau. Makes you wonder what happens to Scottish players who are stars at that young age but then don't make it at a world-class level in later years.

In the final stages, we were based in Pisa and played against East Germany, Czechoslovakia and Austria. We never got through the group stages but it was a great experience for me and I played in every game. I played twelve times for the Scotland Under-18s before I became too old.

Going to that tournament was the first time I had ever been abroad and it meant I had to go up to the SFA offices in Glasgow to fill in the forms to get a passport. There was a young guy there, Bill Richardson, asking me questions as he filled in my passport application form. He said, 'You're not a full-time player, are you?'

I replied, 'No, I'm still at school.'

'OK, then,' he said and continued scribbling on the application form.

When I was handed my passport by the SFA, my occupation was given as 'Schoolboy'. It was a ten-year passport and, for the next decade, every time I went abroad, I had to show a passport that said I was a schoolboy. Right up until I was twenty-seven – having been married, had children, played in the European Cup – any time I was at an airport check-in or immigration point, I would have to show this passport with 'Schoolboy' written on it. It gave some foreign airport staff a few laughs over these years. Normally people are embarrassed by their passport photo – I was mortified every time someone read my occupation.

After that eventful game against England at Newcastle, I was included in about a dozen Under-23 squads although I didn't always get a game. I started four games and for the rest I was on the bench. Apart from that infamous England game at Newcastle, I always got on the park when I was a sub. I was in the squads that got to the semi-final of the European Championships at that level and made an appearance in some of the matches.

Football legend Jock Stein started taking the Under-23 team and he had me on the bench for a game in Romania. He was very good with me and gave me simple but very effective instructions when he was putting me on to replace Willie Pettigrew.

We were winning 2–1 and were desperate to hold on for the win. Big Jock told me, 'I want you to go out there and just run and dribble with the ball. Hold the ball as much as you can and we'll see this one out.' And that's exactly what I did. I had about fifteen minutes where I ran the Romanian defenders ragged.

Jock gave me a hug after the game and said, 'That was brilliant, son. Well done.' That meant a lot to me.

During that European Championship run, Willie Ormond said he would bring me into the full international squad the following year. But, by then, he had been replaced by Ally McLeod as manager and I didn't get a look-in.

That was until 1978 when I was with Rangers and the Ibrox manager, Jock Wallace, was pushing for me to get a full Scotland cap. Ally McLeod called me into the Under-21 squad as the over-age player. We were to play Wales away from home and Ally announced his team. He had me playing up front as a striker and I said to him in front of the rest of the squad, 'You want me to play up front, then?'

'Yes, just play your normal game. The way you play at Rangers,' he replied.

'But I don't play up front for Rangers.'

'Yes you do. You've scored twenty-two goals.'

'That's right – but from midfield. I play centre midfield.'

'Doesn't matter. You're playing up front for us.'

I was thinking to myself, 'Here's the Scotland manager and he doesn't even know what position I play for Rangers.' He was obviously only giving in to the pressure he was getting from the likes of Jock Wallace to give me a game for Scotland.

I played quite well in the Wales match and almost scored an equaliser with a header, which was cleared off the line by a defender. However, we were defeated 1–0. That was the last time I was to pull on a Scotland jersey and I believe an incident on the team bus on the way to the match in Wales had a lot to do with that. Once again, I was standing up against someone who was having a go at me but didn't have any logic in what they were saying.

The players were told to be on the team bus by 6 p.m. on the night of the game. I had been sharing a room with my Ibrox team mate Bobby Russell and it was five to six when we stepped on to the bus. Ally McLeod was already sitting in the front seat and he growled at us, 'Where have you two been?'

I told him we had been in our room getting ready, to which Ally replied, 'But I've been waiting here for five minutes.'

I looked at my watch and told him that it was only five to six and we weren't late as we had been told to be here at 6 p.m. Bobby Russell had seen what was happening and did the sensible thing by heading off to the back of the bus away from the bust-up that was undoubtedly brewing. I didn't do the sensible thing – I stayed for an argument. And Ally wouldn't let up. 'We've all been here waiting for you,' he said.

'But you told us to be here for 6 p.m. and I'm here for 6 p.m. so I'm on time. What's the problem?' I said. 'How am I supposed to know what time you're going to get on the bus?' I continued.

Ally told me to get a seat so we wouldn't waste any more time and as I stormed up the back of the bus I turned to him and said, 'I just can't believe you.' I have always been a stickler for the logic in what people do or say. It was the most stupid thing for Ally to start an argument about. Needless to say, it meant no more call-ups from Mr McLeod either for the Under-21s or the full national team.

Not getting a full Scotland cap was a big disappointment for me. It stopped me realising an ambition as a youngster to be a player on the world stage. I know wee boys think they can be world-beaters at football, but I really did think I could be world class and playing international football was a big part of that. My ambitions in life were all football ambitions and all I wanted to be was successful at the highest level. Compared to where I wanted to be as a little kid and because I never got a full Scotland cap, I never made it as far as I wanted to go.

Obviously, as a part-time player with Kilmarnock, my chances of an international call-up were slim but, when I signed for Rangers and had such a good first season, I thought I would have merited a look-in. People might say I wasn't good enough but I would make the point that I was playing for a team that had just won the domestic treble. I had played in European games and I'd been the club's top scorer with twenty-seven goals – and not one of them a penalty – that season from midfield. Nowadays, if Scotland had anybody who could score twenty-seven goals a season – never mind from midfield – they would walk into the national side.

At that time, in season 1977–78, Scotland were trying to qualify for the World Cup in Argentina under manager Ally McLeod and, every time a squad was named, I'd look at the papers and see my name wasn't there. Each time I wasn't included in the squad, I'd be disappointed but what made up for that was getting international recognition playing in Europe with Rangers.

Every time a foreign team would come to Ibrox, their coach would name me as the Rangers player they most feared – and that includes world-class managers like Giovannni Trapattoni, who was with Juventus. Even the manager of Twente Enschede described me in the media as a 'Mercedes'. When Jock Wallace was asked about this at a press conference, he disagreed. 'Gordon Smith's not a Mercedes – he's a Rolls Royce,' he said.

And when I was playing down south, I met the England manager at the time, Ron Greenwood, who said, 'I just want to say to you, Gordon, that in football there are artists and there are artisans. You're not an artisan – you're an artist. Just keep doing what you are doing and I wish you were English.'

Nowadays I would probably be able to fall back on my mother's father – grandpa Bullock – who was born in Carlisle and was therefore English. If I hadn't played for Scotland at Under-18 and Under-23 level, I could maybe have played for England – and I would have.

Although I'm as Scottish as the next person, without a doubt if it had meant furthering my football ambitions and proving managers like Ally McLeod wrong, I would have played for England. Just like I would have signed for Celtic if Rangers hadn't come in for me. I would go where I thought was best for my football career.

Don't get me wrong, I always supported Scotland and I was at Wembley in 1977 for that great game when we beat England 2–1 and the Scots fans invaded the pitch and took the goalposts and half the pitch back up the road with them. I was sitting in the stand with Marlene so I couldn't even get on the park as a supporter.

Another reason I thought I might have got a shout for the Scotland squad was that some of the most respected managers in the country had wanted to sign me at one time or another. There was Jock Stein, Bill Shankly, Tommy Docherty, Jock Wallace and Billy McNeill. It made me think that, if these guys thought I was a good footballer, then surely I should get the chance to play for my country. It's only now, if people cast up the fact I don't have any full international caps, that it annoys me that I didn't get to play for Scotland because, to be honest, I think I deserved the chance.

There was another team mate of mine at Ibrox who never got a full Scotland cap. Bobby Russell was a very talented and silky player and he should have been given his chance as well. Perhaps the reason neither of us got a game for Scotland was that we weren't the archetypal Scottish player in the eyes of the manager and the fans.

Everyone wanted you to be tenacious, hard and tough tackling. We're the only country in the world where you get a big cheer for tackling someone. You could have a great run, put in a great cross into the box or make an inch-perfect pass and you hardly get any applause. But, if you put in a crunching tackle, it goes down great with the crowd. It was as if you weren't putting in the big tackles so you weren't committed enough. You could describe Bobby and me as more cultured and skilful players and maybe that wasn't what was wanted in the late 70s and early 80s.

In those days, people mistook hard tackling for courage and I would say playing my kind of football against defenders took more courage because I would be at the receiving end of the tackles. The real hard men were players like Jimmy Johnstone, Willie Henderson, Davie Cooper and George Best. They were the guys trying to play football and who were getting kicked all over the place by defenders – but they got up, dusted themselves down and came back for more.

This attitude, that you've got to be a hard tackler first and then we'll see if you're any good at football, still exists today and I'm still being accused of being a coward for not having a reputation as a hard tackler.

A few years ago when Craig Brown was Scotland manager, I went down to the Marine Hotel in Troon, where the squad were staying, to see Paul Lambert. I had written a newspaper column criticising the way Scotland were playing because they were so defensive. I bumped into Craig Brown who tried to take me to task about what I'd said in the column. We were having an argument about this and I told him I was perfectly entitled to express my opinion. His reply was, 'You're one to talk about players – you were nothing but a coward when you were playing.'

'Why was I a coward?' I asked him.

'Because you couldn't tackle,' he said.

'Oh, well,' I thought to myself. 'You can be up against some of the toughest defenders in the world and score goals against them but, because you don't have a reputation as a hard tackler, you're a coward. Somehow I don't think so.'

I've borne the brunt of some hard and wild tackles in my time and have been injured by them but that never stopped me coming back for more and I was never afraid of being tackled.

There is a certain irony that, when I was playing with Basle and moved to sweeper, I was the guy in the team making all the tackles. But, when I was with Rangers and in line for a possible cap call, that wasn't the type of play that was required from me.

And round about that time I thought I might get a Scotland cap after all. When Andy Roxburgh was made Scotland manager I wrote to congratulate him on his appointment because I had got on well with him when I did my coaching B Licence at Largs. Andy replied thanking me and said that, depending on how the next few results went, I might be getting a call-up. Unfortunately that call never came.

I think there were three things that stopped me getting a full international cap. The first was standing up for myself and arguing with Ally McLeod on the team bus over whether I was late or not. The second was that, by the time Jock Stein took over as Scotland manager, I was playing with Brighton – a small English club – and I didn't have the same profile in Scotland as I did when I was with Rangers. And the third was that I didn't really fit into the tough-tackling midfield, terrier-type mould that was expected of a Scotland player in those days. The guys I was up against for a midfield place were the likes of Graham Souness, Archie Gemmell and Roy Aitken.

I've no doubt, if I had been born on the continent, I would probably have won an international cap and, if I was in my twenties today, I would definitely have got the chance to play for my country. No disrespect to the players in the Scotland team now but, when Barry Ferguson scored sixteen goals for Rangers in one season, they were raving about it. But I scored twenty-seven goals in my first season at Rangers and twenty-three goals in my second season.

Nowadays, if you are playing for the Old Firm and you're scoring goals, there's no way you wouldn't be in the Scotland team. And no harm to the lad Craig Beattie, who is a tremendous young prospect, but he had only started five first-team games for Celtic when he made his Scotland debut. The boy may well become a great Scotland player but he has hardly a wealth of experience playing in the top level yet he is in the Scotland squad.

Maybe, when I was hoping to play for Scotland, there were a lot of better Scottish players around but I never gave up hope. In June 1978, I actually put all my wedding arrangements on stand-by in case I got the call to go to Argentina with the Scotland squad for the World Cup. I even told Marlene that, if I was picked, the wedding would have to be postponed. That never happened and Marlene and I married as planned. In hindsight, after the disaster Scotland had in the World Cup that year, I think I got the better end of the deal by getting married rather than going to Argentina with Ally McLeod.

Sure, I'm disappointed – but not bitter – about not getting a full Scotland cap. But what chance did I have when, despite being in Rangers' first team week in, week out, the Scotland manager, Ally McLeod, didn't even know what position I played?

14

THE NEGOTIATOR

The Borussia Dortmund fans had not long left the stadium and their cheers for Paul Lambert after a lap of honour in his farewell match must have still been ringing in his ears as we sat in the club's chief executive's office. On one side of the desk was the chief executive, Michael Meier, and on the other were Paul and me. I was acting as Paul's representative.

This was the moment Paul was to sign the forms which would take him back to Scotland and the start of a new era in his career with Celtic. It wasn't long since Paul had won a Champions League medal with Borussia playing in that defensive midfield position which is now commonly known as the Paul Lambert role. It came as a surprise to everybody that Paul was leaving Dortmund after having so much success in Germany. But his family were unsettled and they were desperate to get back home.

Michael Meier shuffled the bits of paper and made sure they were all in order, turned the sheets to face Paul and pointed to where his signature was to go. Meier's outstretched hand offered a pen but, as Paul leaned forward to take it, the chief executive quickly pulled the pen back from his grasp.

'Now, let me say this,' began Meier, 'I think you're making a big mistake – you shouldn't be leaving here. This is a great club and you have done really well and this is the best part of your career. You're a top player in our team and you should not be leaving.'

This guy wasn't going through the motions and he meant every word. It was literally a last-gasp bid to persuade Paul to change his mind and stay with Dortmund. His impassioned plea had ratcheted up the tension in the room and I had already cracked. If it had been me, I would have been ripping up the papers and telling Meier I'd be in at training the next day.

But Paul stood firm. 'Sorry, he said, 'my mind's made up, my wife's expecting us to go back to Glasgow, the deal's done and already in my mind I'm back in Glasgow. I'll always have a great affection for the club but I'm signing the forms and going to Celtic.' At that, Meier reluctantly gave Paul the pen, he signed the papers and we were off to Parkhead.

If it were totally down to a football decision, I think it was mistake for Paul to leave Borussia Dortmund. He had won a Champions League medal a few months previously, he was playing in the Champions League again that season, he was about to play in the World Club Championship and he was a hero to the fans. But Paul's family hadn't really settled in Germany and wanted back home. His departure was more of a family decision than a football one. Having said that, he has done fantastically well at Celtic since joining them in 1997 and is now on the first step of the football managerial ladder with Livingston.

Paul did so well in Germany that Berti Vogts told me that, while he was manager of the German international team, he thought Paul was one of his countrymen and was considering calling him up to the German squad. He thought Borussia had unearthed a young German player and he phoned the club to ask about him. When he was told Paul was a Scot, Berti recommended to Craig Brown – the then Scotland manager – that he should take a look at him for his team.

While I was with St Mirren, BBC Radio Scotland asked me to become a sports pundit and I did that on a few occasions during big games. And, when I left Love Street, they asked me to do this on a Saturday. At first, it was on a casual basis – I'd just get a phone call every week asking if I could do a game – but I eventually got an annual contract to do both radio and television.

I thought I would be able to find a football coaching job after my time at St Mirren but the only offer I got was to be part-time manager of Albion Rovers. I had to say thanks but no thanks because the money I would have been getting there would have been less than I was getting for working on a Saturday for the BBC. With Albion Rovers I would have been on £80 a week and I was getting £100 a shift for being on the radio.

I often wondered if the reason I wasn't offered a coaching job was because I wasn't a favoured friend of the group of SFA coaches who are often referred to as the Largs Mafia. They are the coaches who take all the SFA football courses at the sportscotland National Centre, Inverclyde, in Largs. I didn't think for a minute that I couldn't have done the job because two of my previous managers – Tony Fitzpatrick and Davie Hay – had recommended me to take over from them. And falling out with Jimmy Bone was probably the last thing I should have done because Jimmy is very much part of that fraternity.

I don't care how many times it is denied but this coaching fraternity does have a major influence in who gets jobs in Scottish football. It's not that they could stop people getting a job but they would put a word in for favoured friends and I was most definitely not one of their favoured friends.

As well as having fallen out with Jimmy Bone, my tendency to be outspoken could also have come back to haunt me because, when I completed my coaching A Licence at Largs in 1988, I had told people that I was disappointed with the standard of training and coaching we had received there. That obviously wouldn't have gone down well with those and such as those. It would probably have been better if I had kept my opinions to myself because that could have put me right out of the scene.

In the spring of 1993, when I realised there wouldn't be any football jobs for me, I took up an offer from the Rangers chairman David Murray to help set up a company called Rangers Financial Services. The idea was to use the club's branding and fan base to sell investments, insurance policies and pensions to the club's army of supporters. Because I had a financial services background and was an ex-Rangers player, they thought I would be ideal to head it up.

We worked out of offices under the Govan Stand at Ibrox and it was strange for me, having been a player at Ibrox, to now be working there outwith the football scene. To a certain degree, I was feeling frustrated because I thought I might have being doing a coaching job at Ibrox instead of selling pension plans, investments and insurance to the supporters. I wasn't enjoying working there and I left in December of that year to work with two friends I had employed at London and Capital, Douglas Morrison and Frame Broadfoot, who had set up a financial advice business.

I carried on as a self-employed financial advisor until 1995 when I was approached by a firm of chartered accountants, Neville Russell, to become their manager in Scotland with offices in St Vincent Street, Glasgow. At the time, I was looking after the financial affairs of some footballers, including Paul Lambert, and I suggested they should also launch a football agency business.

They liked the idea and we set up the Neville Russell Sports Management Company. I was the director and I brought in a former team mate of mine at Manchester City, Jim Melrose, who was already working as an agent.

Things were going well but, in early 1997, Martin O'Neill – who was Leicester City manager at the time – asked Jim Melrose to go there as his chief scout. The lure of football was too much for him and he left for Leicester.

The company asked me to step into Jim's shoes and take over as a football agent but I wasn't that keen. I was enjoying my work as director but they persuaded me that I was the best placed to build the agency business they already had. When Jim left, the company had three players on their books and, within a year of me taking over as agent, we had signed up twenty-five players, including Paul Lambert and fellow-Scots internationalist John McGinley.

Then it began to get wearisome with the company making me write up report after report on who I was speaking to, how much money was coming in and so on. It meant all my time was being taken up with that instead of being out there earning for both our clients and the company. The other problem I had was that they weren't willing to give me any staff to help run the business. All I got from them was the office and I soon realised you don't need an office to run a football agency business. Most of your meetings are outside the office – at football clubs or hotels. So I decided to leave and set up a football agency myself.

To keep everything above board, I wrote to all the players I had represented with Neville Russell and recommended that they stay with that company. But they all had a three month get-out clause in their contracts and, after those three months, every one of them decided they wanted me to be their agent.

I started my own football agency in April 2000 and it meant I had to find a £100,000 bond to lodge with FIFA so I could become a registered agent. I put up £10,000 of my own money and I borrowed £90,000 from the bank. I never set eyes on the £90,000 as it was transferred into a Swiss bank account run by FIFA.

I think the bond was a good idea because it meant that people who were football agents were going to take it seriously. It was a mistake when FIFA stopped the bond system and handed regulation to the individual country's football associations.

Over the years, I have represented players like Jonatan Johansson when he was transferred from Rangers to Charlton, Paul Lambert, of course, Barry Lavety, Jamie Fullarton, Martin Baker, Warren Cummings who went from Chelsea to Dundee United, Kenny Miller when he went from Hibs to Rangers, Ulrik Laursen when he moved from Hibs to Celtic, Craig Burley when he moved from Celtic to Derby County, Scott Severin, Andy Kirk, Hearts captain Steven Pressley and Derek Adams from Mother-well to Aberdeen.

The two biggest deals I've ever been involved in saw Paul Lambert come to Celtic and Craig Burley leave Celtic. And because of the typical Celtic procrastination, Paul could have been a Rangers player instead.

THE NEGOTIATOR

Davie Hay – who was manager at St Mirren when I was an assistant – was now working as Celtic's chief scout and he phoned me one day to ask if Paul Lambert would be interested in coming to Celtic. The Parkhead management team of Wim Jansen and Murdo McLeod had seen Paul play in his holding role and they wanted to use that system at Celtic. I phoned Paul in Germany and he said that, since his wife and family hadn't really settled over there, then, yes, he would like to come home and sign for Celtic. Davie Hay told me that the Celtic general manager at the time, Jock Brown, didn't think Paul was the right signing for the club although Wim Jansen and Murdo McLeod were adamant that he was.

I then contacted the Borussia Dortmund chief executive Michael Meier and told him Celtic were interested in signing Paul and that he would like to come home. Meier told me the club weren't interested in selling Paul but he would speak to him. Having spoken to Paul and getting confirmation that he wanted back home, Meier called me back and said they would only sell at a fixed price of five million Deutschmarks.

I passed this information on to Celtic and left the rest to them, thinking that, if the Parkhead side wanted Paul, all they had to do was pay Dortmund the transfer fee and that would be it. But I hadn't accounted for Jock Brown thinking he could squeeze a lower price out of Dortmund. Michael Meier got on the phone to Jim Melrose and complained bitterly about Celtic coming in with a lower offer when they had already been told that it was a fixed-price transfer fee. Meier was not happy at the way things were panning out.

When this happened I didn't know if Paul's transfer to Celtic would now go through because I knew that Michael Meier wasn't going to budge from his fixed price and here was Celtic trying to negotiate the fee down. What I did know was that Paul had set his heart on coming back to Scotland and the only other club in Scotland big enough to pay the transfer fee and Paul's wages were Rangers.

So I phoned the Ibrox manager Walter Smith and told him that Paul was coming back home, although his Celtic transfer was in the balance, and asked if Rangers would be interested in signing him. Walter told me Rangers had been interested in signing Paul when he was at Motherwell and asked me how much Dortmund wanted for him. He thought the price tag was a bit on the high side but said he would come back to me. When Walter Smith eventually did call me back, it was to say that Rangers weren't in a position to make an offer for Paul.

I suspect that Walter couldn't have made any signings because he had already told Rangers he would be leaving at the end of that season 1997–98, although at that point in October the news hadn't been made public.

I only decided to contact Rangers when the Celtic deal with Dortmund appeared to be stalling and I hadn't told Paul about it. I later let him know that I'd spoken to Rangers but they weren't going to make a bid for him and he accepted that I was only doing this to keep our options open. I didn't phone Rangers to try to upstage Celtic, I was making sure my client had an option. I was worried that Paul's transfer to Celtic was going to fall through because Celtic weren't going to meet Dortmund's asking price.

At the time, Paul had no allegiance to either Celtic or Rangers – all he wanted was a move back to a big club in Scotland. All this is completely inconsequential because, after having been at Parkhead for seven years, Paul is as big a Celtic man as you'll find. It's where his heart lies and Paul is totally Celtic minded. You could say that in his time at the club he has been completely Celtified. In the end, the transfer turned out to be a great move for Paul. And, one day, Paul might even be the Celtic manager. Remember – you read it here first.

The Old Firm derby the following January was quite ironic because Rangers were going for the record-breaking ten-in-a-row and two players I represented scored the goals that won Celtic the game – Paul Lambert and Craig Burley. You sometimes feel that players you represent can be like family and their joy is your joy too. Even though I'm a Rangers supporter, I was very proud that day when Paul and Craig scored these goals.

Here were two players who you've become friendly with and you're looking after their careers – you've got to be proud of the fact they're doing well. In any case, I'm the type of person who thinks that, if you win the league, it's because you have deserved to win. Rangers were going for ten-in-a-row and a memorable season, but Celtic were hot on their heels at that point in the season and the game Paul and Craig got those goals was a big, big win for Celtic.

Craig Burley's transfer out of Parkhead, in December 1999, was a strange affair and seemed to come out of nothing. By this time, Kenny Dalglish and John Barnes were at the club. As far as everyone knew, Craig was doing well at Parkhead until stories started to appear in the papers saying that Craig had rejected a new deal at Celtic. This came as a big shock to both Craig and me because we hadn't been talking to Celtic about an extension to his contract.

When it hit the papers, Craig got on the phone to me asking what I thought was going on and if I thought they were trying to get rid of him. It was as if the club was trying to make out that Craig was a disruptive influence and was causing problems at the club.

The stories continued that Craig had knocked back a new contract and that Celtic couldn't afford his wage demands. Craig was shocked by this. I don't know if an incident in which Craig had words with John Barnes after a game about how the team were playing had anything to do with the stories appearing in the papers. Craig, like me, can be a bit outspoken at times and the row with John Barnes came shortly before it all went wrong for Craig at Parkhead.

Then Kenny Dalglish told Craig that Derby County were interested in signing him. It was becoming obvious there was no future for Craig at Parkhead so he decided to head back down south to Derby. But there was still the outstanding issue of Celtic owing Craig a large sum of money from his signing-on fee when he first came to Parkhead. I phoned the club, looking for Eric Reilly, the director who handled that side of things. He wasn't in so I asked to speak to his secretary instead but she wasn't available either.

Before I knew it, Kenny Dalglish was on the phone asking me what I was doing calling Eric Reilly's secretary. When I told him that I wanted to find out about the money Craig was owed, Kenny said I should deal with him as he looked after everything at the club. Kenny said he would phone me back when he had a copy of Craig's contract in front of him and he did call me. 'It says he's owed the money at the end of the season,' said Kenny. 'So if he takes this transfer he doesn't get to the end of the season.'

There was a touch of déjà vu about this as the same argument had been used against me when I was a player leaving clubs who still owed me signing-on money. 'No, Kenny, Craig is owed that money and he'll only go if he's paid that money.'

'He's not getting it,' said Kenny. 'No chance.'

'He'll not be going then,' I replied.

'Well, f*** him!' was Kenny's riposte.

Three days later, Kenny Dalglish phoned me and offered to pay Craig a third of what they owed him. I had already spoken to Craig about my previous conversation with Kenny and he made it clear he didn't want to leave Celtic in the first place and that he definitely wasn't going if the club still owed him money.

I told Kenny, 'I don't need to speak to Craig about this – I know he won't take a third of what the club owes him.'

'That's the final offer,' Kenny replied. 'If he doesn't take it, then the deal's off.'

'That's OK with me, too.' I said. 'If that's the final offer, the deal's off as far as we're concerned as well.'

A week later, the Derby County manager, Jim Smith, called me and asked about Craig's personal terms and what would he be looking for.

'I don't know if you know this but the deal has fallen through at this end because Celtic owe Craig money,' I said. 'And, if Craig doesn't get the money, then he's not going anywhere.'

'He's getting his money,' Jim Smith said. 'I've been told that Celtic will pay him what he is owed.'

I called Eric Reilly straight way and, to my surprise, he asked me to come into Parkhead and sort out the money. Craig got the signing-on money he was owed, I negotiated a great deal for him at Derby – getting more money than he was getting at Parkhead – and Craig signed for the Rams.

I've never got to the bottom of why John Barnes and Kenny Dalglish wanted rid of Craig. Was he too outspoken for them or did they just want to transfer someone out to get money in so they could buy new players? Mibbes aye, mibbes no.

I got a lot of stick for Kenny Miller leaving Hibs to join Rangers in June 2000. The Easter Road fans blame me for unsettling their young star striker. According to the Hibs faithful, I decided that Kenny Miller was good enough to play for Rangers so I phoned Dick Advocaat or David Murray and persuaded them to sign him. I talked Rangers into paying £2 million for Kenny and then persuaded Hibs, who didn't really want to sell him, to take the £2 million – I must be some negotiator, by the way. Now, if you believe I made all that happen, you'll believe anything.

I thought Kenny Miller would have done well but Dick Advocaat didn't really use Kenny in the first team that much – despite him scoring five goals in one game. I had hoped that Kenny would have flourished at Rangers but he had to go down south to Wolves before he began to realise his full potential. I believe one of the problems was that the standard of coaching he was getting at Ibrox wasn't good enough.

Kenny was an up-and-coming young player so I have to ask myself why he didn't make it as a first-team regular at Ibrox. At the time I didn't know how good Dick Advocaat was as a coach but now I believe he wasn't good enough.

I have since done some research on the former Rangers manager and I would say my opinion of him is that he was a very good football tactician but wasn't a good coach or man manager and that's what lost him the dressing room at Ibrox. I also wonder if Dick Advocaat really wanted Kenny at Rangers because all my negotiations with the club were with David Murray. I maybe should have realised everything was not as it should be because I never once spoke to Dick Advocaat about Kenny's transfer and, when the boy signed on at Ibrox, Dick was nowhere to be seen.

Hibs fans had another go at me when Ulrik Laursen was transferred to Celtic for £1.5 million in August 2002. Normally, the fans say that because I'm a former Rangers player, I try to get the players I represent transferred to Ibrox. Well, even although Ulrik was going to Rangers' greatest rivals, they still had me down as the villain of the piece. I can't make two clubs agree a fee for a player – the clubs decide if they want to buy or sell. I'm just in the middle negotiating the best deal I can for a player.

But try telling that to the Aberdeen fans who claim that, because I'm an ex-Ranger and there is now a bitter rivalry between the clubs, I deliberately encouraged another of the players I represent, David Rowson, to leave Pittodrie for Stoke City in the summer of 2001. The reality of that one was that, the year before, Aberdeen had promised David a rise in wages if he did well. He had a very good season and Aberdeen only offered him an increase of £100 a week. I'd had an offer from Stoke that would double the boy's wages. I told David that, if he wanted to make money out of the game, then he would make more by going to Stoke but it was his decision. It really was a no-brainer for David – double your wages or stay in Aberdeen for an extra hundred quid. I wonder how many Aberdeen fans would change their jobs if someone offered to pay them twice as much as they are getting just now.

Of all the football chairmen I have had to deal with, Rangers' David Murray is by far the easiest – if only for the fact that you can get a decision out of him there and then. When you are talking to other clubs, you have to go through a series of chief executives, directors and board members before you can get a decision. With David Murray he will tell you yes or no on the phone. I've struck a deal with David Murray speaking to him on the hands-free in my car for five minutes. You agree the deal and, within hours, there's a fax from Rangers outlining everything you had spoken about on the phone ready for you to show the player and have signed. It's the same with Eddie Thompson at Dundee United because there's one man in charge.

In my experience, the hardest to deal with was Celtic because of the cumbersome process of decision making that went on at Parkhead. You would speak to the chief executive who would then want to speak to the manager. Then it would have to go to a board meeting and at one stage the board had a subcommittee to deal with transfers. I'm not surprised it takes Celtic so long to bring a player in and you wonder how many they have missed out on because of the way they do business. Give me a tough bastard to negotiate with – but one who can make a quick decision – any day.

During this time, my media career was continuing apace with annual contracts for BBC radio and also appearances as a football pundit on Scottish Television. I was enjoying my media work and eventually I was contracted to BBC Scotland to do television as well as radio. After a while, however, the constant Saturday night working in the studios began to get wearisome as it was interfering with my family life and I wanted a break. In December 2001, I told the BBC that I wanted to stop working on Saturday nights, although I did eventually return to that *Sportscene* slot the next season. My decision to pack in the Saturday night television work led to a ridiculous story in the media that I'd had a fall-out with the new *Sportscene* presenter at the time, Dougie Vipond, and I wasn't happy with the dressing room I had. Despite me telling the reporter doing the story that it was all a load of nonsense, the paper went ahead and ran the story.

Let me make it clear that I didn't stop doing *Sportscene* because of the dressing room I had at the BBC, nor did I have a row with

Dougie Vipond who is one of the nicest guys you could meet. I suspect someone was trying to undermine Dougie and they were using me to do it. Well, they failed and Dougie is still at the BBC and fronting *Sportscene* on a regular basis.

Another accusation levelled at me is that I have a conflict of interest being an agent and working in the media. They suggest that I am promoting my players but my argument is – to whom? The public don't buy or sell players and to suggest that managers would be influenced by what I have said is ludicrous. In reality, my media work has caused me more of a problem because managers and players hear or get to hear my comments about them. This has led to managers refusing to speak to me and players cancelling their contracts with me.

One of the big advantages I have as an agent is the number of people I can phone and find out about players' wages at all levels of the game. Knowledge certainly is power and knowing how much to demand in wages for the player you're representing is vital. I was talking with a chief executive of a Premiership club in England who told me that what he was offering would make my player the highest paid at the club. But, because I knew who really were the highest paid and what they were on, I had a huge advantage and was able to tell him that I knew he was lying to me.

Knowledge is not just about getting a player the highest possible wages. It's about knowing where he really should be in the pecking order and what other players of similar ability and experience are getting at similar-sized clubs.

My ability to find out what players are being paid is down to the fact that I've been a footballer and have met many players who have moved on into management and have been at different clubs. Anything anyone tells me remains confidential but it is very useful to know what the going rate is. Sometimes I don't even need to use the information because clubs know that I know what's going on and they play fair right from the start.

The other negotiating tactic I would often employ is structuring a player's wages so, every time he played a certain number of first-team games, his money would increase. I can appreciate that a club won't want to pay big bucks to someone who is just breaking into a team and they don't know how well he will do. But, at the same time, it's not fair for a player to progress quickly and become a first-team regular and still be on the money he was earning while trying to break through.

Agents are sometimes painted as the pariahs of football, but that's a generalisation and, like most generalisations, it is far from the truth. No matter what walk of life you come from, what business you are in or what your profession is, there will be good and bad people involved. And the world of the football agent is no different.

But, make no mistake, agents are needed to represent players, otherwise the clubs will take advantage of the players. An agent is there to advise players – not just on football matters but also on issues outside football which could affect them. Even when I was a young player I could have done with an agent to negotiate on my behalf.

A perfect example was when I was Manchester City and I spoke to Billy McNeill about extending my contract. He told me he didn't think I had done well enough and I wasn't in a good position to negotiate a new contract. But maybe, if I had a good season, I could come back to talk to him about it. That was on the Thursday but, on the Saturday, Billy was telling me in the dressing room before a game, 'Smudger, the way you have been playing recently, you can win this game for us.' One day I'm not doing well enough to merit a new contract and two days later I'm a match-winner.

But that's football for you. When it comes down to business, the players will always get shafted if there's no one there to protect them and negotiate on their behalf. The last thing a player wants to do is fall out with his manager about money – and maybe I should have heeded that principle earlier in my career when I challenged John Greig about our bonus for beating Juventus!

I don't want to put myself up as a saint here but, when I reluctantly became an agent, I wanted to look after my clients and at the same time protect the spirit of the game as well. There's no doubt, when it comes to transfers, the money changing hands is so huge that the game is getting shady at a higher level and transfers are becoming messy with so many different people getting involved. There are people at all levels of football who do things they shouldn't and they give the whole game a bad name.

In recent years, we've had allegations of clubs and agents paying money for certain players to be given international caps so they can fetch a higher transfer fee in Europe. Over a period there seemed to be a lot of South American footballers – all with just two caps – being hawked around Europe by their agents and some of them just weren't up to the standard you'd expect from an international. Then you've got players coming in from Eastern Europe who are owned or part-owned by rich businessmen who have paid part of their wages at clubs so they can get a cut of the transfer fee when they move to some of the richer leagues in Europe. There's even been the suggestion that the Russian Mafia is involved in this.

I got a phone call from an agent who works abroad, asking if I had any contacts at a particular English Premiership club. When I told him I had, he asked if I would phone them and ask if they would be interested in signing a certain Eastern European player he represented. When I called that club, they told me they were already negotiating with someone to sign the player. I called the agent back and asked what was going on as the club were already talking to the player's agent. 'No, he's not an agent,' he said. 'He's a guy who part-owns the player.'

Here was a Premiership club negotiating with the part-owner of a player and he's neither an official agent nor a representative of the selling club. That particular player was transferred to the Premiership for a large sum of money and, for the standard of player he was, I could never understand why the fee was so high. Needless to say, the player's original agent got pushed aside and never got a penny for his efforts to find his man a new club.

I keep well away from deals like that which aren't straight-forward and transparent and it doesn't pay to ask too many questions either.

If you've seen the movie, *Jerry Maguire*, in which Tom Cruise plays an American football agent, you'll have seen how other sports agents were trying to steal clients from each other. Well, that happens in football as well – and it happened to me.

I represented a young Celtic player who wanted away from Parkhead and had asked me to find him another club. I came back to him and said there were three clubs interested in signing him but he turned round and said that another agent had told him he could get him a better club. The boy wanted to move to that particular agent and I didn't stand in his way.

A few weeks later, the player was at one of the three clubs I had spoken to about signing the boy. That club called me and asked why another agent was now doing the deal after I had made the initial contact and, when I told them what happened, they were shocked.

I was quite sickened by what had happened, but the more I have been involved in the business the less surprised I am when things like that happen. He was a young player who was influenced by someone telling him lies.

Another criticism clubs make of agents is that they unsettle a player so he will want to move to another club and the agent gets another pay day. Sure, that happens but it's with the collusion of everyone concerned – the player, the agent, the manager and the clubs themselves. Nobody is going to tell me that, if a manager complains about this happening, he hasn't, at some point, done the same thing if he wants a particular player to sign for him. And, if a player is told he can make a lot more money by going to another club even though he is still under a contract, he'll want his agent to manoeuvre the deal.

Agents are in touch with clubs all the time, finding out who they are interested in and saying they would be able to get that player away from his club so they could buy him.

I've also known of situations where a player is on a good run of form but has been told another club is interested in buying him. The club he is presently under contract to don't want to sell him so the agent tells him to stop performing at such a high level. I've never understood why a player would do this but agents have told their clients, 'There's no way the club will sell you just now because you are playing so well. You need to start playing badly.'

The other tactic is to have the player come out in the media criticising the team or the manager and I don't know what sports reporters would do to find stories if it wasn't for agents calling them up on the fly and tipping them off that this or that club is interested in such and such a player. Read a story in the sports pages that is not confirmed by official club sources and you can bet your bottom dollar the story has come from an agent. This is how agents create an interest in their players from other clubs if the players want a move. The sports reporters are quite happy to play along with this because it fills their pages with stories about big clubs and players.

I wouldn't call it dirty tricks because everyone is involved and knows what goes on. If players didn't want to earn more money at another club or if clubs didn't want to buy or sell players, then all these things wouldn't happen. What an agent can do is facilitate all these moves so the players and the money in football keeps going round and round.

Everyone is involved and, if any one person involved is to be tarred with a brush, everyone should be tarred with the same brush. Agents couldn't do what they do without clubs being involved.

I have never tried to create a transfer for a player because I'm still a football person and I feel a responsibility towards the game. Maybe that's why I'm not as rich as some of these agents. I'm also very upfront about what money I make being an agent – I work on a maximum fee of five per cent of the player's guaranteed income, which doesn't include bonuses – just his basic wage.

However, there are people said to be making money out of transfer fees who shouldn't be – and they are some of the football managers we have in the game. I have to say first and foremost that I have never been asked by a manager for a backhander to make sure a transfer goes through, nor have I offered a manager cash. But the game is rife with stories of managers getting money from an agent to make sure the agent's player is signed to that manager's club. And sometimes for a fee which is more than the player is worth.

People have said to me that agents have been told there is no chance of getting their players into certain clubs as the managers will only deal with particular agents. And that is because those agents will give the manager a cut of the deal. I've been told what's involved is hundreds of thousands of pounds being transferred into offshore bank accounts. It's sad that these stories surround the game of football and I welcome the fact that the authorities want to investigate these allegations.

I've been told that players have been signed by a club on the basis of who the agent was – and the backhander involved – and not what the player can do for the team. I've no doubt there is corruption in football – but it's not just the fault of the football agent because everyone is involved.

There was one record-breaking, big-money transfer – worth £12.6 million – I was inadvertently involved in and I never made a penny from it. In August 1998, while I was working as an agent, my old pal from the Brighton days, John Gregory, called me. He had been made manager of Aston Villa and he wanted to talk to me about a new scouting system he wanted to introduce. I said I would write a paper for him on how everything should be organised. I sent my paper to him and John handed it to some of the directors at the club. When they asked him who wrote it, he told them he had.

Two weeks later at a board meeting, the new scouting system

was discussed and John was told they liked what was in the paper but they needed to bring someone in to put it into practice. John said, 'I'm thinking of bringing in my old Brighton team mate, Gordon Smith.'

As soon as my name was mentioned, one of the directors said, 'Gordon Smith wrote this paper, didn't he?' John then admitted that it was me who had written it and, straightaway, the directors agreed that I should be interviewed for the job.

At the time, I was also working on a software package for football scouts which would contain all the information needed to monitor the progress of youngsters any club was interested in. So, with that going on, I was very interested in the Villa job.

I met with John and the directors and they offered me the assistant manager's job. I naturally asked them what the wages were going to be but, when I told them I was working as an agent, doing television and writing a newspaper column, they said they couldn't afford me. I was a bit surprised that they decided they couldn't afford me, even before knowing what I was earning, but I left it at that and came back to Scotland.

It wasn't long before John was back on the phone, saying that the chairman Doug Ellis was very impressed with me and he wanted to do a deal so I would come to the club. I asked about money again and John said he didn't know what Doug Ellis would offer but I should come back down to the Midlands and have a meeting with him.

John and I were due to meet Doug Ellis at his home but, before going there, the two of us had a meal. In the restaurant, John's mobile phone rang and he left the table to take the call. When he came back he told me that it had been the Manchester United manager, Alex Ferguson, calling about his bid to buy the Villa striker, Dwight Yorke. United wanted the deal tied up by the following lunchtime so the player could be registered in time to play in Europe. John said Fergie's first offer was £8 million but he had managed to get him to up his offer. Now here was Fergie phoning to offer £11 million.

After the meal, we were heading to Doug Ellis's house and, by the time we got there, United's chief executive, Martin Edwards, had been on the phone to the chairman offering £12 million for the player. Doug Ellis couldn't believe how much money United were willing to pay for Dwight Yorke as he had been willing to accept £8 million. It was only John Gregory's insistence they could get more that had stopped him agreeing to that price.

There were other Villa directors sitting in Doug Ellis's lounge and all the talk was about United's £12 million offer but John Gregory said, 'Tell them no. We want £13 million.'

Doug Ellis called Martin Edwards back and told him he wanted £13 million for Dwight Yorke. Doug held the phone away from his ear and we could all hear Martin Edwards at the other end of the line saying, 'We told you the most we would pay was £12 million and you said that would be acceptable. We're not paying £13 million.'

At this point, John Gregory butted in and said to his chairman, 'Tell him we'll take £8 million plus Ole Gunnar Solskjaer.'

When Martin Edwards heard this he said, 'I can't believe this. We've had a £5 million bid for Solskjaer from Tottenham. If we give you £8 million and Solskjaer that would be £13 million anyway and we're not paying you that – it's too much.'

Doug Ellis said he would call Martin Edwards after he'd had a word with John Gregory. But he turned to us all in the room and said, 'Did you hear all that from Martin Edwards?'

When we said yes, he picked up the phone again and dialled the Spurs chairman and owner Alan Sugar. 'Hello, Alan, Doug Ellis here. Just want to check something with you. Have you put in a £5 million bid for Solskjaer?'

Alan Sugar must have asked why he was asking because Doug Ellis continued, 'We've got a deal on just now with Manchester United and they told us you bid that for him . . . Oh, you did. OK, that's fine.' And Doug Ellis put the phone down and said, 'Spurs did bid for Solskjaer but they were told he's not for sale.'

I had been sitting in the background, taking all this in, when suddenly, Doug Ellis turned to me and said, 'Gordon – you're going to be the assistant manager so what would you do?'

'I don't really think I should get involved here,' I said.

But Doug Ellis insisted, 'No, it's OK. You're coming here, you're the new assistant manager and we can talk about that in a minute – what would you do?'

'What I would do is this,' I told him. 'You want £13 million. They've offered £12 million. The transfer deadline is tomorrow at noon so it's a case of who calls each other's bluff first. I would wait as late as possible tomorrow before you phone Manchester United and say you'll take the £12 million and who knows, you might get a call from them with an increased offer before that if they cave in first.'

'That's a great idea,' said Doug Ellis. 'We'll wait until 11 a.m. tomorrow and decide what to do then.'

Then he started talking about my position and asked if I could start in a few weeks' time, on 1 September; but I told him I had other work commitments and it would have to be the beginning of October if I was coming to Villa. That was OK with him and when I asked what the wages would be Doug Ellis said, 'We'll rent you a house in Sutton Coldfield, you'll get a Jaguar car, you'll get the bonuses the team gets and the wages will be £65,000 a year.'

Now, that might seem like a lot of money but I knew of another assistant manager at a club no bigger than Aston Villa who was on £250,000. I told Doug Ellis that I was already earning more than that and I would be giving up a lot moving my family to the Midlands. But he said £65,000 was all they could afford so I told him I couldn't accept his offer. I had it in my mind that, if they'd offered £100,000 a year, I would have moved to Aston Villa but their offer never came near that mark.

The following day, I was driving back to Scotland when I heard on the radio that Manchester United had paid Aston Villa £12.6 million for Dwight Yorke. I had a wry smile to myself at the thought of my advice getting Villa £600,000 more than they were going to accept. That would have paid my wages for six years if they had made me the offer that would have tempted me to come to the club. And, because of my advice, I would have made the deal self-financing. I thought I would have had a phone call from Doug Ellis but that didn't happen.

I later spoke to John Gregory about the job offer and he said the chairman would call me to talk about it but that call never came either. So, I didn't go to Aston Villa and sometimes I regret that decision. It would have meant I had got back into football at a high level and you don't get much higher than the English Premiership. However, I might have ended up being frustrated at Villa because, although I would have had the title of assistant manager, my role didn't involve coaching players – it was mostly on the business side of the club.

I would still like to get back into football as a coach or a manager in the Scottish Premier or First Division. I would even go to the English League Two because the standard is decent at that level. I believe I could do a decent job as a manager because, if you look at my CV, I've played at the highest level in four countries, I've got my coaching A Licence and I've got the Professional Footballers Association football management certificate. I'm also a graduate with a BA in Business Studies, which means I understand finance, I've worked in management outside the game, which has given me skills in dealing with people, and I've got fifteen years of media experience. Wait a minute . . . I've just realised I might be overqualified!

With all that, allied to the stuff we all learn from the University of Life, I reckon I could do some football club a right good turn.

Perhaps, if Albion Rovers had offered me a bit more money to become their manager when I left St Mirren, I might have had them in the Champions League by now. Well, then, again – maybe not!

15

JUST HOW DO WE MANAGE?

Some of the boys came out of the office heads bowed and in tears. Others came out punching the air and whooping with delight. The ones who were in the depths of despair had just been told they weren't getting a contract with Chelsea and, well, the others who were on cloud nine had been told they were being kept on. The whole scene, from the boys waiting nervously outside the office at the end of the season, to being told the good or bad news by the club's head of youth development, Graham Rix, and the emotional aftermath, had been filmed for a television documentary.

I was amazed by the number of people who spoke to me about the programme and said it was really good and how it portrayed football as it really is. I had watched that programme with my brother, Billy, who is a director with one of the country's top insurance companies and we both thought that all it did was show exactly what was wrong with football.

These boys had no idea whether they were going to be kept on or whether their dreams were going to be shattered in a conversation that would take less than a minute. Frankly, it's disgraceful management practice that a boy hasn't a clue if he is going to have his contract renewed or not. If the club had been doing the proper monitoring, assessments and training of these lads, they would have been already aware if they had made the grade or not.

During the programme Graham Rix told one of the boys that he was being let go because his ball skills weren't good enough.

What had the coaches been doing for the past year? If the boy needed to improve his skills, they should have been coaching him all through the year and he shouldn't be hit with a surprise like that on the day he's kicked out of the club.

But that, I'm afraid, is what football is like – even in the twenty-first century. The game is still in the dark ages and needs to be modernised with proper coaching – and I don't mean on the football field – for managers, so they know how to manage properly. The way some of the kids and even older players are treated nowadays is like something out of the era of dark satanic mills. And that's not how to get the best out of people, no matter what trade or profession you are in.

I would definitely recommend that football managers attend the same skill-building and man-management courses that people from other walks of life attend. I can just hear the snorts of derision from some of the people I know in football when they read this but they are the very people who need to modernise their way of thinking and open their minds to new ideas on how to get the best out of their players.

What we have just now is a total lack of training for would-be managers. Sure, some of them may have had great football careers but scoring great goals and putting in last-ditch tackles is not the ideal preparation for dealing with finance amounting to millions of pounds and being able to handle the complexities of human nature and the different characteristics of every one of their players.

Some managers will say they have learned at the feet of their gaffers when they were players and they have taken bits of what they were like, added their own tuppenceworth into the mix and that's what makes them a manager.

Of course, there are exceptions – the intelligent, natural-born leaders who have come into football – but they are few and far between. Most of the time, young would-be football managers are learning from other managers who are just as much in the dark about man management as they are.

I call it the science of 'muddling through' and that's exactly what we are doing in this country. We've got managers who have been taught by people who really don't know much better and some of them will eventually get it right but only after making a lot of costly mistakes along the way. What we need is better-trained managers and there are many lessons we can learn from outside football.

When I worked in financial services, I attended a management conference and was asked, 'What's the difference between training and coaching?' I said that I thought it was exactly the same thing but, after hearing what the lecturer had to say, I soon realised that there is a world of a difference between training and coaching and the difference in results can be just as startling.

I was taught that training is all about telling people what to do. Coaching is when you ask someone about what they are doing. When all you're doing is training someone, you're telling them that when they get the ball they should be in a certain position and they then pass it into a certain area.

Coaching is when you ask questions of people and help them think for themselves about what they should be doing when they get the ball. If what they tell you isn't right, you then ask them why they chose to play that particular pass or take up a certain position and if they think they could have done something better.

By asking questions and having the footballer find the correct answer himself you pass on the responsibility to the player. He has to tell me what he is doing and why he is doing it. When a player takes on the responsibility for finding the correct way of doing things, the learning process is far more effective.

During that course, we were shown a film to prove the point. There was a group of people who were asked if any of them played golf. One of the guys who raised his hand said he was a four handicap and he was asked to teach a non-golfer in the group to play the game. A woman who hadn't played golf before was also chosen to go on to the driving range for some coaching from the instructor.

The golfer with the four handicap was telling the non-golfer, 'Hold the club like this . . . swing the club like that . . .'

The woman who was being coached was told to swing the club at the ball the way she thought it should be done. Of course, she was all over the place, never having done it before. But, every time she took a shot, she was asked to analyse what she had done and think how she could improve. At the end of the session the woman who was being coached was hitting the ball far better than the guy who was being trained.

Coaching is about getting people to teach themselves and to take responsibility for their own development and that's a very important factor in learning or improving at football or any other sport for that matter. It's also a motivational tool when you can get a person into the frame of mind that they are learning for themselves and have responsibility for their own improvement. That's far better than going through the motions of doing what someone tells you to do.

There's obviously a place for training where people have to do exactly as they have been told – like in the military – but once you put a team of people together who are thinking about what they should be doing as opposed to doing something because they have been told to do it, then you'll start getting places.

Football can definitely learn from the world outside. If I was in charge of a club, I would send the coaches and managers on the same type of courses that managers from other professions attend. I would want them to learn about psychology, man management and financial dealings. These are skills the modern-day manager needs – and are more important to their career than whether or not were they able to trap a ball, tackle, shoot and head when they were players.

This might go a long way to stop the madness of managers being sacked on a regular basis because the board have decided that they made a mistake in the first place and the guy wasn't really the right one to deliver the goods after all.

Because managers aren't properly trained as managers,

directors can sometimes have no idea who is going to be a good manager or not and they're risking a lot of money when they bring the new boss in. If the applicant has a good track record that's fine – you can base your judgement on that – but there's a certain mystique around the professional game of football at times. Some directors are afraid – or perhaps don't know – to ask the right questions They feel embarrassed that their knowledge of football will be shown up by this professional who is sitting in front of them describing how many goals he's scored and how many international caps he's got. Unfortunately, being a good footballer doesn't make you a good manager.

Sometimes in today's game being intelligent is a drawback – particularly if you're a player. Managers fell out with me because they couldn't take someone answering them back and, worse than that, answering back with a logical argument. An intelligent footballer will also think too much about things whereas, if you're the type of player who goes through life without a clue about what's really going on, you will survive all the abuse you get from fans, coaches and managers.

This theory was backed up by an Italian study showing that being intelligent is a drawback for professional footballers.

I've had the parents of young players ask me why their kids are being treated so badly at clubs and I just have to tell them quite often there's no logic or sense to football and how people behave in the game. Outside football, managers are trained to deal with people and certain circumstances but, in football, there's no training like that at all.

Football managers retain a great control over their charges. The good managers have authority over the players while others have power. This was something I learned when I studied sociology as part of my degree. Power is when you have control over subordinates through the strength of what you can do to them – fear, basically. Authority is when the people working for you give you respect and do things for you on the basis that you are the boss and what you're doing is right. Authority is given to you by the people who are your subordinates. Power is when you just take control over subordinates, regardless of how they feel.

Although there are certain exceptions, football management is all about power. The managers I have worked under who had authority rather than power were Jock Wallace at Rangers, Joe Royle when I was at Oldham for a short period and Gustl Starek, at Admira Wacker. The players respected what they were doing and that respect was reciprocated from the managers to the players.

The biggest power in football is that there is a pool of football labour at a club but, each Saturday, there are only eleven jobs to go round and, by playing on a Saturday, you could receive appearance money and win bonuses. And added to that was the power of a football club in the pre-Bosman days when the club held on to a player's registration and could effectively stop someone playing, either for his own team or another one.

Another aspect about football management is the myth that a manager can motivate a player and, sadly, directors, managers, players and fans all seem to buy into this idea that a coach or manager can motivate a player ten minutes before a game. That's nonsense because motivation is something that has to come from an individual – people have to be self-motivated. What a manager can do is create the environment in which players motivate themselves. It's not the manager who motivates, it's the environment in which the player is working that is most important.

Jock Wallace was said to be one of the game's great motivators but he never once motivated me as an individual. I was motivated by the atmosphere and environment Jock had created at Ibrox, how he treated the players and how he brought home to you the responsibilities you had to the team. Creating the right environment is the way to motivate players, not jumping up and down on the touchline waving your arms about and bawling at players on the park who either can't hear you or just ignore you anyway.

I used to get a lot of stick from St Mirren fans for not shouting enough at players from the touchline. If I failed to motivate these St Mirren players, it was because I failed to create the right environment at the club during the week and not because I didn't make myself hoarse shouting at the players for ninety minutes every Saturday.

People like Jock Stein, Bill Shankly and Matt Busby were all natural leaders and had the intelligence to think about how they were going to approach different players in different ways. Unfortunately, their likes are few and far between these days.

There's a great story about sports management and motivation, which I tell in my after-dinner speeches and attribute to Jock Wallace. Jock never actually said this but it's exactly what he would have been thinking. The story comes from an American football coach, Vince Lombardi, who had a reputation for being able to get the best out of his players. He was giving a press conference and the reporters were asking him how he became such a good motivator. He drew breath and said, 'OK, this is the first time I have ever revealed what the secret of my motivational skills are. I go into the dressing room at the beginning of the season, talk to all the players and find out which of the boys need to be motivated. The reporter then asked, 'Then what do you do?' and Lombardi replied, 'I get rid of the bastards.'

The reporters were shocked at what he said but the guy was absolutely spot on – if you need to motivate a player, you should get rid of him because if he's not motivated himself, there's nothing you can say or do to motivate him.

When youngsters would come in to Love Street with their parents to sign on, I would say to them that the only question for a young player is how he thinks he'll become a footballer. I would tell them the answer is ASK – Attitude, Skill and Knowledge. Skill is what they've already got and that's what they are bringing to the table. The right attitude is what I want them to give me in the future and, in return, I will give them knowledge. That's the best relationship a coach can have with a young player – you've already got skill, give me the right attitude and I'll give you knowledge to improve your ability.

Even players can learn from modern management techniques. At the highest level of football on both sides of the border, I have helped players I was representing to get themselves back into the first team after being out in the wilderness.

I represented a player who was with a Scottish Premier League club at the time and was out of favour with the manager. He wasn't even getting in the first-team squad and he asked me what he could do as he didn't know why he wasn't getting picked because the manager wasn't speaking to him.

I told him he should do some extra training over the next few days, then ask if one of the young boys could wait behind after training to give him some heading practice. I told the player that the manager will start to wonder what's going on and will be impressed by the effort being put in with the extra training. Within a fortnight, the player was back in the first-team squad. That was the end of stage one.

Stage two began when the manager started to speak to the player and I told my player that he should tell the manager he is doing the extra training to try to get back in the first team. The player then asked the manager his opinion on what his best position was and what role he could play if he got back in the first team. I told the player to continually engage the manager in conversations about how he was playing and what he thought he could do for the team. Before long, my guy was back in the first team and he kept the rapport going with the manager and, before the end of the season, he was captain. My player went from sitting in the stand to being the team captain.

What happens is that sometimes players don't know why they are being left out in the cold but, if they start to react in a different way from what the manager expects – by doing extra training – the manager will start to take an interest. He'll be impressed by the player putting in the extra work and, once the player engages the manager by asking his views on how he should play and showing that he respects the manager's opinion, the manager will be more favourably disposed towards him.

The final stage is that the manager ends up becoming a mentor to the player and thinks that he has pulled the boy out of nowhere and made him a player worthy of a place in the first team. The manager becomes proud of what the player has achieved because he has been made to feel it's all down to him and he has taken responsibility for the player's improved form.

I used exactly the same method with a player I represented in the English Premiership. The manager hardly said a word to the player but, by the time the player had gone through the same process, he was back in favour and the manager ended up speaking to him more than anyone else.

The quality of the manager in football is one thing but another problem, which poses a threat to the game if not dealt with sensibly, is players' wages. Some people say that the blame for players' wages being too high should be laid at the door of football agents – but that is total nonsense. Wages are high because clubs agree to pay those wages.

When I am negotiating a player's wages, I am taking it on good faith that a club can afford what they are offering. It's not the role of the agent to ask to see the club's books to see if they can afford what they have offered the player. A lot of the time, people running football clubs – many of them sensible and successful businessmen – get carried away with the emotion of being in charge of a football club. They try to keep up with the Joneses and bow to fan pressure by making big signings which the club can't afford.

I wouldn't go to a club like East Stirling and ask for £2000 a week for a player because I know they couldn't afford that and the player probably doesn't represent value at that kind of money in the first place. The club should set the wages at a level they can afford and, if I don't accept their offer for the player, it means I must have an alternative, which will offer better money. That's just market forces.

I admit that wages were too high at clubs that couldn't afford it and that even goes for the Old Firm who have been trying to reduce their wage bill to a more affordable level. There is no doubt the wages are coming back to a more sensible level because, if they didn't, many more clubs would be going into administration.

Although this process of reducing the wage bill is being carried out by individual clubs, I would go further and say there should be a link between a club's turnover and the amount they pay in wages. An overall wage cap based on income and a club's wage bill should be no more than 70 per cent of their turnover.

Whatever the turnover of the previous year was should be used to set the figure for the following season's wage bill unless there are very good reasons for that not to be the case. To break the wage cap, a club would have to put their case to the SFA or the SPL who would also be responsible for making sure clubs comply.

If clubs are found to be paying more than the 70 per cent of turnover on wages, then they should have points docked. This system wouldn't stop clubs deciding to pay big money for a big-time player as it only sets a limit to the overall wage bill. A club could have lots of players on a smaller wage or a smaller squad with a few players on big money.

It would make the game a lot healthier and protect clubs from themselves by stopping them spending money and make contract commitments they can't afford to honour. Take the case of Craig Burley coming to Dundee. A deal was struck and he got his first month's wages, didn't get paid the second and, by the third, month the club was in administration. At the end of the day, Craig only received a tiny percentage of what he was due from that contract.

Now, I negotiated that deal and I had to take it on good faith that Dundee could afford to pay what they had agreed to pay Craig. If there had been a limit on Dundee only spending 70 per cent of their turnover, then perhaps they wouldn't have gone into administration with a threat hanging over the existence of one of Scotland's senior clubs. And players wouldn't have been shown the door because the club couldn't afford to pay them.

I can hear the clubs outside the Old Firm claiming that the overall wage-cap system would mean they couldn't compete with Rangers and Celtic. Well, they can't compete with them just now, so it would make no difference to that situation.

While clubs wouldn't have the same money as the Old Firm or other better-supported teams, it doesn't mean to say that they can't compete with them. These clubs would just have to get better at others areas of the game like having a better scouting system where players in lower leagues could be brought in and developed and better coaching to get more out of the players available. This would give young Scottish players more opportunity of breaking though because clubs would have to develop their own talent but, most importantly, clubs wouldn't be allowed to dive headlong into the kamikaze trait of spending money they don't have and putting themselves at risk.

It wouldn't just be down to buying your way to success. Managers would have to up their game and show they can do a good job by being better coaches, tacticians, man managers, negotiators and talent spotters instead of getting away with merely spending even more money on bringing in new players on big wages when they are looking for success.

Some clubs in Scotland are already tackling the problem of players' wages being too high. Teams like Aberdeen, Hibs and Livingston have a system of wage categories. They will decide which players are in which category as follows: Category A – the guys who are expected to play all the time; Category B – the players who are liable to get a game and there wouldn't be a problem fitting them in; Category C – those who have still to reach their full potential and would need to show some real form to get in the team; and Category D – the players who are really on the fringes and who would only be used in an emergency.

By doing this, the clubs have introduced a bit of structure into the wages they pay players. The clubs call them categories but they are really just wage bands that make managers think more about the finances and who they really want to keep at the clubs by paying them bigger money in Category A. This system also stops the situation of players who are well away from getting a first-team spot being paid the same money as someone getting a regular game. A lot of players are still getting really big money for kicking their heels in the reserves or sitting in the stand every week.

The Old Firm will probably always be top dogs in Scotland but both clubs struggle financially compared to the clubs in the English Premiership and the rest of Europe. Rangers and Celtic are criticised by supporters for not going out and spending big. Sure, they've got tens of thousands of season ticket holders and lucrative sponsorship deals but what is missing is the big Sky TV money that the English Premiership clubs have. The lack of this money is a major factor in why the Scottish game is so far behind England in financial terms. And that's why Rangers and Celtic want to play there.

By having a system of wage capping, Scottish clubs will be more secure in the long term and the standard of management and coaching will improve. It could also mean that some of the pressure from fans on directors to spend money the club doesn't have will be relieved. It could also stop the directors taking daft decision themselves when they are caught up in the emotions of wanting to do all they can to help the team gain success. Chairmen and directors get hooked and, before you know it, they are making decisions that don't turn out to be the right ones. They are so keen to fulfil people's hopes and dreams that they do things that they wouldn't dream of doing in their own business lives.

Another major change is needed to improve Scottish football and that is when we play the game. I am in favour of a two-month winter break during January and February. Traditionally, we play between August and May and I don't think there is any other country that plays professional football in worse winter conditions than we do. Playing through the winter months detrimentally affects the standard of training, coaching and the quality of the football on offer to the fans, who also have to endure the worst of the weather to watch a game.

Along with other people in the game, I have been calling for a winter shutdown for many years and it now appears to be getting through to the administrators. There's talk about stopping youth football during the winter and as far as I am concerned that is a good start.

We should start the season as normal in August and play through to the end of December. We shouldn't play any games during January and February and continue the rest of the season in March through to the end of June. Some people against a winter shutdown say that no one knows when the worst of the weather will be, but 90 per cent of the games that have been postponed or abandoned because of the weather have been in January and February. When the football returned in the spring, the conditions for both playing and spectating would be a lot better. When I was playing in Austria and Switzerland, the winter shutdowns meant the pitches were in good condition all season long.

Another argument used by those who are against a winter shutdown is that World Cups and European Championships are played in the summer months. But I don't see the problem there because countries like Sweden, Denmark, Switzerland, Austria Norway and Russia all manage to play in these international tournaments as well as having a winter shutdown. Even if we do ever manage to qualify for the final stages of either of these tournaments, there would be nothing wrong with shortening the winter shutdown to six weeks and finishing the season a fortnight earlier – leaving our national team to go on and win the World Cup. I wish!

In 2001, I was asked by the SPL to write a paper on winter shutdowns and, not long after being asked for this, I submitted it to them. It took the SPL four years, right enough, but, eventually, in 2005, they came back to me and asked if I would present what I had written to their Football Board. The members of the board are Campbell Ogilvie of Rangers, Jim Duffy from Dundee, Terry Butcher of Motherwell, Steve Walford, formerly of Celtic, and Aberdeen's Willie Miller. My views were received better than I thought they would be and I thought there would be lots of arguments put up against what I was saying. But the Football Board members recognised it was an issue which they had to address.

Football is Scotland's most popular sport and we should ask ourselves if we are creating the best conditions for that sport to be played and watched at all levels. The answer to that is obviously no. We should be playing our national sport in the best possible conditions and these don't occur in January or February.

I've seen it so often – the referee comes out to inspect the pitch and he sees that it isn't frozen or flooded so the game goes on. It doesn't matter what the overhead conditions are like – the game goes on. I was at a Livingston versus Morton Scottish Cup tie in season 2004–05 and we were on the edge of what was described by the weather experts as a hurricane. It was farcical and neither the players nor the fans got the best out of what could have been a good game.

When I was assistant manager at St Mirren, one of the things we would take account of during training sessions was how to keep the players warm during the harsh winter months. Proper coaching was impossible because you couldn't have the players standing around in the bad weather trying to show them what you wanted them to do in things like set-pieces. All we could do was keep them running to prevent them from freezing to the spot.

Having a better-quality playing surface because of a winter shutdown would also improve the quality of the football and, in turn, improve the entertainment value for the supporters. It's almost impossible to play good, skilful football when the pitch is a quagmire, the rain is teeming down and the wind is howling up the park. Players would go in, make the tackle, win the ball and then just hump it up the park.

I always tried to play good football but there were days when the weather was so bad that I knew I just wouldn't have a good game. The playing surface wasn't conducive to bringing the ball down, spraying the passes around or going on a run with the ball at your feet. Sometimes all you could do was watch as the ball was punted up and down the park from one defence to the other.

When was the last time you saw a World Cup played on a muddy, cut-up pitch with the wind and rain howling round the stadiums? If that happened, people would soon be saying that is no way to play the beautiful game of football. So why should we put up with that in Scotland for most of our football season? I rest my case.

16

MY MATE, PAUL . . .

I'm sitting on the couch of one of the world's greatest songwriters and he's gone off to get his guitar. I've just told Paul McCartney – yes, *that* Paul McCartney – I could play one of his more complicated Beatles songs on guitar and he seems mightily impressed.

In the minute or so he's out the room, dreaded thoughts race through my head. 'I hope he's not going to ask me to play it for him,' I'm saying to myself. 'Oh no . . . what have I let myself in for?'

The ex-Beatle bounces back into his living room and sits down beside me again. He starts playing and singing his fabulous song, 'Blackbird', and it's not just a chorus or two – it's the whole song. The final chord is dying away when Paul asks me, 'Is that how you play it?'

I hesitate and nod my head in amazement before replying, 'Aye, something like that.'

This is one of the most bizarre and at the same time wonderful moments of my life. Sitting chatting to Paul McCartney – my musical hero since boyhood – is one thing but now he's giving me a one-man concert in his living room.

And that's not all. My wife, Marlene is chatting away to Linda McCartney in her kitchen and my three-year-old son is playing a new game – jumping on and off Paul's grand piano.

Just how can all this be happening? After all, I'm just a boy from a council house in Stevenston, North Ayrshire.

*****

To borrow a Beatles song title, 'The Long and Winding Road' to Paul McCartney's door began twenty years earlier when, as an eight-year-old, I stood on the doorstep of another pal of mine, Davy Patterson, waiting for him to come out to play. Then, in 1963, I was at a house in the Hayocks council estate in Stevenston and not the rambling countryside of East Sussex where Paul McCartney stayed in a place called Peasmarsh.

So, there I was, waiting for Davy's mum to go and fetch him from upstairs as I stood at the front door. At first, it was just a bit of background music coming from the radio playing in Davy's living room but suddenly a song caught my attention. At that point in my life, I had no real interest in music and had no idea what the song was or who was singing but I did know I liked it. Davy was taking his time coming downstairs, but that didn't bother me as I was captivated by the sounds from that radio. I thought the song was brilliant and, for the first time, I was able to appreciate good music. Davy bounded downstairs and we headed off for a game of football with our pals, the words and music of that song from the radio still kicking around my head even though I still hadn't a clue who or what it was.

Fast-forward to later that year. Beatlemania was really taking off and I bought my first single record – 'She Loves You' by the Fab Four. Shortly after that, my dad's brother, Uncle James, bought me a Beatles EP and I couldn't believe it when I heard a track on that EP – 'Please, Please Me'. I was knocked out by it for a second time and stunned to discover it was the song I had heard on the radio earlier that year while I was at Davy's house waiting for him to come out. That sealed it for me – I had been a Beatles fan and didn't even know it.

From that point on I was a massive fan of The Beatles and in particular Paul McCartney. I read about them in the papers and magazines, went to see their movies – *A Hard Day's Night* and *Help* – and bought every Beatles record I could get my hands on, which led to many an argument with my older brother, Matthew, who was a Cliff Richard and The Shadows fan.

I would also have arguments with my dad over The Beatles. He liked the old crooners and could just about suffer Elvis but Beatlemania was not for him. 'They'll only last six months,' he would say. Even when we watched The Beatles on television, during the Royal Variety Performance, he wouldn't agree with me that they had arrived as a top act. 'Nothing of the sort,' he would say. 'They'll not last much longer.'

My mum and dad had bought a Dansette record player for Matthew and me to share. It was fabulous – the red leatherette top and the big spindle in the middle that could take ten singles piled on top of each other and the arm that came across to hold them in place before the records dropped down on to the turntable one at a time. The record player was our Christmas present in 1963 and we kept it in the bedroom Matthew and I shared. And that's where the battle of the bands took place. Matthew would want to play Cliff and I would want to play The Beatles. How we ever heard any music over the noise of us arguing, I'll never know.

The more I heard and learned about The Beatles, the more it became apparent to me that Paul McCartney's music was what I really liked. For me, The Beatles' song 'Yesterday' was what made me think they had gone to another level. It appeared to me that, all of a sudden, they had come out with this beautiful ballad and I could appreciate that they weren't just a pop band who attracted thousands of screaming girls to their concerts.

My pal Davy Patterson was also a big Beatles fan and, at one point in our early teens, we spoke about getting into music and forming a band. There was only one drawback and we recognised we would struggle a bit since neither of us could play a musical instrument. We had a laugh about it, but I suppose it's that working-class thing about finding a way out of the council estates. For some people, music is how they make it big and, for others, it could be sport. I knew that The Beatles came from a working-class background just like ourselves and we were thinking maybe music was our way out. Thankfully, I was able to take the football road out of Hayocks and, even though I was into music in a big way, football was the main priority in my youth – a good choice since I'll always be a better footballer than guitarist.

Davy was a great musical influence on me when I was a teenager and he would get me listening to progressive rock bands like Led Zeppelin and Yes. Still, I was really disappointed when The Beatles split up in 1970 but I soon realised Paul McCartney was my favourite when he began to release his own material with his new band, Wings. The more I heard each of the Fab Four's solo material, the more I realised it was Paul McCartney's music which had drawn me to The Beatles.

I was so into Paul McCartney that, when I was seventeen, I tried to copy his hairstyle and grow a beard like him. I was able to get the hairstyle spot-on – long at the back but short at the sides so your ears were showing. But Paul had a full beard at the time and, despite all my efforts, there was no way I was able grow a beard like his when I was still a teenager. A few years later, I was still trying to look like McCartney and I eventually managed to get that beard. It made me look older then than I do now!

I was twenty years old when I first saw Paul McCartney and Wings live at Glasgow's Apollo Theatre, in September 1975. I was with my girlfriend Marlene and, on the drive up from Ayrshire, the band's songs were blasting from the speakers. Marlene had got used to this by then as I would make up tapes of my favourite McCartney tracks and constantly play them on the car stereo. Worse than that, I would sing along as well. I couldn't have been that bad because, not only did Marlene encourage me to sing, she suggested I learn how to play the guitar and I thought it was a great idea – except that I didn't have a guitar.

That all changed a few months later on my twenty-first birthday. I had gone to visit Marlene at her home in Kilmarnock and she handed me one of the best presents ever – my first guitar. She knew how much I loved singing and that I really wanted to learn to play guitar so she went out and bought me a Fender acoustic guitar. It was just what I needed – not just a guitar but also the incentive to learn how to play.

At the time, I was playing for Kilmarnock but also going to college for my Business Studies degree. As part of the degree, we had a year getting work experience and I was with a company called the Planning Exchange, in Bath Street, Glasgow. As luck would have it, one of the guys in the office was a reasonable guitar player and, in our lunch hours, he would teach me chords and how to play. It's not quite what you would expect in the administration and finance department but I managed to cope with a mixture of balance sheets and barre chords at the same time.

I worked hard and practised a lot and soon I was ready to put all the chords together and play a song. That's when I went out and bought my first songbook. And, of course, it had to be *The Beatles Complete*. Some of the chord structures of The Beatles' songs that I wanted to learn are not that simple and they are difficult to work out – even with the aid of a chord book. So I found myself a guitar teacher from Paisley – Davy Shaw. He was a great guitar player, songwriter and teacher but, sadly, these days, he's suffering from Multiple Sclerosis. He taught me a lot and I used to give him an album which had a song on it I wanted to learn and ask him to work out the chords for me. One of my favourite Beatles songs was 'Blackbird' and, for the life of me, I couldn't work it out.

I left it with Davy and it must have been a real difficult one to work out because the next week Davy said he needed more time to work out exactly how Paul McCartney plays the song. But, in the words of another Beatles hit, 'We Can Work It Out', Davy did just that and, the following week, he was teaching me how to play 'Blackbird'. For all you guitar players out there, although the song is in the key of F, McCartney tunes his guitar down a tone and plays the song using chord shapes in the key of G. Now, remember that bit because, as you'll find out, Paul McCartney couldn't believe I knew how to play that song!

AND SMITH *DID* SCORE

The next time I saw Wings play was in December 1979 and again they were at the Apollo in Glasgow. By this time, I was playing for Rangers and I took a box in the theatre for Marlene, my younger brother, Billy, and my sister, Elaine. We were sitting in the box, waiting for the show to start, when this guy came up and said, 'Sorry to bother you but I'm a big Rangers fan. Can I have your autograph?' I said it wasn't a problem and, as he was about to leave he asked me, 'Are you a big fan of McCartney?'

I answered, 'You better believe it. Been a fan of his for years.'

'Do you want to meet him then?' he said.

I must have had that blank look you get on your face when you just can't believe what someone has said. He asked again, 'Do you want to meet him?'

'Are you kidding?' I replied.

'No,' he said, 'I'm head of security. All you have to do is come round to the side door after the concert and I'll take you to meet him.'

It was a brilliant concert and, after it was over, Marlene and I were debating whether the guy was serious or not. We weren't sure if we were going to get to see Paul McCartney, but we decided to give it a go just in case, although Elaine went home immediately after the concert.

So, Marlene – who was pregnant with our son, Grant, at the time – my younger brother, Billy, who was sixteen, and I trooped round to the side door and joined about forty other fans hoping to get a glimpse of the great man. It was freezing cold and we weren't properly dressed for standing outside the stage door in the middle of winter.

For twenty minutes, we huddled together and stamped our feet trying to keep warm and, eventually, Marlene said, 'Come on, we might as well go. Nothing's going to happen.'

'Hang on a bit longer,' I pleaded. 'Nobody's come out yet. McCartney is obviously still inside.'

Just then, the door burst open and one of the other security guys came out and asked the small crowd, 'Who's Gordon Smith?'

'That's me,' I replied.

'Right,' said the security guy. 'You've to come in and meet Paul McCartney.'

As the fans around the door gasped, I said, 'Brilliant.'

And, as I was about to head through the door, Marlene said, 'Hang on a second – I'm his wife – have I to come as well?'

The security guy looked at her, pointed at me and said, 'No. It's just him.'

But Marlene was having none of that. 'Hold on here,' she said. 'I'm expecting a baby and there's no way I'm going to be left standing here in the freezing cold. I'm coming in as well.'

The guy was a bit taken aback and said, 'OK, OK, in you come then.'

We had to leave Billy outside and, when we got through the door, we climbed some stairs and could hear the chatter of lots of people. Obviously there was a bit of a party going on. I expected that when we got to the top of the stairs, there would be someone who would usher us into a room and introduce us to Paul McCartney. But, when we got near the top, we lifted our heads and there they were waiting for us – Paul and Linda McCartney.

'How are you doing, Gordon?' said Paul. 'Nice to meet you.'

I introduced Marlene to Paul and Linda and started chatting away. Paul asked, 'Did you enjoy the concert?'

'Yes, it was great. But how do you choose which songs to play? You don't do that many Beatles numbers but a lot of fans would want to hear them, wouldn't they?' I asked.

Paul told me that he had lots of new material he wanted to play and said, 'At the moment, I don't want to go down that route. Doing just Beatles stuff, people would think I was cashing in on the fact that I was in The Beatles. I've got my solo career and I've got plenty new material without having to play the old Beatles stuff.'

After a few minutes, I said, 'It's been lovely meeting you.'

I was about to head back down the stairs when Paul asked, 'Where are you going?'

263

The place was full of people and I could see Billy Connolly and I didn't want to outstay my welcome. I said, 'Well, it's really made my night getting to meet you but you must have lots of other people you want to talk to.'

But Paul asked, 'Why do you need to go?'

'I don't need to go,' I said.

And Paul replied, 'Well, if you don't need to go, just stay.' Then he started asking me about playing football for Rangers. 'I've never seen the football up here,' said Paul. 'When we come up to live on the farm, we're a bit isolated. I'm a Liverpool fan but I don't get much chance to see them.'

Marlene and Linda were getting on great and were talking away to each other but, after a few more minutes, I said again, 'Look, it's great meeting you but we'd better go.'

But Paul said, 'Don't worry about it. I go to other people's concerts and, when you're backstage, you always feel a little bit like why are you there? I've invited you up, you're obviously a fan, you enjoy the music, so stay as long as you want.'

I said to Paul, 'You know something? My brother will be really disappointed he didn't get to meet you.'

'Why? Where is he?' asked Paul.

'He's downstairs outside the stage door,' I explained.

'So why did he not come in?' asked Paul.

I told him that the security guy wouldn't let him in and Paul asked, 'Who wouldn't let him in?'

I pointed across the room to where the security guy was standing and Paul shouted him over.

'What's your brother's name?' Paul asked me.

'Billy,' I answered.

So Paul turned to the security guy and said, 'Right, go downstairs and bring a Billy Smith up here.'

The next thing I noticed was Paul looking over my shoulder and, when I turned round, there was Billy at the top of the stairs.

'Billy, how are you?' said Paul. 'In you come.'

Billy just couldn't believe it. He had just walked up the stairs to see his big brother and his sister-in-law talking to Paul and Linda McCartney!

Then Paul started winding Billy up. 'So you didn't want to meet me?' said Paul.

'I did!' protested Billy.

'No, you didn't. I had to send for you. I had to send a security man to bring you here.' The look on Billy's face was priceless.

Linda went away and brought back a Wings T-shirt, which she gave to Billy. After about twenty minutes talking to Paul and Linda, I said, 'We really do have to go now. This has been a watershed moment for me considering how much of a fan I've been over the years. I can't believe it.'

Paul replied, 'You never know – some day, I might get to see you playing football.'

We shook Paul's hand, gave Linda a kiss and headed downstairs and out into the street. When we came out there was still a crowd waiting outside and they asked me, 'Did you meet Paul McCartney?'

When I told them I had, you could tell by the poor souls' frozen faces they were gutted that they hadn't got to meet him – just like I would have been if I was in their shoes.

The following summer, I was transferred to Brighton, which is not that far from where Paul lives in East Sussex. Brighton were playing in the same league as Liverpool so I found out the address of Paul's management company and wrote a letter offering to get him tickets for our next game against the Merseyside club.

I got a letter back from Paul wishing me good luck with my new club, saying he would like to come to a game and that he would be in touch. But I never heard anything until the following year when, completely out of the blue, Marlene and I received an invitation to the opening of Linda McCartney's photographic exhibition in London, in October 1982. I couldn't believe it – we'd only met him for twenty minutes or so, a couple of years ago, and now we were getting invited to Linda's exhibition.

When I was at Brighton, we were sponsored by BMW so I had a fancy 5-Series car which looked quite flash. When we drove up to the art gallery and pulled in to the pavement, someone was there to park your car for you so it looked like a real celebrity had turned up. There was a wee red carpet on the pavement leading to the art gallery entrance and the crowd was being held back by a rope barrier. As we got out of the car, you could hear a murmur of anticipation as people were thinking we must be big celebrities. But, when they saw Marlene and me, you could see the disappointment on their faces as they didn't a have a clue who we were.

When we got inside, there were quite a few real celebrities already there looking at Linda's photographs round the walls. We spoke to Billy Connolly and spotted the pop group Bananarama and the Liverpool entertainer Kenny Lynch. Marlene and I had a good look round the exhibition and we bought the book of the photographs which were on show.

Suddenly there was a bit of a kerfuffle at the door as Paul and Linda were arriving and I said to Marlene that we should get Linda to sign the book before we left. Paul and Linda were doing the rounds, talking to everyone there, so we left it for a while before we approached Linda. Eventually I went up to her and said, 'Excuse me, Linda, would you mind signing the book for me?'

Linda turned round to face me and said, 'Oh, hello there. How are you getting on?'

'Fine,' I replied but saying to myself that she thinks I'm somebody else as there was no way she would remember me. Linda tapped Paul on the shoulder and said, 'Look who's here.'

Paul turned round, smiled and said, in a broad Scottish accent, 'Aye, how are you getting on? You alright?' Then he started talking about football and said, 'Sorry I haven't been down to a game yet – I've been so busy.'

Marlene and Linda were having a conversation about kids and Marlene told her that she'd had the baby she was pregnant with when we last met in Glasgow. I asked both Paul and Linda to sign the book and Paul's signature had a cartoon-like character face at the end of it. I asked Paul if I could get a photograph taken of the four of us together and he said that was no problem.

We were just about to walk away when Paul asked, 'How's your brother, Billy, then?'

I was gobsmacked and managed a surprised, 'Oh, he's doing great, thanks.' It was amazing that he could remember someone he'd met for a few minutes that far back. Later, when I phoned Billy to tell him Paul McCartney was asking for him, he wouldn't believe me.

There was an official photographer there for the launch and Marlene and I hovered around just waiting for our chance to get the photograph of Paul, Linda and ourselves. But all of a sudden the photographer had disappeared outside and Paul and Linda were saying their goodbyes to everyone.

As Paul walked by me he stopped and said, 'You were meant to get a picture, weren't you, Gordon?

'Don't worry about it,' I said. 'It would have been nice to get a picture but there's no harm done. It was great meeting you again.'

Paul replied, 'No, I can't believe that we didn't get a picture taken. I'm really sorry about that.' And then he said, 'You live not far from us – you know where we live don't you? Come and visit us.'

I blurted out, 'What do you mean "Come and visit us"?'

'Just come and visit us any Sunday. Just come down and see us. Alright?' At that, Paul disappeared though the crowd, leaving me wondering if I had really heard what I thought I had heard. Paul McCartney inviting me to his house? Marlene and I just looked at each other.

On our way home that day, I couldn't make up my mind if Paul had really meant what he said. On the one hand, I was thinking, he said it with a sincerity that made me believe that he did mean it. But, on the other hand, he hadn't given me a date – like next Sunday or the Sunday after that – so there wasn't any definite arrangement and maybe he didn't expect me to do anything about his invitation.

I decided that there was enough sincerity in how he had invited us that he did mean us to visit him. Well, it's not often Paul McCartney invites you round to his house and the fact that I was desperate to meet him again may have had some bearing on my conclusion.

I was thoroughly impressed by Paul. You idolise someone all your life and you wonder if they are going to live up to your expectations. Paul and Linda turned out to be down-to-earth and friendly. It's a shame that Linda had taken all that criticism about her being stuck-up when she first married Paul. That couldn't have been further from the truth as she was a lovely person.

In the following weeks, I would talk to Marlene about going to see the McCartneys and she would reply, 'There's no way we can just turn up at Paul McCartney's house out of the blue.'

But, one Friday months later, in February 1983, I said to Marlene, 'Do you know where we're going on Sunday? We're going to see the McCartneys.' Marlene didn't think I was serious but I insisted and she decided she would bake some scones and a cheesecake and we would pick up a bottle of wine to give to Paul and Linda.

About midday on the Sunday, we all piled into the car – me, Marlene, Grant, who was almost three, and our daughter Leigh-Anne who was about eighteen months – and headed off for Peasmarsh. We drove down country roads surrounded by trees, hedges and fields, passing the odd big house and a few farmhouses and steadings. When we got into Peasmarsh we stopped about six different locals and asked them where Paul McCartney lived. Not one of them said they knew.

The people there were obviously very protective about the McCartneys because the conversation with one of them went like this, 'Can you tell me where Paul McCartney lives?' I asked.

'Has he invited you to his house?' came the reply.

'Yes.'

'And you don't know his address?'

'No. He just told us to come along.'

'And he didn't tell you his address? Sorry, mate, I don't know where he lives.'

We spent an hour driving up and down every country road and lane we could see. Then we passed a country lane with a sign at the entrance which said, 'Beware of the children.'

I drove on and said to Marlene, 'Did you see that sign? Isn't that the kind of quirky thing people like Paul and Linda McCartney would think of?'

I stopped the car and reversed to the entrance of the lane where the sign was. We drove along the lane for about a mile with nothing in sight apart from grass and trees. Suddenly, there was a little round gatehouse on the left-hand side and we thought that there would have to be a big mansion further down the road. We were a hundred yards or so past the gatehouse when we saw a woman and three kids walking along with their dogs. I stopped the car when I recognised the woman as Linda McCartney and that's when I started to get really nervous. Thoughts like 'Holy shit! What am I doing here?' and 'Who am I to be turning up at Paul McCartney's house unannounced?' were racing through my head.

Linda was about to pass the car when I wound down the window and was about to say, 'Hi!' when she said, 'It's yourself. How are you getting on?'

I was trying to play it cool. 'Oh, we were just out for a drive and we were passing . . .'

'No problem,' said Linda. 'We said to come and visit. Paul's in the house so park the car and come on in.'

I asked Linda where the house was and she pointed to the tiny gatehouse we had just passed. 'That's it there?' I asked and Linda said, 'Yeah, that's where we live.'

I couldn't believe this was where Paul and Linda McCartney – one of the world's most famous and richest couples – stayed. When you walked in the door, you came into a room that was so small the grand piano took up most of the space. There was an L-shaped settee, a television on a shelf above the fireplace and a stand with lots of cassette tapes and videos on it.

Through another door you could see there was a dining room. It was very tight with a lovely oak table and eight chairs. But there was also a bed – or, to be more precise, a mattress – squeezed between the dining table chairs and the wall. This was where Paul and Linda's youngest – their son, James – slept.

Next on the ground floor was a WC with a shower and a tiny kitchen. I was stunned at how small the kitchen was. It was smaller than the kitchen in my mum and dad's council house in Stevenston where I grew up. Upstairs were a couple of bedrooms and a bathroom. That was where Paul, Linda and their three daughters – Heather, from Linda's first marriage, and their own girls, Mary and Stella – slept.

When I sat down beside Paul, he explained that they'd been living in this house for about seven years while a big house with a recording studio was being designed and built further into their estate.

Paul said to me, 'You probably think this is very small.'

And I replied, 'Yes, I can't believe someone as famous as you lives here.'

'You're right,' he replied. 'Most people wouldn't believe we live here – they think this is the gatehouse. But we move between here and the farm on the Mull of Kintyre which is also quite small.'

While Paul and I were sitting on the settee, Marlene handed over the scones, cheesecake and bottle of wine and chatted to Linda in the kitchen while she made the Sunday dinner. Grant and Leigh-Anne were playing with the McCartney kids and, at one point, Paul asked if I would take Grant's shoes off.

I hadn't noticed what was going on behind me. Apparently, Grant and James were jumping on and off the grand piano. James was in his bare feet but Grant still had his shoes on. 'It's not a big deal,' said Paul, 'but could you just take his shoes off if he's going to be climbing on to the piano?'

The television was on and the football highlights of Saturday's game came on. As we were watching the television, Paul said,

'You know I'm a Liverpool fan? You don't happen to know Kenny Dalglish, do you?'

'As a matter of fact, I know Kenny quite well,' I told him. Paul was really impressed that I knew Kenny Dalglish so well.

'Really?' he said. 'You know Kenny Dalglish? Wow, that's brilliant.'

At that point, Marlene and Linda had come into the room and heard that part of the conversation. 'Do you know who I like?' said Linda. 'Gordon McQueen. Big Gordon McQueen – he's lovely.'

I couldn't believe Linda had picked the Scots-born centre half who was playing for Manchester United as her favourite and I said, 'You're kidding me on – I know Gordon as well.'

Linda and Marlene went back into the kitchen and Paul and I continued talking about football. I mentioned that Brighton had drawn Liverpool at Anfield in the quarter-finals of the FA Cup. Paul reckoned we would have no chance against Liverpool on their home ground but said he would come to see me play if Brighton got into the final. 'You come and see me when I'm performing so I'll come and see you,' he said.

I then asked Paul about his relationship with John Lennon and how he felt when his former songwriting partner was shot just over two years earlier, outside his New York apartment.

Paul admitted that John was very bitter when The Beatles broke up. 'But I had been trying over time to dispel that bitterness because we should have been like brothers,' Paul said. 'But there were times John could be really annoying.'

Paul added, 'I was making my peace with John and getting friendly with him again before he was shot. But there were still a lot of things unsaid between us when he was killed.'

I asked him if he had got more security guards looking after him when John was shot but I was surprised, to say the least, when he said he didn't have any bodyguards at all.

At the time we visited him, Paul was recording the music for *Give My Regards to Broad Street*. He was also doing the filming for

271

the movie in London and he told me, 'I go on the train from Hastings to London myself every day I'm filming and I don't have any security guards with me. It's quite funny because I notice people glancing at me and then they say to themselves that it can't possibly be Paul McCartney sitting on a train by himself. It's amazing – I don't get any hassle at all. I go on the underground in London and walk about the streets and nobody bothers me.'

I asked Paul if that wasn't a bit dangerous considering John Lennon had been shot in the street. But he said, 'John had security and he still got shot so maybe it's better just being ordinary. I just get around and people think it can't possibly be Paul McCartney. You never know the moment or how it's going to happen so what's the point in worrying about it?'

We then started talking about music and I told him I played the guitar a bit. I wanted him to know that I had a real appreciation of his music because I could play. He asked me what songs I usually play and I told him I'd learned quite a few Beatles songs along with some of Paul's newer material with Wings. I told him one of my favourite Beatles songs to play was 'Blackbird', from *The White Album*. Paul looked at me quizzically and said. 'You can play "Blackbird"?'

I assured him I could and he asked, 'Honestly? How do you play it then?'

I told him about tuning the guitar down a tone and playing the song with chords in the key of G, but the song is actually in F.

Paul said, 'Well done. That's brilliant – I'm really impressed. I've had loads of people in the music industry come to me and say they had no idea how to work out how to play "Blackbird" and I've had to show them.'

Paul asked me if I had worked it out myself but I had to be honest and tell him it was a pal of mine from Paisley who had shown me.

'Well, I'll tell you what,' said Paul, 'he's good. Lots of people have never been able to work that one out.'

You've no idea how good that made me feel. So, well done,

Davy Shaw, and can I get that Beatles album back now? Only kidding!

I thought that was that until Paul suddenly got up and disappeared out of the room without saying a word. I was sitting there wondering what was coming next when Paul re-appeared with a guitar in hand. Fortunately for me, Paul plays left-handed and I play right-handed so he couldn't ask me to play one of his guitars. But the thought had crossed my mind that someone else may have left a right-handed guitar at Paul's house and he was going to hand it to me and say, 'Right, let's see you playing "Blackbird", then.'

But Paul sat back down and started playing the intro chords for 'Blackbird' and I thought he would stop after a few seconds. But he carried on and played the whole song to me. It was an amazing few moments and it's difficult to describe it – bizarre, eerie, incredible, all those things. I'm sitting on the couch with one of The Beatles and he's singing me one of his songs.

He finished the song and that was when he asked me if that was how I played it. Like I said, all I could do was nod my head and mutter, 'Aye, something like that.'

Paul put the guitar away and I said it was really time we were heading home but he asked if we would like to stay for something to eat. I decided to thank him but say no as I didn't want to encroach.

We gathered up our kids and Paul and Linda waved us off as we drove back down the road heading for home. In the car, Marlene and I talked about how stunned we were by how tiny their house was but what had really struck me was how friendly and down-to-earth they were towards us. They even sent back the ceramic dish Marlene had used for the cheesecake she made for them. Linda had put the dish in a padded bag and posted it back to us.

Several weeks later, Brighton had, indeed, made it to the FA Cup final. I remembered what Paul had said about coming to see me playing if I ever got to the final at Wembley and there I was. Paul had given me his home phone number so I called him up and offered to get some tickets for the final against Manchester United. I sent him six tickets but about a week before the game Linda phoned our house with some bad news and then even more bad news. 'Afraid we can't come to the game,' she said. 'We're recording in Montserrat and it's the only chance we have of getting into the studio there. And we've got other bad news for you. You sent us the tickets and we've lost them. We can't find them anywhere – we're really sorry about that.'

Paul then came on the phone, apologised for the tickets getting lost and wished me all the best for the cup final.

Fortunately, I had kept the serial numbers of the lost tickets and I was able to get vouchers from the Football Association as replacements. I gave the vouchers to friends of ours – twin brothers, Jamie and Roger Heal, from Brighton. I explained to them that the original tickets had been lost but they would be allowed into Wembley with the vouchers. I had told them the tickets were originally meant for someone else but they couldn't go. Jamie and Roger asked me, 'What will happen if these other people turn up and want their seats?'

'You'll get a real shock then,' I replied. 'These seats were for Paul and Linda McCartney.' They didn't believe me and to this day they still reckon it was a wind-up.

The last time I spoke to Paul McCartney was the phone call about the Wembley tickets. I'd like to catch up with him again because a lot has happened in our lives since then. And that might have happened in April 2003 if Paul hadn't had a bad throat and cancelled a concert in Sheffield.

My son Grant was playing for Sheffield United at the time and Marlene, Grant and I had tickets to see Paul play at the Hallam Arena. We were going to watch the concert and go round to the stage door like we did in Glasgow twenty years earlier and ask to see Paul. It would have been great for Grant and Paul to meet since Marlene was pregnant with him the first time we met the McCartneys.

We were in a restaurant round the corner from the arena and Grant went off to check what time the show started. When he came back, he told us the concert had been cancelled. When the gig was rescheduled Marlene couldn't make it so I went on my own. It was a strange feeling sitting in the audience listening to one of the world's great musical icons and remembering how I'd sat in his house and he'd played a Beatles song for me. I never did go to the stage door that night and, in the words of another famous Beatles song, I thought I'd just 'Let It Be'.

I did meet another member of The Beatles in bizarre and rather more uncomfortable circumstances. This time it was their original drummer, Pete Best, who is probably the most unlucky guy in the history of popular music. Pete was in The Beatles from 1960 to 1962, playing in Hamburg, Germany, and the famous Cavern Club gigs in Liverpool. But shortly before The Beatles recorded their first chart single 'Love Me Do', he was replaced by Ringo Starr.

It was only due to a madcap American lawyer who went around inviting people to my house for dinner that I met Pete Best. I was playing for Manchester City at the time and had met this lawyer Don Burris when I was doing some football coaching in the States in the summer of 1983.

I had stayed with Don and his family in California while I was over there and got on well with him. The following year, I got a call from Don saying he was coming over to England with his wife on business and asking if I could fix him up with some tickets for the Liverpool versus Manchester United game that was taking place at Anfield while he was over. I called my pal, Mark Lawrenson, who was playing for Liverpool at the time, and he said he would leave me three tickets in an envelope at the door of the stadium. Now, this is where it all started to go wrong for me that day. Don was late arriving at Anfield and, when I got to the main door, there was no envelope for a Gordon Smith and no one knew anything about tickets. Fortunately, one of the officials recognised me and let us in. The game was well under way and, as bad luck would have it, we were right in the middle of a row. The fans were growling at us as we squeezed by them, blocking their view.

After the game, I took Don and his wife into the players' lounge to meet Mark Lawrenson and, of course, to ask him what he'd done with our tickets. With a daft grin on his face, he reached into his inside pocket and pulled out the envelope with my name on it. 'Oops,' he said. 'I forgot to leave them for you.'

Don was chatting to Mark when I overheard my American visitor saying, 'We're staying with Gordon tonight. Why don't you and your girlfriend come to dinner at his house?'

Mark said, 'That'll be great!' and I scrambled find a phone – no mobiles in those days – to call Marlene and tell her there would be another two people for dinner that night. Mark said he'd be round at my place for 7.30 p.m. and we headed to the car park.

We were driving along and Don said, 'You need to take me to the Adelphi Hotel.'

I said, 'You're joking! We've got to get home – Marlene is expecting us.'

'You've got to take me,' replied Don. 'I've arranged to meet Pete Best there.'

'Pete Best? As in The Beatles' drummer?' I asked in amazement.

'Yeah,' said Don. 'That's the guy. I'm a huge Beatles fan and I've been getting in touch with people in Britain and I've arranged to meet him at the hotel.'

We trooped into the hotel and, sure enough, there was Pete Best and his wife, waiting to meet Don. We were talking away and then Don pulled the same stunt again.

'What are you doing tonight, Pete?' he asked.

'Nothing much.'

'Well, why don't you and your wife come to Gordon's for dinner?'

Here we go again – find a public phone and call Marlene to break the news that Don has invited Pete Best and wife to dinner. We now had a full-blown dinner party on our hands.

Marlene was fine about it but she asked, 'Who's Pete Best?'

'I'll tell you the full story later but he used to be the drummer for The Beatles and got sacked to make way for Ringo,' I explained.

At 7.30 p.m., everyone, apart from Mark Lawrenson and his girlfriend, was sitting around the dinner table and we started the meal.

Now, as you can imagine, Pete Best must be really fed up with people asking him what it was like playing with The Beatles and then missing out on the fame and fortune when they made it big. But all Don wanted to talk about was exactly that. At the hotel, it had been question after question about The Beatles and it was the same at the dinner table. You could see Pete Best was getting more and more fed up with this and he began to get very morose as the grilling continued. I was really embarrassed for the guy as Don just wouldn't let up despite me trying to change the subject at regular intervals.

After a while, Mark and his girlfriend arrived and when I introduced them to Pete Best, Don chipped in, saying, 'Pete was the drummer with The Beatles before Ringo.'

Mark said, 'Oh, were you? How are the lads? Do you still keep in touch with all The Beatles?'

And Pete replied, rather dryly, 'I haven't spoken to them since 1962.'

I said to myself, 'Oh God! Can this get any worse?' For a start, Mark was obviously not up on The Beatles because he had just asked Pete if he still kept in touch with *all* The Beatles and John Lennon had been dead for nearly four years by that time.

The atmosphere was terrible with Don continually quizzing Pete about a time he'd obviously decided he didn't want to talk about any more. I felt really sorry for the guy and it wasn't long before Pete made his excuses and left.

17

BOXING CLEVER

The bell rang and the two boxers came out of their corners into the middle of the ring and sized each other up, waiting to see who would make the first move. Bright lights flooded the canvas and ropes and, in the giant function room, hundreds of people sat at tables waiting to see the night's top-of-the-bill fight.

The noise would have been deafening if I had been listening but I was so intent on staying focused and concentrating on the game plan my trainer had drummed into me, I didn't notice the din.

Here was me in a boxing ring taking part in a charity fight against the Scottish Socialist MSP, Tommy Sheridan, in a Glasgow hotel in February 2003. We were raising money for Yorkhill Hospital in Glasgow and never in my life did I think I would end up doing something like this.

I had trained very hard for the fight and had to learn how to box from scratch. Like everything I do, I wasn't going to do it in a half-hearted manner. This was just as well because it was only after I had agreed to take part in the celebrity boxing match that I discovered that Tommy was ten years younger than me and that, for years, he had been doing boxing training to keep fit.

The former European, Commonwealth and British Welterweight champion, Gary Jacobs, started my boxing training and then former Commonwealth champion Ian McLeod took me for the last couple of weeks. I didn't have a very good right hook at that stage and concentrated on getting as many jabs in as possible to score points. I won the first round and, in the second round, I came out and hit Tommy with a good punch but, as I went in to finish him off, I lost my balance just as Tommy caught me with a glancing blow and I ended up on the canvas. At the end of the second round, Gary Jacobs, who was refereeing, came over to my corner and told Ian McLeod he was giving the second round to Tommy. Despite our protestations that I had fallen and not been knocked to the floor, Gary said he was counting it as a knockdown. I won the third round – and the fight – on points and it was a great feeling to achieve something you have never tried before.

Tommy Sheridan turned out to be one of life's good guys. I had never met him before and I don't think I could have fought him after getting to know him so well. It's easier to go into the ring and punch someone when you don't know your opponent.

Taking part in that boxing match just about sums up my feelings about life – don't be afraid to try something new and, when you do, prepare as best you can. And, if you do happen to get knocked down, as I did in that fight – although I still say it was more to do with me losing my balance – always get back up and battle on. I enjoyed the boxing so much that I have continued my training at a gym in the Pollok area of Glasgow.

Looking back at my life, I have to confess I'm disappointed that I didn't achieve as much as I wanted to in my football career. But it has been a great experience for me – it prepared me for other things and gave me a great resolve to succeed at whatever I do. I would have liked to have been a football manager but, who knows, I still might get the chance – I'm still only fifty.

I really enjoy my work in the media because I love football and I always try to be objective – honest! I always like to have an input into how the game is run because I realise it is not all glamour and it's tough for most players as they try to make a living from football. Players suffer because managers and directors often make wrong decisions and I, like many others have suffered by those decisions.

My family life has been wonderful. I am close to all my family and I've been married to a wonderful woman for twenty-seven years – aren't I glad Marlene saw my picture in the newspaper all those years ago?

My son Grant is a professional footballer with Bristol City and he's doing well, although he hasn't had any lucky breaks so far. He has been in the Scotland squads at Under-18 and Under-21 level and, who knows, he might just beat his dad and win a full international cap.

My older daughter, Leigh-Anne, has graduated from university and has opened up her own business – a gift boutique in Glasgow called La Coco. She's got a great entrepreneurial spirit and is very independent, which is something I admire in her.

And my younger daughter, Libby, is at the Glasgow Academy of Musical Theatre Arts – the stage school for singing, acting and dancing. It's great that she's got such strong ambitions to make it in her chosen profession.

I'm also close to my mum and dad, brothers and sister and that's good because families are important.

I do as much charity work as I can – especially now, after working in the media, because I understand why charities are so keen to use well-known people to help raise funds and further their cause. That was one of the reasons I agreed to put myself through the rigours of the celebrity boxing match. And let me leave you with an anecdote from that night which will stay with me forever.

There had been a slight delay and I was waiting in a side room for the fight to start. As I was walking through the hotel reception a lot of the spectators saw me and were shouting that they had put their money on Tommy Sheridan to win the fight. I shouted back that so had I. The doctor who was on duty for the boxing matches that night was sitting in the corner of reception and appeared to be a really nice, polite, mild-mannered person. As I was passing him he said, 'How are you feeling, Gordon?'

'I'm OK,' I replied.

'Do you think you can win?'

'I do, actually, but it appears I'm the only one.'

'You're right. Everyone I've spoken to doesn't give you a chance but, if you think you can do it, that's a good thing. And, if you do win tonight, don't forget the toast after the fight.'

'What's that?' I asked him.

'F*** the begrudgers!' he said.

Well, who am I to argue with that?